"Cushion's *Beyond Mainstream Media* ... masterfully written. Given its international scope and provocative ..., the book promises to become a key text within political communication and journalism studies. I urge my colleagues to read and engage with it."

Victor Pickard, *University of Pennsylvania, USA*

"Cushion's work is invaluable to understanding how the evolution of alternative news is intrinsically tied to mainstream politics and professional journalism. This book suggests the future of news could look brighter with more commingling of alternative and mainstream approaches."

Jennifer Rauch, *Linfield University, USA, author of* Resisting the News: Engaged Audiences, Alternative Media, and Popular Critique of Journalism

"A fascinating and much needed empirical analysis of the production, content and user engagement of 'alternative political media' in the UK that helps us to understand why people trust mainstream media (and politics) less and how alternative news media have evolved in relation to them. Dispelling myths of alternative media and their users as either amateur journalists or political activists, Cushion reveals distinctive content with increasingly professionalised processes used by critical news consumers with diverse media diets. Crucial reading for those seeking to understand 'alternative' media and politics."

Natalie Fenton, *Goldsmiths, University of London, UK*

"By delving into the mainstreaming of alternative online political media, this book offers a nuanced understanding of their impact on contemporary politics and journalism. Cushion's rigorous empirical research, including content analysis, interviews, and surveys, provides a solid foundation for his arguments. This work challenges the traditional categorization of alternative media and sheds light on the diverse perspectives and ideologies that these platforms now encompass. It is a thought-provoking and thoughtfully executed study that will undoubtedly shape future scholarly discussions in the field."

Frank Esser, *University of Zurich, Switzerland*

BEYOND MAINSTREAM MEDIA

Offering one of the most comprehensive assessments of alternative media to date, *Beyond Mainstream Media* examines the rise of alternative media over the last decade, analysing their changing content and editorial strategies, and exploring why many people go beyond the mainstream media for news and information.

Considering the differences in agenda between alternative and mainstream media coverage, Cushion sheds light on why right-wing alternative media have become a more prominent part of national media systems than left-wing sites in the Western world. In doing so, he argues that alternative left-wing media should place less emphasis on attacking professional journalism and focus more on converging into the world of mainstream news to promote their politics. This book draws on over 3,500 articles and 17,000 social media posts produced by alternative media, extensive interviews with editors and contributors, and a survey of over 2,700 media users. It develops a comparative international perspective by explaining how findings and concepts can be applied to understanding much broader issues, such as public distrust in the mainstream media or the influence different media and political systems have on the production of alternative media.

Providing both an introduction to and a critical analysis of the state of alternative media today, this book is written in clear, jargon-free language and is recommended reading for advanced students undertaking courses in Alternative Media and Political Journalism.

Stephen Cushion is Professor at the School of Journalism, Media and Culture, Cardiff University, UK.

Communication and Society

Series Editor: James Curran

This series encompasses the broad field of media and cultural studies. Its main concerns are the media and the public sphere: on whether the media empower or fail to empower popular forces in society; media organisations and public policy; the political and social consequences of media campaigns; and the role of media entertainment, ranging from potboilers and the human-interest story to rock music and TV sport.

BEYOND MAINSTREAM MEDIA

Alternative Media and the Future of Journalism

Stephen Cushion

LONDON AND NEW YORK

Designed cover image: cundra / iStock VIA Getty Images

First published 2024
by Routledge
4 Park Square, Milton Park, Abingdon, Oxon OX14 4RN

and by Routledge
605 Third Avenue, New York, NY 10158

Routledge is an imprint of the Taylor & Francis Group, an informa business

British Library Cataloguing-in-Publication Data
A catalogue record for this book is available from the British Library

ISBN: 978-1-032-42025-7 (hbk)
ISBN: 978-1-032-42026-4 (pbk)
ISBN: 978-1-003-36086-5 (ebk)

DOI: 10.4324/9781003360865

Typeset in Times New Roman
by Deanta Global Publishing Services, Chennai, India

For James and Catherine Cushion. Thanks for all your alternative perspectives.

CONTENTS

TABLES

INTRODUCTION

This book examines the rise of alternative political media over the last decade. It systematically tracks their online and social media content over time, exploring first hand with editors and contributors their production strategies and editorial goals. But perhaps most importantly, the book investigates why many people have gone beyond the mainstream media for news and information over recent years. In doing so, it considers the role and influence alternative media have in increasingly fragmented media and partisan political environments, against a backdrop of growing hostility towards mainstream news outlets. Professional journalists, after all, have faced fierce criticism over recent years for being out of step with the public or, worse still, mispresenting public opinion (Cushion 2018), and failing to reflect or understand people's alienation from or anger with the political establishment. The acronym the 'MSM' is now a widely used pejorative term broadly characterising legacy news media, representing professional journalists as distant, elitist, and collectively pursuing a narrow agenda that perpetuates the political status quo. It has become a social media hashtag associated with spreading 'fake news' and disinformation, with high profile politicians, notably Donald Trump in the United States (US), using the term to attack journalists and undermine public confidence in mainstream media.

In 2019, the BBC's former Director-General, Tony Hall, delivered a speech claiming "The phrase, 'mainstream media', is now a term of abuse – used by people of all political persuasions. Traditional journalism is painted as part of the problem rather than the solution" (BBC 2019). He argued that two major forces – the rise of disinformation and use of social media – accounted for this shift in popular opinion. In doing so, he alluded to the pernicious influence of new alternative media sites because audiences were increasingly turning to information sources

DOI: 10.4324/9781003360865-1

that reflected their ideological perspectives: "More and more people are becoming loyal to particular news services – and sometimes quite niche services – that reflect their worldview" (BBC 2019). He then argued that "social media has turbo-charged this trend, exacerbating our sense of polarisation as we all live within our filter bubbles or echo chambers" (BBC 2019). While not referencing alternative media sites, the subtext was clear: the emergence of new online and social media sources represented an existential threat to mainstream media and politics.

However, a senior BBC news broadcaster, Nick Robinson (2017) went further than Hall by criticising specific alternative media sites in the United Kingdom (UK). Writing in *The Guardian*, he argued that:

> Those who see themselves as fighting the establishment … have not just complained about the MSM. They have established their own alternative media sites – Wings over Scotland, Westmonster, The Canary, the Skwawkbox, Novara Media and Evolve Politics – or, in the case of pro-EU supporters, a new newspaper, the New European (Robinson 2017).

Robinson further opined that:

> Their [alternative media sites] most shared and liked stories are attacks on the MSM and the BBC in particular. They share a certainty – fuelled by living in a social media bubble – that we reporters and presenters are at best craven, obeying some diktat from our bosses or the government, or at worst nakedly biased.
> *(Robinson 2017)*

This book examines these claims as well as other critical assertions about alternative online political media. It questions many of the assumptions behind the role and influence of alternative media sites, and develops an evidence-based assessment about their impact on mainstream media and political debates. It asks, for example, if there is any systematic evidence of alternative media routinely spreading disinformation about mainstream media, or if editors are driven purely by activism and partisanship, and devoid of journalistic standards. And whether alternative media users live in ideological bubbles, divorced from the 'real world' of mainstream media and politics.

The rise of new left-wing and right-wing alternative media

Alternative media have been thrust into the limelight in recent years because of their impact on political events and issues. Alternative right-wing media in the US, for instance, have been viewed as critical to Donald Trump's Presidential success in 2016 (Benkler et al. 2017; Thompson and Howley 2021). Meanwhile, alternative left-wing media in the UK were considered central to Jeremy Corbyn's rise as leader of the Labour Party and his relative electoral success during the 2017 election campaign (Waterson 2017). New sites such as Another Angry Voice, Evolve Politics and The Canary were in the top 25 most shared election news stories online during the campaign (Booth 2017). But across Europe, alternative media have been on the march. In Sweden, far-right sites have grown in prominence, including Fria Tider, Nyheter Idag, and Samhällsnyt. Likewise, right-wing sites in Germany, such as Junge Freiheitand and Compact online, have been attracting many users, as they have in Austria with Unzensuriert, Contra Magazin, and Info Direkt. While the rise of alternative media have become aligned with new populist, right-wing politics, their dominance is context specific, with some new sites having been launched in Denmark – Den korte avis, for instance – but not as many as other parts of Northern Europe (see Holt et al. 2019). But beyond Europe, in Latin America, for example, alternative media have been on the ascendency, with their editorial characteristics shaped by the wider national media environment (Harlow 2023). To different degrees, alternative media sites around the world have had an impact on national, and sometimes international, political debates. They can help fuel public conversations, pressure mainstream political parties, and redirect the agenda of how professional journalists report what is happening in the world.

But as this book will explore, the agendas of alternative media can vary significantly, as well as their editorial standards, such as the degree of objectivity and partisanship in their news content. The wider influence of alternative media, in this sense, can be is difficult to isolate and interpret collectively. For example, a survey of users regularly consuming far-right-wing alternative media in the US discovered many held some striking beliefs and conspiracy theories, such as 40% agreeing with the statement that "the government, media, and financial worlds in the US are controlled by a group of Satan-worshipping paedophiles who run a global child sex trafficking operation" (Cillizza 2021). In other words, the consequences of alternative media can be profound if they spread misleading or outright false information.

However, the role and reach of alternative media should not be overstated. As the 2022 Reuters Institute annual survey based on data from six continents and 46 nations dryly put it:

> In many countries, new partisan/alternative brands have entered the market, but because their audiences are typically small and because most people still gravitate towards established outlets, their influence on aggregate patterns of audience behaviour is minimal – and in some cases is offset by increasingly mixed/centrist audiences for larger brands.
>
> *(Newman et al. 2022: 41)*

For instance, the far-right respondents who believed in a global child sex trafficking operation conspiracy represented a tiny fraction of the US population, with this specific set of beliefs rejected by the vast majority of the American public

(Cillizza 2021). One of the best antidotes of 'fake news', conspiracy theories and disinformation, in this respect, has been professional journalism, the mainstream media, and in particular public service media, because they have mitigated the rise and impact of blatantly false information. Over many years, representative surveys have consistently shown most people across the world continue to rely far more heavily on mainstream media for news and information than alternative media (Newman et al. 2022). This was particularly evident at the start of the coronavirus pandemic when sites such as the BBC and The New York Times were considered more trusted and reliable sources of health information than alternative media (Newman et al. 2020, 2021).

Studying alternative media and their wider influence

Despite the long-held influence of mainstream media, the rise of alternative political media represents a challenge to their journalistic authority and power into the 21st century. After all, the relentless attacks against professional journalism over the last decade could help cultivate negative perceptions of mainstream media, undermine public confidence and trust in professional journalists, and have an impact on people's knowledge and understanding of politics and public affairs (as explored in Chapter 9). But, to date, there has been little sustained analysis of what role alternative media play in shaping public perceptions of journalism and politics. While alternative media have grown in stature and prominence over recent years, this book makes the case that more empirical scrutiny and theoretical understanding of their content across online and social media platforms, their editorial aims and strategies, and their relationship with users and the mainstream media is needed. Recently launched alternative online political media have not been subject to any sustained academic research, particularly from an audience and production perspective (cf. Rauch 2021).

However, alternative media have long been researched and theorised (Comedia 1984; Downing 1984), particularly around the turn of the 21st century (Atton 2002, 2004; Bailey et al. 2007; Downing et al. 2001; Couldry and Curran, 2003; Rodriguez 2001). In more recent years, the *Journal of Alternative and Community Media* was launched and a Routledge *Companion to Alternative and Community Media* (Atton 2018) was published. In 2022 and 2023 a double special issue devoted to new alternative media was published in the academic journal, *Digital Journalism* (Frischlich 2023; Ihlebæk et al. 2022). It contained 18 contributions from right around the world, developing cross-national analysis and drawing on a wide range of methodological approaches to study alternative media (Frischlich et al. 2023; Ihlebæk et al. 2022). While alternative media studies has progressed, the concept of alternative media itself remains highly contested in how it is theorised and empirically understood. As Rauch (2016: 757) has pointed out, "scholars have employed a wide range of cognate adjectives to describe such [alternative] media, including radical, citizens, autonomous, activist, independent, participatory and community media". Indeed, across many recent studies, labels such as "alternative and partisan news websites" (Newman et al. 2019: 23), "hyperpartisan news" (Rae 2021: 1117), "alternative news media" (Holt et al. 2019: 860), and "alternative online media" (Schulze 2020: 6) have all been used to represent alternative political media. In doing so, it raises questions about the classification of online political sites and what type of source they should be labelled. After all, scholars have drawn on broad terms such as media, journalism and news interchangeably with alternative and (hyper)partisanship to describe a wide array of online political sites. Needless to say, while media represents an all-inclusive label, news and especially journalism reflect terms that have normative value (Christians et al. 2004). Pursuing a highly partisan agenda, for example, could be seen as inimical to how news or journalism *should* be produced (Strömbäck 2023). At the same time, while scholars should be rigorous and precise when classifying different media, in reality the fluidity of today's media and political environment means most people do not necessarily distinguish between the information they receive from mainstream media, alternative media or political communication more generally (Broersma 2018; Schwarzengengger 2022).

This book adopts a broad conception of alternative media, recognising it as relational term that interacts with the wider media system. As outlined in Chapter 1, it draws on Holt et al.'s (2019) definition of alternative media, which refers to sites that, in one form or another, *self-identify* as being alternative to mainstream media. In their words:

> alternative news media position themselves as correctives of the mainstream news media, as expressed in editorial agendas or statements and/or are perceived as such by their audiences or third-parties. This counter-hegemonic alternativeness can emerge on the macro-level of societal function, the meso-level of organizations and/or the micro-level of news content and producers.
>
> *(Holt et al. 2019: 860)*

Using this conception of alternative media, this book draws on the latest international scholarship in the field, and a series of original UK case studies, in order to provide a normative and empirical understanding of *alternative online political media*. Needless to say, this does not reflect the wide and diverse range of alternative media sites that exist around the world. It excludes media formats such as film or magazines, or in subjects like religion and music. By narrowing the focus to *alternative online political media sites*, the aim was to develop a comprehensive analysis of how politics was reported over time, how content was editorially constructed and understood by self-identified producers and users of alternative media. In various chapters, the book allows producers and users to interpret alternative political media for themselves rather than imposing a definition of what alternative media should represent.

The scope of the book

The book is informed by one of the largest studies to date of alternative online political media, examining both left-wing and right-wing alternative online political media sites in the UK between 2015 and 2021. This research was supported by a large ESRC Grant award (ES/S002510/1), which funded a content analysis of alternative media sites, interviews with editors and contributors, and surveys with media users.[1]

Overall, for left-wing sites, the book includes analysis of The Canary, The Skwawkbox, The London Economic, Evolve Politics, Another Angry Voice and Novara Media. It also includes analysis of Byline Times, which was labelled left-wing because the site tends to address more liberal than conservative topics. For right-wing sites, the book examined Guido Fawkes, Breitbart London, Westmonster, The Conservative Woman and Unity News Network (UNN). The sample was chosen on the basis of identifying – at the time the analysis took place – the most influential alternative online political media sites in the UK. 'Influence', in this respect, was measured by the reach of their online political sites and social media platforms (Booth 2017). Sites such as The Huffington Post and Indy 500 were not included because they are tied to traditional media ownership structures. Sites affiliated to a political party, such as Labour List or Conservative Home, were also excluded. The focus of analysis was on *independently funded alternative media that self-identified as being alternative and/or a corrective to mainstream media.* How sites financially supported their editorial operations varied, from raising funds by user subscriptions and donations to billionaires bankrolling editorial sites. As Chapters 5, 6, and 9 explore, the relative funding revenues and ownership models shape how alternative media editorially operate. How alternative media are more widely understood should also not be taken for granted. As subsequent chapters acknowledge, this book's conception of alternative media may not reflect how the wider public define and understand what is meant by alternative media (c.f. Rauch 2021). This makes it essential that any research with audiences is clear about what specific media outlets they are being asked about in order to avoid any misunderstanding.

In total, the book draws on an analysis of 3,692 articles, 17,207 social media posts, 40 interviews with editors and contributors, and a survey with 2,751 people about their relationship with media, including a targeted survey with 303 regular alternative media users. This primary data from the UK is combined with secondary data around the world in order to provide a comparative perspective throughout the book. Taken together, it represents a reflection of the latest (English language) international scholarship in the field at the time of writing, including a series of original UK-based case studies.

The book asks the following questions:

- What is the editorial agenda of alternative political media and has this changed over time? Is alternative political media content distinctive from mainstream media coverage?

- How do editors and contributors select and frame content, including on social media platforms? To what extent do they seek to discredit the mainstream media? How do they explain their site's own editorial agenda and values?
- Why are people (dis)engaged by alternative and mainstream media? Do they trust or question their content? What motivates them to go beyond the mainstream media for news about politics and public affairs?

In exploring alternative media, the book engages with wider debates about trust and (dis)engagement with different media platforms, including the existence of so-called filter bubbles and echo chambers in social media, and more broadly about media systems, regulation and journalism standards. It is split into nine chapters that, taken together, examine the changing nature of alterative media content, the editorial production of online and social media output, and how users engage with and understand both right-wing and left-wing sites, as well as their relationship with mainstream media.

Chapter by chapter outline

Chapter 1 begins by exploring how alternative media have been theorised. In doing so, a definition of *alternative online political media* is outlined in order to set the analytical lens of the book. A comprehensive assessment of the most recent academic literature is then carried out, examining the content of alternative media, their production and engagement of users, and identifying how original research can build on and develop new lines of inquiry. Overall, the chapter argues that scholars and researchers need to go beyond case studies of a specific outlet, and focus on both right-wing and left-wing sites in order to develop a more international and comparative approach to understanding the production, content, and user engagement of alternative media.

Chapter 2 analyses the latest scholarship examining the content of alternative media and, more specifically, how they have interpreted the editorial characteristics of new alternative online political media. Many recent studies have focussed on a specific right-wing media site, often at a critical moment in time, such as during an election campaign. To develop an original perspective, the chapter then develops a typology of alternative media in the UK based on a systematic analysis of editorial output. Over time, it found coverage blurred into a hybrid mix of reporting and commentary, with a strong editorial focus on mainstream media. Overall, the chapter argues that alternative media should be viewed as fluid and dynamic, shifting in content, style and format that responds to the vicissitudes of national media and political systems. The editorial influence and evolution of alternative media, in other words, should not be isolated from mainstream politics and professional journalism because they are intrinsically tied to their developments.

Chapter 3 considers how alternative media have adapted their editorial practices to the new digital environment. It shows there have been few systematic studies around the world examining how social media has been used by alternative media, or how they compared with the practices of mainstream media. Drawing on a UK case study of how Twitter was used by alternative media, the chapter discovers little conformity in how sites used social media initially, but over time they followed a broadly similar approach to posting content. The collective use of social content is interpreted as a response to the changing political environment and how mainstream media editorially operate. More broadly, the chapter argues the shifting use of social media represented a mainstreaming of alternative media, a shift towards professionalised practices and standards of professional journalism.

Chapter 4 focusses on how alternative media portray mainstream media and professional journalism more generally. It explores how editorially significant mainstream media are to the agenda of alternative media across different nations. It then draws on a quantitative and qualitative case study of UK alternative media sites, which reveals that hostility towards professional journalism increased over time, especially among left-wing sites which often focussed on attacking BBC news reporting. The chapter argues that the portrayal and criticism towards professional journalism is a reflection of the broader national media environment. Or, put differently, in order to understand the portrayal of mainstream media in alternative media there is a need to understand the changing characteristics of national media systems.

Chapter 5 switches the focus of book to the production of alternative media. It argues that alternative media have long been narrowly studied through the prism of their activist aspirations. The growing international scholarship of alternative media has demonstrated increasing hybridity of alternative media, challenging long-standing binary oppositional definitions between mainstream media and alternative media. Informed by 40 interviews with editors and contributors of UK alternative media sites, the chapter shows they were not cynically creating news through an activist lens, but producing distinctive content through a professionalised process that was aligned with their editorial and ideological goals.

Chapter 6 continues the focus on the increasingly sophisticated production of alternative media, in particular the use of social media. It explores how recent academic scholarship has begun to more fully recognise the shifting continuum in the editorial practices of alternative and professional journalism. Interviews with 40 alternative media editors and contributors in the UK reveal that the motivations for their agenda, including acting as a corrective to ideological biases within the media system. For instance, some interviewees explained that the framing of coverage was due to how social media algorithms worked in ways that might undermine the impact of their sites. The strategic importance of social media to reach people and convey their agenda was viewed by many producers as central to them being able to influence their readers' understanding of the world.

Chapter 7 begins the book's focus on alternative media audiences. It explores how users of alternative media users have been characterised as blindly partisan in their consumption habits, driven by ideological goals, and detached from mainstream media and politics. It reviews recent large-scale national and cross-national studies that have helped paint a broad picture of alternative media users, and argues more qualitative understanding of audiences is needed. Drawing on two original UK surveys and the wider international literature, the chapter then challenges conventional wisdom that alternative media users are solely partisan activists divorced from the 'real world'. Across several countries, research shows many users demonstrated they were highly curious and critical news consumers, displaying media literacy skills, with many still reliant on mainstream media.

Chapter 8 further explores fears about alternative media users inhabiting so-called filter bubbles and echo chambers that reinforce rather than challenge their ideological convictions. While a perception has grown that alternative media users have become disenfranchised from mainstream media and driven by populist beliefs, the chapter finds that there is limited evidence to support this assertation. It argues that their attitudes need to be understood in the wider media and political context in which they inhabit, which varies considerably between different countries around the world. The UK survey with alternative media users found, for example, that the national media system informed how they interpreted mainstream media and professional journalists.

Finally, Chapter 9 goes beyond the key findings of the book to consider broader questions about the importance of national and media political environments in understanding alternative media comparatively. In doing so, it explores the wider ideological influence of alternative media and what future role they will play in the world of politics and journalism. It first argues for a de-Westernisation of alternative media studies because many nations have political structures that limit or entirely censor critical journalism. It also makes the case for a decentring of alternative media studies away from the US because America has an exceptional media and political system that creates more opportunities for (right-wing) alternative media to thrive than most other Western nations. The chapter then examines how exposure to alternative media is likely to cultivate public disaffection with mainstream media, particularly public service journalism. Finally, it asks why right-wing alternative media have become more influential than alternative left-wing media, comparing their funding streams and media ownership models. The book concludes by arguing that alternative left-wing media need to converge into the world of professional journalism – rather than operate at a critical distance from it – in order to extend their ideological reach and influence on the mainstream stage.

Note

1 The research would not have been possible without the support of an ESRC grant award (ES/S002510/1) entitled 'Beyond the MSM: understanding the rise of online alternative political media'. This grant was developed with Professor Richard Thomas at Swansea University and was carried out over a four-year period (between 2019 and 2023). Professor Thomas helped develop and lead the research study, providing much-needed

energy and creativity throughout the project. I am also grateful to Dr Declan McDowell-Naylor, a research associate employed on the grant, who had a critical role in managing the coding of the content analysis, carrying out the interviews, and developing the findings. In addition, there were a number of research assistants who spent many productive hours coding online content including Andy Nelmes, Dr Marina Morani, Luke Roach, Ben Foster, Lizzy Wilmington, and Claire Thurlow, while Sophie Timmermann, Marta Silvia Viganò, and Andy Nelmes helped enormously with the analysis of audience survey data.

References

Atton, C. (2004) *An Alternative Internet. Edinburgh n Alternative Internet*. Edinburgh: Edinburgh University Press.

Atton, C. (2002) *Alternative Media*. Thousand Oaks: Sage Publications.

Atton, C. (2018) (ed.) *The Routledge Companion to Alternative and Community Media*. London: Routledge.

Bailey, OG., Cammaerts, B. and Carpentier, N. (2007) Understanding Alternative Media. Maidenhead: Open University Press.

Broersma, M. (2018) 'Epilogue: Situating journalism in the digital: A plea for studying news flows, users, and materiality' in Eldridge, S. and Franklin, B. (eds.) *The Routledge Handbook of Developments in Digital Journalism Studies*. London: Routledge.

BBC (2019) 'The BBC and the future of news', 20th March, https://www.bbc.co.uk/mediacentre/speeches/2019/tony-hall-lords

Benkler, Y. Faris, R. Roberts, H. and Zuckerman, E. (2017) 'Study: Breitbart-led right-wing media ecosystem altered broader media agenda', *Columbia Journalism Review*, March 3, https://www.cjr.org/analysis/breitbart-media-trump-harvard-study.php

Booth, R. (2017) 'DIY political websites: New force shaping the general election debate', *The Guardian*, 1st June, https://www.theguardian.com/politics/2017/jun/01/diy-political-websites-new-force-shaping-general-election-debate-canary

Christians, C.G., Glasser, T.L., McQuail, D. Nordenstreng, K., White, R.A. (2004) *Normative theories of the media: Journalism in democratic societies*. University of Illinois Press.

Cillizza, C. (2021) 'This is how dangerous right-wing media *actually* is', *CNN Politics*, 27 May, https://edition.cnn.com/2021/05/27/politics/far-right-media-conspiracies-trump-qanon-poll/index.html

Comedia (1984) 'The alternative press: The development of underdevelopment', *Media, Culture & Society*, Vol. 6(2): 95–102, https://doi.org/10.1177/016344378400600202

Couldry, N. and Curran, J. (2003) *Contesting Media Power: Alternative Media in a Networked World*. Lanham and Oxford: Rowan and Littlefield.

Cushion, S. (2018) 'Using public opinion to serve journalistic narratives: Rethinking vox pops and live two-way reporting in five UK election campaigns (2009–2017)', *European Journal of Communication*, Vol. 33(6): 639–656, https://doi.org/10.1177/0267323118793779

Downing, J (1984) *Radical Media: The Political Experience of Alternative Communication*. Boston, MA: South End Press

Downing, J.D.H., Ford, T.V., Gil, G. and Stein, L. (2001). *Radical Media: Rebellious Communication and Social Movements*. Thousand Oaks: SAGE Publications.

Frischlich, L., Ihlebæk, K.A., Figenschou, T.U., Eldridge, S.A., Cushion, C. and Holt, K. (2023) 'Contesting the Mainstream: Understanding the Audiences of Alternative News Media', *Digital Journalism*, Forthcoming.

Harlow, S. (2023) *Digital-Native News and the Remaking of Latin American Mainstream and Alternative Journalism*. London: Routledge, https://doi.org/10.4324/9781003152477

Holt, K. Figenschou, T.U. and Frischlich, L. (2019) 'Key Dimensions of Alternative News Media, *Digital Journalism*, Vol.7(7): 860–869, https://doi.org/10.1080/21670811.2019.1625715

Ihlebæk, K.A., Figenschou, T.U., Eldridge, S.A., Frischlich, L., Cushion, C. and Holt, K. (2022) 'Understanding Alternative News Media and Its Contribution to Diversity', *Digital Journalism*, Vol. 10(8): 1267–1282, https://doi.org/10.1080/21670811.2022.2134165

Newman, N. Fletcher, R., Robertson, C.T. Eddy, K. and Nielsen, R.K. (2022) *Reuters Institute Digital News Report 2022*. Oxford: Reuters, https://reutersinstitute.politics.ox.ac.uk/digital-news-report/2022

Newman, N. Fletcher, R., Schulz, A., Andı, S., Robertson C.T. and Nielsen, R.K. (2021) Reuters Institute Digital News Report 2022. Oxford: Reuters, https://reutersinstitute.politics.ox.ac.uk/sites/default/files/2021-06/Digital_News_Report_2021_FINAL.pdf

Newman, N., R. Fletcher, A. Schultz, A. Simge and R.N. Nielsen (2020) *Reuters Institute Digital News Report 2020*. Oxford: Reuters,https://reutersinstitute.politics.ox.ac.uk/sites/default/files/2020-06/DNR_2020_FINAL.pdf

Newman, N. Fletcher, R., Kalogeropoulos, A. and Nielsen, R.K. (2019) *Reuters Institute Digital News Report 2019*. Oxford: Reuters, https://reutersinstitute.politics.ox.ac.uk/sites/default/files/inline-files/DNR_2019_FINAL.pdf

Rae, M. (2021) 'Hyperpartisan news: Rethinking the media for populist politics', *New Media & Society*, Vol. 23(5): 875–1338, https://doi.org/10.1177/1461444820910416

Rauch, J. (2021) *Resisting the News: Engaged Audiences, Alternative Media, and Popular Critique of Journalism*. New York: Routledge.

Rauch, J. (2016). Are there still alternatives? Relationships between alternative media and mainstream media in a converged environment. *Sociology Compass*, Vol. 10(9): 756–767.

Robinson, N. (2017) 'If mainstream news wants to win back trust, it cannot silence dissident voices', *The Guardian*, 27 September, https://www.theguardian.com/commentisfree/2017/sep/27/mainstream-news-win-back-trust-dissident-voices

Rodriguez, C. (2001) *Fissures in the Mediascape: An International Study of Citizens' Media*. Cresskill, NJ: Hampton.

Schulze, H. (2020) 'Who uses right-wing alternative online media? An exploration of audience characteristics', *Politics and Governance*, Vol. 8(3): 6–18.

Schwarzenegger, C. (2022) 'Understanding the users of alternative news media: Media epistemologies, news consumption, and media practices', *Digital Journalism*, https://doi.org/10.1080/21670811.2021.2000454

Strömbäck, J. (2023) 'Political alternative media as a democratic challenge', *Digital Journalism*, Forthcoming.

Thompson, J. and Hawley, G. (2021) 'Does the alt-right still matter? An examination of alt-right influence between 2016 and 2018', *Nations and Nationalism*, Vol. 27(4): 1165–1180

Waterson, J. (2017) 'The rise of the alt-left british media', *Buzzfeed*, May 6, https://www.buzzfeed. com/jimwaterson/the-rise-of-the-alt-left

1
RESEARCHING THE BOUNDARIES OF ALTERNATIVE AND MAINSTREAM MEDIA

Alternative media have long been researched and theorised by scholars. But academic debates about conceptualising alternative media have intensified in recent years, with the fast-changing media environment prompting new ways to understand what is 'alternative' to 'mainstream' media. After all, the development of online media and then social media into the 21st century has made it far easier technologically and economically to launch alternative media sites and reach audiences locally, nationally, and internationally. This chapter explains how alternative and mainstream media will be analysed throughout the book. It focusses on three key areas, which include examining the content, production and consumption of alternative media, along with how users engage with mainstream media. But the chapter begins by setting out how alternative media will be conceptualised throughout the book. It pinpoints a number of disagreements and junctures in conceptual debates about their meaning and outlines a definition of alternative media, which centres on *alternative online political media*. The chapter then makes the case for a more international, comparative approach to the study of alternative media. Since empirical research about alternative media often focuses either on single case studies of specific outlets or nations, it argues more cross-national analysis is needed. This book draws on original research in the UK's media and political system but interprets the findings in the context of wider, conceptual debates and empirical studies relevant to understanding alternative media around the world.

In reviewing relevant academic literature, two broad categories of alternative media research were identified. First, the most recent scholarship which, much like other areas of political communication, has contextualised the study of alternative media within post-2016 concerns about digital threats to democracy,

DOI: 10.4324/9781003360865-2

including concerns about the rise of so-called 'fake news', conspiracy theories, and disinformation. There has been a condensed area of research on alternative media, with many new empirically rich studies published since 2016. The themes of this research focus closely on the classification of what is seen as a new genre of media outlet (see Holt et al. 2019; Rae 2021) and in exploring issues of hyperpartisanship and mainstream media criticism (McDowell-Naylor et al. 2021; Cushion et al. 2021). The second broad area of research dates back to the 1980s and into the late 2000s, covering the key work of leading scholars in the field, such as John Downing and Chris Atton. While this body of scholarship reflects a wide range of case studies, they all broadly focus on the democratic contribution of alternative media and the progressive left-wing causes they champion. This chapter draws mainly on the most recent academic literature but engages with older scholarship, at times, when discussing the conceptualisation of alternative media.

Conceptualising alternative media: towards a more inclusive understanding

Historically speaking, mainstream media have been narrowly classified by alternative media scholars. Above all, they have been characterised as reflecting the elite interests of the business and political class, in binary opposition to more radical alternative media information sources (Downing 1984). From this perspective, alternative media were viewed as being more democratic and accountable to the public than mainstream media, more independent of commercial and political influences, and more focussed on addressing a largely left-wing brand of politics that championed social changes in society.

Indeed, according to Rauch (2021: 1), alternative media have long been "widely presumed to have a liberal or progressive disposition toward issues such as civil rights, women's equality, pacifism, and environmental protection". It followed that much of the academic literature about alternative media in the 1980s and subsequent decades was centred on left-wing publications and political struggles. The book titles of John Downey and his colleagues' pioneering work about alternative media at the latter end of the twentieth century into the 21st century – *Radical Media: The Political Experience of Alternative Communication* (1984) and *Radical Media: Rebellious Communication and Social Movements* (2001) – reflected the emphasis on social movements and political resistance. Meanwhile, Atton's (2002) influential writing about alternative media centred on not just the content but the organisational systems shaping sites, the participatory role of users, and the wider relationship between consumption and a shared goal of achieving progressive political victories. He argued that alternative media "provide readers with access to other readers' (activists') lived experiences and on occasion offers these as part of a network of sociocultural and sociopolitical projects (often aimed at social change through extra-parliamentary means)" (Atton 2002: 153). In doing so, Atton (2002: 153) concluded that "alternative media can provide empowering narratives of resistance for those counter-publics that are written by those very counterpublics". But, as explored throughout this book, over recent years the focus has swung to the agenda of right-wing alternative websites and social media accounts. From a US perspective, Rauch (2021: 1) has observed that "the U.S. presidential campaign of 2016 revealed the extent to which a right-wing media ecosystem bolstered by nontraditional sources like partisan blogs, niche publications, and conspiracy websites could dominate the mainstream news agenda and shape electoral outcomes". But across Europe, too, far-right alternative media have become a more prominent part of the media ecosystem, with more academic attention paid to understanding their influence than left-wing alternative media.

Over time, scholars have moved away from constructing a binary opposition between mainstream and alternative media by characterising a far more complicated and multi-layered relationship between them. Indeed, 17 years after Downing published his seminal book about radical media with colleagues, he reflected on his own "binarism" when differentiating mainstream media from alternative media (Downing et al 2001: ix). He acknowledged that explaining the political significance of alternative media led him "to define radical media more tightly, in strict opposition to mainstream media, to a greater degree than I now believe possible for most conjunctures in political history". In doing so, Downing et al (2001: ix) conceded: "It simultaneously led me to write off major commercial media as permanently part of the problem, except on rare and good days. That was my slippage toward binarism … it … seriously simplified both mainstream and alternative media" (Downing et al 2001: ix). More than two decades into the 21st century, academic debates about the differences between mainstream and alternative media have become highly nuanced and sophisticated. Holt et al. (2019) suggested there have been two critical interventions in alternative media literature in recent years. First, alternative and mainstream media have now been conceptualised along a continuum, rather than in direct opposition to each other. Second, rather than celebrating alternative media, there have been more critical analyses of them, pointing out their limited reach with the public and the structural constraints they operate under which restrict their output and editorial goals. As a result of this reconceptualisation, scholarly typologies of what represents alternative media have become complex in scope and scale (Holt et al. 2019).

Today's new digital alternative media are conceptualised differently from past accounts in the 20th century. This is because of the increasingly blurry lines between what constitutes mainstream and alternative forms of media. Holt et al. (2019), for example, have suggested that the emergence of new online political sites does not necessarily meet the kind of normative ideals scholars have previously invested in alternative media. They argued that scholars have largely moved on from "debating whether right-wing alternative media can live up to the previous, largely normative interpretations of alternative media" (Holt et al. 2019: 862). Instead, they "propose a non-ideological umbrella definition, accounting for different levels or key dimensions on which news media can differ along the mainstream—alternative continuum" (Holt et al. 2019: 862). This was developed according to three levels: the micro, mesmo, and macro. At a micro level, this involves analysing content producers, as well as the output produced including their style and format. At a mesmo level, it includes production processes, such as understanding editorial norms and routines, as well as organisational procedures, from the political economy to the culture of manufacturing output. At a macro level, this considers alternative media sites within the wider media system and how they interact with the broader information environment. This book will examine these different levels of analysis, as well as explore how audiences regularly engage with alternative and mainstream media.

Central to this new conceptual framework – in particular at a macro level – is empirically understanding the relationship alternative media have with mainstream media, rather than relying on normative constructions of what is considered to be 'mainstream'. This represents a significant shift in focus because alternative media were previously theorised as being alternative to rather than interconnected with mainstream media. As Rauch (2016: 757) has put it, the relationship between alternative and mainstream media has always been "interdependent, antagonistic, fluid and contingent". Throughout this book, the analysis of alternative media will be grounded in the contexts of the wider media and political systems that shape production, content, and audience engagement. This is informed by systematic and rigorous research that interprets both the similarities and differences between alternative media and mainstream media. In other words, the analysis in the chapters that follow is empirically driven rather than normatively imagined. In this sense, the book shares Holt's (2018: 50) perspective that there is a "discrepancy between the dominant theories about alternative media and alternative media as they actually are". Or, as Schulze (2020: 8) has observed, stable conceptual definitions will remain debatable "in the absence of further content specific analyses".

Holt et al. (2019) have developed an inclusive set of criteria that reflects contemporary alternative media and their opposition to mainstream media. This takes into account the diverse range of platforms and content that can express their alternativeness to what is perceived as either traditional, legacy, or mainstream news. Their perspective is worth quoting at length:

Alternative news media represent a proclaimed and/or (*self-*) perceived corrective, opposing the overall tendency of public discourse emanating from what is perceived as the dominant mainstream media in a given system. This stated "alternativeness" can emerge on and should be studied on multiple different levels: Alternative news media can publish different voices (*alternative content creators*) trying to influence public opinion according to an agenda that is perceived by their promoters and/or audiences as underrepresented, ostracized or otherwise marginalized in mainstream news media, alternative accounts and interpretations of political and social events (*alternative news content*), rely on *alternative publishing routines via alternative media organizations* and/or through channels outside and unsupported by the major networks and newspapers in an *alternative media system.*

(Holt et al. 2019: 860; their emphasis*)*

At the core of this definition of alternative media are sites *self-defining* as being in opposition to mainstream media. How this manifests itself in alternative media output may, of course, vary, given the size and scope of sites around the world. The book draws on original analysis of alternative online political media sites in the UK throughout Chapters 2, 3, and 4, empirically exploring how often and in what ways they oppose mainstream media, such as providing correctives to professional journalism. For example, it examines two alternative media sites in the UK – The Canary and Evolve Politics – which have explicitly defined themselves *in opposition to mainstream media.* In the following chapters, different self-concepualisations of alternative online political media will be compared with the output they produced between 2015 and 2021. In doing so, the book will assess whether there was a broadly shared agenda of focussing on being a self-appointed corrective to mainstream media or whether other editorial characteristics were more dominant.

Rae's (2021) analysis of the contemporary digital journalism environment diverges from Holt et al.'s 2019 inclusive conceptualisation of alternative media. Drawing on sites such as The Canary in the UK and Breitbart in the US, she connects their rise in prominence to a broader growth in political populism and partisan coverage. Rae (2021: 1120) argued that many new alternative media sites represented hyperpartisan reporting and reflected characteristics of

personalisation (bias towards a political leader); bad manners, emotionalisation and simplification (transgressive style); polarisation (shuns objectivity and facts to be overtly partisan), intensification (the elevation of partisan journalism to a "hyper" extreme) and anti-establishment (openly hostile towards mainstream media and political parties while appealing directly to the "people" as content consumers and distributors through social media).

But she conceded more systematic empirical research was needed to understand how far these editorial agendas and conventions represented new alternative media, including interrogating the production of sites and how audiences interpreted them in the context of wider political and media systems.

The following three chapters consider this conceptualisation of alternative media, assessing scholarship internationally about whether these hyperpartisan characteristics reflect the routine agendas of new alternative media, their social media use, and the level of hostility towards mainstream media, including drawing on original research from a UK perspective. As explored in the next chapter, it is often normative ideals rather than systematic empirical investigations that have conceptualised alternative media (Holt et al. 2019). The book develops a typology of alternative online political media sites in the UK based on a detailed analysis of their editorial content between 2015 and 2021. This can be used as an analytical framework for future studies which aim to understand alternative media content. Chapter 4 also examines coverage qualitatively in order to assess the portrayal of mainstream media and professional journalism across alternative media sites. In doing so, it explores claims that alternative media spread disinformation (Robinson 2017) by questioning the credibility of their critiques and by examining the style, language, and use of evidence that supports their analysis.

But before the editorial agendas of new alternative media sites will be examined, this chapter begins by exploring how scholars have researched alternative media over recent years, from the content of sites to their production and audience reception. In doing so, it identifies how this book will build on and develop a holistic understanding of new alternative political media.

Researching alternative media: towards an international agenda

As explored in the following sections, studies about alternative media have often focussed on the content, production, and audiences in *specific* nations, rather than developing an international understanding of alternative media. There has been research exploring alternative media sites with international scope and aims, such as the Indymedia movement (Pickard 2006; Stengrim 2005), but they still often focus on case studies within one organisation rather than across different media organisations. In many ways, the focus on single case studies within a nation is understandable given the often idiosyncratic ways alternative media operate, responding to national political issues and concerns. But, in doing so, it arguably limits an understanding of the global role and impact of alternative media, including identifying the similarities and differences that shape the content, production, and audience reception of alternative media sites and their relationship with mainstream media. As Rauch (2016: 265) has observed: "Additional work is needed to more fully understand the wide range of goals, motivations and practices of people producing and consuming media on the alternative–mainstream continuum in diverse global contexts".

While UK-based case studies of alternative media will be drawn upon throughout the book, the analysis in each chapter will be developed through a comparative lens, interpreting the findings in the wider context of academic debates and developing an international picture of alternative media. In doing so, they examine the relationship between alternative media and mainstream media cross-nationally, including asking whether they are distinctive from professional journalism, comparatively examining the strategies editors and contributors employ compared to mainstream media and, critically, exploring how audiences respond to alternative media and mainstream media. The original research drawn on throughout this book, then, is used to develop a wider discussion about alternative media cross-nationally, leading towards an international research agenda of issues brought together at the end of the book. It broadly follows Holt et al.'s (2019: 866) call to scholars that "International comparative studies of alternative news media in different media systems would help refining our knowledge about the general characteristics of alternative news media across contexts".

To introduce the scope of the book, the following sections draw together the latest alternative media scholarship, examining empirical studies that have focussed on content, production, and audiences. This review of (English-language) academic literature is limited to the last decade or so in order to reflect the most recent scholarship in alternative media that interpreted their development in a contemporary digital media environment. After all, online and social media have transformed media systems, making it far easier financially to launch alternative media, connect with audiences, and share content locally as well as nationally and internationally. In exploring the most recent academic literature, the chapter identifies where more research is needed in order to enhance knowledge and understanding of alternative media in the 21st century.

Content: developing left-right comparative and longitudinal analysis of online and social media output

The vast majority of studies recently published about alternative media have focussed on their *editorial content and character*, rather than examining the production of sites or the audiences who consume them. Drawing on either content analysis or some form of textual analysis, these studies have addressed a wide range of topics and issues and have explored the content of sites including their social media profiles, such as the role played by hyperlinks or tweets. However, there has often been a lack of integration between the analysis of websites and social media output. Or, put differently, there has often been limited analysis of how online content has been produced and compared with how it is editorially framed and shared across social media sites, such as Twitter or Facebook. Many studies examining newly launched alternative media have been cross-sectional in focus, comparing a particular moment in time, such as an election campaign, rather than adopting a longitudinal perspective which captures the evolution of alternative media over time.

In recent years, the role alternative media play in producing 'fake news' and spreading disinformation has foregrounded many analyses of content (Marwick and Lewis 2017), such as a US study that found alternative news created false narratives about mass shootings (Stairbard 2017). But debates often centre on the boundaries between what constitutes so-called 'fake news' and alternative media output. For example, Robertson and Mourão (2020) identified 50 fake news sites in the US, and discovered that their design replicated the editorial style and format conventionally pursued by alternative media. In doing so, they argued that "fake news producers should be understood as hybrid actors mimicking features of both mainstream and alternative journalism in a manner that results in interpretive partisan news communities" (Robertson and Maurao 2020: 1011). Whereas traditionally scholars were preoccupied with debates about interpreting the boundaries between alternative and mainstream journalism, studies have now begun to develop typologies that differentiate between sites of disinformation and alternative media (Holt 2018).

But beyond exploring the relationship between alternative media, so-called fake news and disinformation, the most prominent trend in academic studies is related to the rise of right-wing alternative media websites, their social media power and opposition to mainstream media. While alternative political media have traditionally been associated with producing a left-wing, radical, and progressive brand of political content, today there is far more attention paid to partisan, conservative right-wing sites and their ideological impact (Holt 2019). In the US especially, the influence of highly partisan, conservative sites such as Breitbart News, have become widely studied in the context of whether they helped Trump become electorally successful or elevated far-right-wing perspectives to the mainstream news agenda (Kaiser et al. 2019). But worldwide, far-right-wing sites have been credited with helping to propagate a populist brand of politics that have enhanced the prospects of electing right-wing governments. Heft et al.'s (2019: 20) study – provocatively subtitled "Beyond Breitbart" – examined the websites and social media accounts of right-wing sites in Sweden, Denmark, Germany, Austria, the UK, and the US, and discovered "cross-national heterogeneity of news sites, ranging from sites with a 'normalized' appearance to more radical sites that clearly set themselves apart from legacy news outlets in terms of their thematic categories, their funding strategy, and their organisational transparency, leading to various types of digital right-wing 'alternatives' to mainstream news". But they also credited each of the nation's media and political systems with shaping the editorial character of the right-wing sites examined.

A special issue of *The Journal of Alternative and Community Media* exclusively focussed on exploring the rising phenomena of alternative right-wing media from four different countries – Brazil, the US, Germany, and Finland – all with distinctive media and political systems (Haller et al. 2019). All but one focussed on the content of online coverage or across social media platforms in order to compare and contrast their ideological messaging and the wider impact of alternative media. The editors of the special issue concluded that while the studies identified clear editorial differences in content between countries, their shared success was "based in large part on the denunciation of the traditional media as allegedly misguided and/or untrustable" (Haller et al. 2019: 5). As explored in Chapter 4, a small but significant number of empirical studies in the US and across Europe have documented how alternative media have sought to attack mainstream media, undermining their journalistic legitimacy in a variety of ways.

This book will build on and develop an understanding of contemporary alternative media in three main ways. First, it will carry out a comparative analysis of both left-wing *and* right-wing media content, understanding any similarities and differences in the context of their national media and political contexts. Second, the analysis will be longitudinal in scope, examining the editorial character of newly launched alternative media and assessing whether they changed over time and, if so, understanding why content has shifted in style or focus. Third, it will examine any editorial shifts between online and social media platforms, asking whether the medium changes the message of alternative media.

Production: from single case studies of activism to comparative analysis of alternative media

Few studies have comprehensively explored the production of alternative political media *comparatively*, examining the actors who create content and, importantly, understanding their editorial choices and motivations. There have been some sustained studies exploring the production of particular sites, notably Indymedia (Pickard 2006). But the focus is often on a particular mission of a site within a national political and media context, rather than examining a broader range of alternative media production practices. There are, of course, logistical reasons that mitigate the comparative analysis of how alternative journalism is produced. After all, many sites do not last long and their diverse formats make it difficult to select similar samples of alternative media to compare and contrast.

But despite the increasing academic interest in alternative media at the turn of the century, Atton (2007: 24) observed that

> we need studies that ask questions about the nature of journalistic practices in alternative media. We need to examine the ways in which practitioners work. How do they learn to become journalists or editors? How do they identify and choose their stories? How do they select and represent their sources? Are alternative journalists truly independent, or are their working methods influenced by the practices of mainstream journalists?

Over the last decade or so, more studies have sought to understand the production of alternative media by interviewing or surveying editors and contributors. Forde's book, *Challenging the News* (2011), for example, stood out for its focus on production processes. She carried out interviews over a 15-year period with US, UK, and Australian independent journalists, as well as surveys and focus groups of editors and managers of various community media. She found they viewed themselves as distinctive from professional journalists because of their stronger journalistic ideals to serve democracy. Forde also interviewed mainstream journalists, who – she suggested – emphasised technical skills or the thrill of being a professional reporter. Most strikingly, the research with alternative media practitioners empirically reinforced previous understanding of their values and roles in the production process. For instance, many viewed themselves as activists rather than objective journalists, producing a distinctive news service compared to mainstream media.

As explored in Chapters 5 and 6, this is at odds with more recent production studies of alternative media which suggested a shift from a position as an activist writer to more professionalised journalistic mindsets and ambitions. Forde (2011) showed how alternative media contributors shared similar practices and exhibited the same pressures as professional journalists, but attempts to robustly police editorial standards had been hampered because of financial precarity.

Harcup (2013) carried out a qualitative survey with journalists who worked for alternative and mainstream media sites in the UK, along with follow-up interviews with them in order to explore their experiences and to reflect on their roles. He discovered that many contributors did not view their experience of working at either alternative or mainstream media sites in a binary way. Instead, a continuum of practices was identified across sites that were seen to represent varying levels of professionalism. Harcup (2013) also found journalists felt more liberated by alternative rather than mainstream media, and they participated more freely in their production processes and felt able to speak their mind on democratic issues that mattered to them. This empowerment was viewed as central to their own journalistic identity and editorial motivations.

Over more recent years, a number of single case studies of alternative media sites – well beyond what can be unpacked in this chapter – have, in different ways, painted a similar picture of production processes and editorial aims. For example, Farinosi and Treré (2014) explored the motivations of people producing information after an Italian earthquake in 2009. They found a desire to be distinctive from Italian mainstream media by giving a localised perspective and bringing together communities in the aftermath of the earthquake. But achieving these goals – Farinosi and Treré (2014) discovered – were mitigated by structural issues, such as limited funding, and a lack of journalistic skills. Similarly, Heikka and Carayannis (2019) examined how citizens responded to public school closings in Chicago by initiating media production independent of news organisations in order to challenge the local government's decision.

But with some caveats (e.g., Forde 2011; Harcup 2013), much of the research about the production of alternative media has emphasised their distinction from mainstream media, including their reporting practices, their funding streams, and, perhaps above all, their activist goals. This has often meant studies examining the production of alternative media have been quite narrowly classified, excluding many sites that may not have conventionally been interpreted as alternative to mainstream media (e.g., Downing 1984). This shift was recognised in Atkinson et al.'s (2019) edited book *Alternative Media Meets Mainstream Politics: Activist Nation*. Taken together, the chapters demonstrated that contemporary alternative media should not be placed on the margins of mainstream media because they can play a critical role in setting the mainstream media and political agenda. However, the chapters included limited research from the producers of alternative media, asking editors and contributors about their editorial ambitions and relationship with mainstream journalism.

This book will follow this direction of travel in alternative media scholarship, interviewing 40 journalists from several sites that played a major agenda-setting role during the 2017 UK election campaign, with many of their articles shared on social media more widely than those produced by mainstream media (Waterson 2017). More generally, Chapters 5 and 6 move beyond the focus on single case studies of production processes and develop a more holistic analysis of the motivations of recently launched right-wing and left-wing alternative media sites from the perspectives of both editors and contributors.

Audiences: identifying alternative media users and understanding their relationship to mainstream media

Academic studies examining alternative media audiences have historically been limited in size and scope. Even at the turn of the millennium, when new independent, alternative online media were becoming more prominent and influential, Downing (2003: 626) identified a "virtual absence of alternative-media user research". As with production studies, deeper into the 2000s, academic research about alternative media audiences grew, but once again it was largely focussed on single case studies of particular media formats or political issues, such as new political blogs or activist causes. Harcup (2013), for example, examined readers of a community blog in the UK and discovered that they found more informative localised news than mainstream sites offered, while Atkinson (2010) revealed that alternative media users wanted corporate interests and values challenged, playing an activist role in co-creating content. Based on these and other studies, this body of evidence provided largely qualitative insights, identifying the specific needs and thoughts of audiences, but in sometimes quite niche media formats and on specialised social issues.

However, in very recent years, there have been a few large-scale national and cross-national studies exploring alternative media based on representative surveys. Taken together, they have painted a broad picture of alternative media users, understanding their shared and distinctive values and attitudes across media and political systems. For example, drawing on surveys from Denmark, Italy, Poland, Switzerland, and the US, Steppat et al. (2021) found that users have contrasting perspectives on what constitutes alternative media. They ranged from legacy outlets to more conventionally defined alternative media sites. But perhaps most revealing was some mainstream media sites were considered alternative sources of news in politically polarised media environments. In other words, in highly partisan news environments, audiences have begun to interpret what scholars label alternative media as mainstream sources of information. Anderson et al.'s (2021) four-wave panel survey of alternative media use in Sweden supported this perspective because it found people with declining levels of trust in mainstream media were more likely to turn to alternative media sources. But despite losing faith in mainstream media, many respondents in the study continued to use various legacy news sources in combination with alternative media. Meanwhile, Reiter and Matthes's (2021) two-wave survey in Austria compared the relationship users of alternative and mainstream media had with political interest. They discovered that regularly using alternative media was associated with greater political interest while undermining trust in mainstream media. In effect, this meant that mainstream media audiences were more likely to become less politically interested the more they regularly relied on alternative media. In sum, recent large-scale representative surveys have begun to demonstrate some specific characteristics of alternative media use in the context of people's broader relationship and engagement with mainstream media.

Klawier et al.'s (2021) survey of German internet users revealed that while many people stated they used alternative media – 43% in total – when asked to name specific sites that were defined as being an alternative media site only 5% could do so. Based on the findings, they recommended that researchers should "avoid using the term alternative media in surveys altogether and to refrain from self-reported measures of generalized exposure to them" (Klawier et al. 2021: 13). In other words, when researching alternative media sites, it cannot be assumed the public share the same definitions of alternative media as academics or, indeed, alternative media sites themselves. As discussed throughout this chapter, the boundaries between what constitutes mainstream and alternative media are not clear cut and have arguably become fuzzier in high-choice media environments across broadcast, online, and social media platforms. Klawier et al. (2021: 13) acknowledged this point in the conclusion of their study, advising researchers that "it is important not only to focus on alternative media in isolation, but also to investigate common notions of established, legacy, or mainstream media, and how citizens make use of them". But despite an emerging agenda in quantitative studies about alternative media use, Rauch (2021: 7) remarked that: "Nearly two decades after Downing's call, little empirical attention has been paid to the perspectives and practices of people who choose to read, watch, or listen to alternative-media products". Likewise, Holt et al.'s (2019) review of alternative media users stated: "our knowledge about audiences of alternative media and especially their motivations and gratifications is still scarce" (Holt et al. 2019: 866).

As previously acknowledged, along with the conceptual challenges of researching alternative media users, several practical issues have mitigated the production of alternative media audience studies. Above all, identifying who is an alternative media user can be highly challenging given the diversity of news sources as well as engaging with them if audience reach is limited. Once that has been established, it can be costly to find and pay people to participate in either qualitative or quantitative research, and funding field work, survey, or transcription costs, along with the analysis of large and small data sets.

The analysis of alternative media users in this book addresses many of the methodological and conceptual issues associated with researching audiences. It draws on both quantitative and qualitative research to identify users of specific sites and to explore their understanding of and engagement with alternative media in the context of their use of mainstream media. In other words, this book adopts a bottom-up perspective that ensures definitions of alternative media are not imposed but articulated through the voices of participants. This analysis explored, in detail, alternative media users' understanding and engagement with different sites and mainstream media more generally in open-ended questioning. This also meant the scope of the research went beyond the sometimes crude quantitative approach to understanding audiences when relying solely on representative survey designs. After all, alternative media audiences represent a relatively minor segment of the population meaning people who self-define as consuming alternative media may constitute a very small sample size. The multiple-choice format of survey questioning in quantitative polls can also limit the kinds of insight qualitative research can generate.

Conclusion: towards a holistic understanding of alternative media

The chapter began by engaging with long-standing conceptual debates about defining alternative media. Given the fast-changing media ecology, the hybrid nature of media systems, and the blurring of lines between alternative and mainstream media, it drew on the latest scholarship to develop an inclusive definition of alternative media. In doing so, the chapter introduced the empirical focus of this book – what was labelled alternative online political media. It then developed the case for a more comparative, international approach to studying alternative media. While many of the chapters that follow will draw substantially on original UK case studies, the analytical lens will go beyond national concerns and be international in scope, engaging with cross-national debates in alternative media, especially in online political media.

The chapter then examined how the book will analyse alternative media content, production, and audiences by first reviewing the most recent academic scholarship and then identifying how original research can build on and develop new lines of inquiry. To summarise, the analysis of content throughout this book will examine both right-wing and left-wing sites over time, exploring any editorial shifts in online and social media output. This is counter to the prevailing research agenda that focuses largely on alternative right-wing media at a notable point in time, on specific sites, and which often overlooks the interaction between online and social media platforms. With production studies, this chapter identified a limited set of academic studies that engaged directly with alternative media practitioners. But even when they did there was a relatively narrow focus on particular alternative media sites and single-issue case studies. By contrast, this book will draw on interviews with 40 contributors and editors from a range of online political sites, and develop an international, comparative analysis of production processes in alternative media, assessing their motivations and relationship with mainstream media. Finally, the chapter established that historically audiences have been under-researched in alternative media studies, partly due to a range of both practical and conceptual issues that make it difficult to access regular users and to explore their engagement. But, in recent years, scholars have begun to develop a greater understanding of alternative media audiences in survey-based research, which has helped characterise users. But often the findings of studies have been limited in scope given many were largely based on multiple-choice survey questioning. In order to develop a bottom-up, in-depth knowledge of alternative media users, this book draws on a large-scale survey, which identified regular alternative media users. It then asked them about their editorial preferences and explored qualitatively their consumption practices, attitudes towards specific sites, and more general (dis)engagement with mainstream media.

Taken together, the aim of the book is to develop a holistic understanding of alternative media, systematically assessing the content of political online media over time, interviewing those involved in their production, and, perhaps most importantly, understanding how and why regular users engaged with a range of sites and their relationship with mainstream media more widely. The next chapter analyses the content of alternative media by developing typologies of online political media and interpreting their wider significance.

References

Andersen, K., Shehata, A. and Andersson, D. (2021) 'Alternative news orientation and trust in mainstream media: A longitudinal audience perspective', *Digital Journalism*, https://doi.org/10.1080/21670811.2021.1986412

Atkinson, J.D. (2010) *Alternative Media and the Politics of Resistance: A Communication Perspective*. New York: Fordham University Press

Atkinson, J. D, Kenix, L.J. and Andersson, L. (2019) *Alternative Media Meets. Mainstream Politics: Activist Nation Rising*. Lanham: Lexington Books.

Atton, C. (2002) *Alternative Media*. Thousand Oaks: Sage Publications.

Atton, C. (2007) 'Current issues in alternative media research', *Sociology Compass*, Vo. 1(1): 17–27, https://doi.org/10.1111/j.1751-9020.2007.00005.x

Cushion, S., McDowell-Naylor, D. and Thomas, R. (2021) 'Why national media systems matter: A longitudinal analysis of how UK left-wing and right-wing alternative media critique mainstream media (2015–2018)', *Journalism Studies*, Vol. 22(5): 633–652. https://doi.org/10.1080/1461670X.2021.1893795

Downing, J (1984) *Radical Media: The Political Experience of Alternative Communication*. Boston, MA: South End Press.

Downing, J. (2003) 'Audiences and readers of alternative media: The absent lure of the virtually unknown', *Media, Culture & Society*, 25(5): 625–645. https://doi.org/10.1177/01634437030255004

Downing, J.D.H., Ford, T.V., Gil, G. and Stein, L. (2001) *Radical Media: Rebellious Communication and Social Movements*. Thousand Oaks: SAGE Publications.

Farinosi M, Treré E. (2014) 'Challenging mainstream media, documenting real life and sharing with the community: An analysis of the motivations for producing citizen journalism in a post-disaster city', *Global Media and Communication*, Vol. 10(1): 73–92. https://doi.org/10.1177/1742766513513192

Forde, S. (2011) *Challenging the News: The Journalism of Alternative and Community Media*. London: Palgrave Macmillan.

Haller, A., Holt, K. and de la Brosse, R. (2019) 'The "other" alternatives: Political right-wing alternative media', *Journal of Alternative and Community Media*, Vol. 4(1):1–6, http://urn.kb.se/resolve?urn=urn:nbn:se:lnu:diva-81994

Harcup, T. (2013) *Alternative Journalism, Alternative Voices*. London: Routledge.

Heikka, T. and Carayannis, E.G. (2019) 'Three stages of innovation in participatory journalism: Co-initiating, co-sensing, and co-creating news in the chicago school cuts case', *Journal of the Knowledge Economy*, Vol. 10: 437–464, https://doi.org/10.1007/s13132-017-0466-0

Heft, A., Mayerhöffer, E., Reinhardt, S., & Knüpfer, C. (2019) 'Beyond breitbart: Comparing right-wing digital news infrastructures in six western democracies', *Policy & Internet*, Vol.12(1): 20–45, https://doi.org/10.1002/poi3.219

Holt, K. (2018) 'Alternative media and the notion of anti-systemness: Towards an analytical framework', *Media and Communication*, Vol. 6(4): 49–57, https://doi.org/10.17645/mac.v6i4.1467

Holt, K. (2019) *Right-Wing Alternative Media*. Abingdon: Routledge.

Holt, K. Figenschou, T.U. and Frischlich, L. (2019) 'Key dimensions of alternative news media', *Digital Journalism*, Vol.7(7): 860–869, https://doi.org/10.1080/21670811.2019.1625715

Kaiser, J. Rauchfleisch, A. and Bourassa, N. (2019) 'Connecting the (far-)right dots: A topic modeling and hyperlink analysis of (far-)right media coverage during the US elections 2016', *Digital Journalism*, Vol.8(3): 422–441, https://doi.org/10.1080/21670811.2019.1682629

Klawier, T., Prochazka, F. and Schweiger, W. (2021) 'Public knowledge of alternative media in times of algorithmically personalized news', *New Media & Society*, https://doi.org/10.1177/14614448211021071

Marwick, A. and Lewis, R. (2017) 'Media manipulation and disinformation online', Data & Society Research Institute, https://datasociety.net/library/media-manipulation-and-disinfo-online/

McDowell-Naylor, D., Cushion, S. and Thomas, R. (2021) 'A typology of alternative online political media in the United Kingdom: A longitudinal content analysis (2015–2018)', *Journalism*, https://doi.org/10.1177/14648849211059585

Pickard, V. (2006) 'United yet autonomous: Indymedia and the struggle to sustain a radical democratic network', *Media, Culture & Society*, Vol. 28(3): 315–336. https://doi.org/10.1177/0163443706061685

Rae, M. (2021) 'Hyperpartisan news: Rethinking the media for populist politics', *New Media & Society*, Vol. 23(5): 875–1338, https://doi.org/10.1177/1461444820910416

Rauch, J. (2016) 'Are there still alternatives? Relationships between alternative media and mainstream media in a converged environment', *Sociology Compass*, Vol. 10(9): 756–767.

Rauch, J. (2021) *Resisting the News: Engaged Audiences, Alternative Media, and Popular Critique of Journalism*. New York: Routledge.

Reiter, F. and Matthes, J. (2021) 'Correctives of the mainstream media? A panel study on mainstream media use, alternative digital media use, and the erosion of political interest as well as political knowledge', *Digital Journalism*, https://doi.org/10.1080/21670811.2021.1974916

Robertson, C.T. and Mourão, R.R. (2020) 'Faking alternative journalism? An analysis of self-presentations of "fake news" sites', *Digital Journalism*: 1–19. https://doi.org/10 .1080/21670811.2020.1743193

Robinson, N. (2017) 'If mainstream news wants to win back trust, it cannot silence dissident voices', *The Guardian*, 27 September, https://www.theguardian.com/commentisfree /2017/sep/27/mainstream-news-win-back-trust-dissident-voices

Schulze, H. (2020) 'Who uses right-wing alternative online media? An exploration of audience characteristics', *Politics and Governance*, Vol. 8(3): 6–18.

Starbird, K. (2017) 'Examining the alternative media ecosystem through the production of alternative narratives of mass shooting events on twitter', *Proceedings of the International AAAI Conference on Web and Social Media*, Vol. 11(1): 230–239 https:// doi.org/10.1609/icwsm.v11i1.14878

Stengrim, L.A. (2005) 'Negotiating postmodern democracy, political activism, and knowledge production: Indymedia's grassroots and e-savvy answer to media oligopoly', *Communication and Critical/Cultural Studies*, Vol. 2(4): 281–304, https://doi.org/10 .1080/14791420500332527

Steppat, D. Castro, L. and Esser, F. (2021) 'What news users perceive as "alternative media" varies between countries: how media fragmentation and polarization matter', *Digital Journalism*, https://doi.org/10.1080/21670811.2021.1939747

Waterson, J. (2017) 'The rise of the alt-left british media', *Buzzfeed*, May 6, https://www. buzzfeed. com/jimwaterson/the-rise-of-the-alt-left

2

THE EVOLUTION AND INFLUENCE OF ALTERNATIVE MEDIA IN NATIONAL MEDIA AND POLITICAL SYSTEMS

When scholars have examined alternative media over recent years, the empirical focus has mostly been on their editorial output, rather than how they are produced or how audiences engage with them. These content-based studies have largely been designed to understand the format, style, and nature of new forms of alternative media across online and social media platforms (see Chapter 1). The novelty of a whole range of recently launched sites considered to be distinctive from mainstream media has led to reconceptualisations about what constitutes alternative media and the development of new typologies of alternative media sites (Holt et al. 2019; Rae 2021). The focus of this book is on developing an understanding of relatively new *alternative online political media*, which scholars have largely examined in the context of interpreting their objectivity, assessing whether they are partisan in character and, if so, understanding what brand of politics they promote in contrast to mainstream media (Holt et al. 2019; Nygaard 2019; Rae 2021). Particular attention has been paid to the rise of right-wing alternative media and their growing impact on mainstream politics and their agenda-setting power (Thompson and Howley 2021; Roberts and Wahl-Jorgensen 2021). This is especially the case in the US since the 2016 election campaign, when sites such as Breitbart News were credited with mobilising public opinion in support of Donald Trump and, it is claimed, helping him become president (Benkler et al. 2017; Thompson and Howley 2021).

This chapter explores the latest scholarship examining the *content* of alternative media and, more specifically, how they have interpreted the editorial characteristics of new alternative political media. To develop an original perspective, this chapter will draw on a longitudinal study of alternative online political sites in the UK between 2015 and 2021, tracking their editorial character in the immediate

DOI: 10.4324/9781003360865-3

years after many new sites were launched. It is based on a content analysis study of 3,452 articles across nine right-wing and left-wing sites (McDowell-Naylor et al. 2021). To understand the editorial characteristics of coverage, every article was assessed according to whether it focussed primarily on either news or commentary, its level of policy analysis, and the degree of partisanship on display. Based on a systematic, comparative assessment of coverage over time, typologies of alternative political media sites in the UK were developed, which reflected their editorial character in four overlapping areas: electoral hyperpartisans, cultural partisans, political cycle specialists, and vernacular macro-blogs (McDowell-Naylor et al. 2021). The chapter concludes by arguing that more *comparative* empirical analyses of alternative media content are needed. It further suggests more academic attention should be paid to how media and political systems shape the editorial character and ideological focus of different alternative media cross-nationally.

Interpreting the characteristics of new alternative online political media

As Chapter 1 outlined, debates about alternative media have historically been tied to various progressive and democratic movements over recent decades (Atton 2002; Downing et al. 2001) and the early internet (Couldry and Curran 2003), with definitions centred on political activism, championing social causes, and in direct opposition to the values of mainstream media. But, in more recent years, alternative media have been re-conceptualised in a new era Rae (2021: 1118) has labelled a "distinct, digital-first subculture of media". This has been connected with debates about digital natives more generally, which represent media born in the age of online and social media. As a consequence, it is claimed, they adopt specific media norms and logics but which overlap with mainstream, legacy media (Thomas and Cushion 2019). In doing so, alternative media have been labelled in new and distinctive ways, particularly sites dedicated to the world of politics. For example, over recent years scholars have used terms such as "alternative and partisan news websites" (Newman et al. 2019: 23), "hyperpartisan news" (Rae 2021: 1117), "alternative news media" (Holt et al. 2019: 860), and "alternative online media" (Schulze 2020: 6) to describe a similar set of political sites cross-nationally. As explained in the previous chapter, this book adopted the definition *alternative online political media* to characterise alternative political sites in the UK. This represented a relatively neutral definition which was not ideologically driven or tied to a set of normative ideals previously used to police the boundaries of what constitutes alternative media.

But while similar terms have been used interchangeably in academic studies, there have been few systematic studies of alternative media that editorially characterise the content of alternative media. Rae (2021), for example, recommended that political online sites, such as the Young Turks, The Canary, and Breitbart

News, should be relabelled hyperpartisan news rather than alternative media. She argued that

> while both alternative and hyperpartisan news evolve on the periphery of the journalistic field, hyperpartisan media is much more transgressive in style. Far from serving as an "endangered species", it both mimics and challenges – even demands it takes its place at the "legitimate" centre alongside established media.
>
> *(Rae 2021: 1128)*

Rae (2021: 1128) concluded that once the boundaries of hyperpartisan media were better established, "future research may then focus on empirical factors such as newsroom practices and content analysis".

Heft and colleagues (2019, 2021) carried out a cross-national content analysis of six nations – Sweden, Denmark, Germany, Austria, the UK, and the US – to interpret new forms of alternative online political media. One of their studies examined the content of 70 European and US right-wing news websites sites along with their social media accounts. Their analysis identified a "systematic variation" (Heft et al. 2019: 31) in the digital infrastructures of right-wing sites. They concluded that across the six different nations of alternative media sites, there were "different patterns of supply and demand, as well as distinct funding structures, organizational strategies, and thematic tendency" (Heft et al. 2019: 38). The "heterogeneity" of content, they argued "provides an important corrective to simplistic interpretations of hyperpartisan media as mere "fake news media" or "junk media" (Heft et al. 2019: 38). However, their analysis was limited to measuring the volume of articles and tweets, rather than understanding content in any detail, such as comparing the editorial diversity of sites or their degree of partisanship.

In another of their studies, Heft et al. (2021) examined the use of hyperlinks across 65 right-wing sites in the same six countries (Sweden, Denmark, Germany, Austria, the UK, and the US). Overall, they concluded that "legacy news outlets primarily serve as transnationally shared reference points for the alternative news ecologies on the right" (Heft et al. 2021: 498). However, they found important differences between nations in hyperlinking practices, which they argued could only be explained by specific national political and media system characteristics. For example, national right-wing sites in Germany and Sweden drew heavily on domestic right-wing sites, whereas others across Europe – notably Denmark – were mostly transnational with their source preferences. The only outlier, Heft et al. (2021: 499) found, were right-wing sites in the US, which were "firmly and homogeneously domestically interconnected, but they also function as hubs drawing transnational connections from the other sampled countries". Among other factors, Heft et al. (2021) concluded this might represent the fact that alternative media sites have been thriving in the US for many years, and their editors and journalists will have cultivated close ties to international media organisations. American exceptionalism in alternative media is an issue explored more thoroughly in Chapter 9. As well as finding diversity among hyperlinked sources across Western right-wing sites, Heft et al. (2021) also concluded that all the sites they examined drew heavily on mainstream news sources. But they acknowledged their analysis could not assess whether these links were used to undermine and delegitimatise legacy media and professional journalistic sources or if they were used as accurate and credible sources of news and information.

Beyond the limited number of cross-national studies exploring alternative media content, there have been some national studies of largely right-wing media sites, including understanding their news agendas. Nygaard's (2019) content analysis of right-wing media found significant differences across Scandinavian countries in how articles conveyed anti-immigration messaging in their news reporting. The analysis of 68 articles in total discovered Swedish alternative media sites were largely descriptive in their style, whereas Danish sites provided normative judgements about the dangers of immigration, with Norwegian right-wing sites adopting a mix of both. But while the study provided some qualitative insights into the contrasting stylistic approaches to reporting, Nyhgarrd (2019: 1161) conceded that "future research on this topic should apply quantitative measures to determine whether the articles published under the news banners by the outlets have become more descriptive in recent years." In other words, there is a need for more systematic, rigorous research to assess any changes in alternative media content over time.

In summary, over very recent years, alternative media *content* has been subjected to more sustained scholarly analysis, including cross-national quantitative studies, and qualitative assessments of national sites on specific issues, particularly from right-wing sites. To develop new lines of inquiry, this chapter now draws on a detailed quantitative analysis of left-wing and right-wing sites in the UK, which both examined the editorial detail of articles and explored whether they had changed over time (McDowell-Naylor et al. 2021). In doing so, a typological framework is developed that characterises the editorial nature of alternative media sites in the UK.

Understanding the editorial character of UK alternative media

To assess alternative media in the UK, nine sites in the UK were chosen and examined between 2015 and 2018. They were analysed in four sampling periods (5–25 October 2015, 9–29 October 2016, 30 April–7 June 2017, which was during the UK general election campaign, and 8–28 October 2018). The extended six-week sampling in 2017 (rather than three weeks) was designed to study the whole period of the UK election campaign when new alternative media were viewed as having a major impact on the political agenda (Waterson 2017). Overall, the content analysis study generated 3,452 articles to analyse in detail. An intercoder reliability test

TABLE 2.1 The frequency of articles published in alternative media sites in the UK between 2015 and 2018

Alternative media site	2015	2016	2017	2018	Total
Left-wing sites					
Another Angry Voice	4	6	119	7	136
Evolve Politics	1	22	56	23	102
Novara Media	3	7	15	4	29
The Canary	62	105	421	138	726
The Skwawkbox[a]	–	31	210	88	329
Right-wing sites					
Breitbart London	135	135	263	93	626
Conservative Woman	33	48	110	75	266
Guido Fawkes	130	136	410	173	849
Westmonster[a]	–	–	242	147	389
Total	368	490	1846	748	3452

[a]Westmonster was launched in 2017, while The Skwawkbox did not publish content in October 2015.

was carried out on 10% of all content. It found all variables had a high level of reliability (McDowell-Naylor et al. 2021).

Above all, the findings demonstrate a disparity in the amount of content produced by different alternative media sites (see Table 2.1). This difference in the amount of content relates to the balance of text-based articles, audio, and video content between sites. The content analysis study focussed on articles to develop a quantitative comparison of coverage. But that, at face value, underestimated the level of output produced by Novara Media, which often only published a relatively small number of articles per week yet featured far more audio and video features than other sites. All of which reinforced Heft et al.'s (2019: 31) observation of a "systematic variation" in right-wing Western alternative media. The analysis of left-wing alternative media sites also revealed different levels of production and content variation.

The comparative content analysis of alternative media sites examined the main topics of articles, whether they were opinion-based or fact-driven, and their degree of coverage about policies, political parties, and levels of partisanship. Table 2.2 shows there was a clear divide between alternative online political sites that produced either news or opinion-led articles, as well as shifts in editorial focus over time and especially during the 2017 election campaign period.

With the exception of Conservative Woman and The Skwawkbox, it was right-wing sites that prioritised news reporting over political commentary, while left-wing sites were more opinion-driven. In terms of the subjects editorially pursued by alternative media sites, there was a range of topics addressed over the four years of analysis. As Table 2.3 demonstrates, coverage of party politics or the media reflected just over half of all topics, while EU affairs and social affairs

TABLE 2.2 The percentage of fact-driven (news) and opinion-driven (commentary) articles in alternative media sites in the UK between 2015 and 2018 (frequency in brackets)

Outlet	Fact-driven news articles					Opinion-driven news articles				
	2015	2016	2017	2018	Total	2015	2016	2017	2018	Total
Left-wing sites										
Another Angry Voice	/	16.7% (1)	10.9% (13)	/	10.3% (14)	100% (4)	83.3% (5)	88.2% (105)	100.0% (7)	89.0% (121)
Evolve Politics	/	72.7% (16)	32.1% (18)	30.4% (7)	40.2% (41)	100.0% (1)	22.7% (5)	60.7% (34)	69.6% (16)	54.9% (56)
Novara Media	/	14.3% (1)	/	/	3.4% (1)	100% (3)	85.7% (6)	100.0% (15)	100.0% (4)	96.6% (28)
The Canary	48.4% (30)	41.0% (43)	13.3% (56)	43.5% (60)	26.0% (189)	50.0% (31)	56.2% (59)	85.7% (361)	51.4% (71)	71.9% (522)
The Skwawkbox	–	32.3% (10)	50.0% (105)	80.7% (71)	56.5% (186)	–	54.8% (17)	44.3% (93)	15.9% (14)	37.7% (124)
Right-wing sites										
Breitbart	80.7% (109)	83.0% (112)	87.5% (230)	91.4% (85)	85.6% (536)	18.5% (25)	14.8% (25)	12.5% (33)	7.5% (7)	13.6% (85)
Conservative Woman	–	2.1% (1)	1.8% (2)	1.3% (1)	1.5% (4)	60.6% (20)	60.6% (20)	76.4% (84)	66.7% (50)	69.9% (186)
Guido Fawkes	75.4% (89)	75.0% (102)	81.0% (332)	77.5% (134)	78.4% (666)	17.7% (23)	16.9% (23)	13.4% (55)	15.6% (27)	15.1% (128)
Westmonster	–	–	84.7% (205)	96.6% (142)	89.2% (347)	–	–	14.9% (36)	2.7% (4)	10.3% (40)
Total	64.4% (237)	58.4% (286)	52.1% (961)	66.8% (500)	57.5% (1984)	29.1% (107)	34.1% (167)	44.2% (816)	26.7% (200)	37.4% (129)

All percentages in tables throughout the book have been rounded up and may not add up to 100.0%.
Material coded as 'other' (n = 178), which includes satire, readers' letters, and fundraising appeals, were excluded from this table.

TABLE 2.3 The percentage of different topics covered by alternative media sites in the UK between 2015 and 2018 (frequency in brackets)

Alternative media site (period of 2017 election campaign in italics)[a]	Party political	Media	EU affairs	Social affairs	All other	Total
Left-wing sites						
Another Angry Voice	45.6% (62)	8.1% (11)	5.1% (7)	6.6% (9)	34.6% (47)	100.0% (136)
Another Angry Voice during 2017 election	*48.7% (58)*	*7.6% (9)*	*5.0% (6)*	*6.7% (8)*	*31.9% (38)*	*100.0% (119)*
Evolve Politics	51.0% (52)	15.7% (16)	2.0% (2)	3.9% (4)	27.5% (28)	100.0% (102)
Evolve Politics during 2017 election	*67.9% (38)*	*16.1% (9)*	–	*1.8% (1)*	*14.3% (8)*	*100.0% (56)*
Novara Media	31.0% (9)	3.4% (1)	6.9% (2)	6.9% (2)	51.7% (15)	100.0% (29)
Novara Media during 2017 election	*46.7% (7)*	–	*6.7% (1)*	–	*46.7% (7)*	*100.0% (15)*
The Canary	40.9% (297)	20.9% (152)	2.1% (15)	7.3% (53)	28.8% (209)	100.0% (726)
The Canary during the 2017 election	*54.6% (230)*	*23.5% (99)*	*1.0% (4)*	*3.8% (16)*	*17.1% (72)*	*100.0% (421)*
The Skwawkbox	61.7% (203)	12.8% (42)	1.2% (4)	3.3% (11)	21.0% (69)	100.0% (329)
The Skwawkbox during the 2017 election	*61.9% (130)*	*11.9% (25)*	–	–	*26.2% (55)*	*100.0% (210)*
Right-wing sites						
Breitbart	18.7% (117)	7.0% (44)	23.6% (148)	11.5% (72)	39.1% (245)	100.0% (626)
Breitbart during the 2017 election	*22.1% (58)*	*6.8% (18)*	*16.3% (43)*	*11.0% (29)*	*43.7% (115)*	*100.0% (263)*
Conservative Woman	26.3% (70)	21.4% (57)	11.3% (30)	14.7% (39)	26.3% (70)	100.0% (266)
Conservative Woman during the 2017 election	*41.8% (46)*	*23.6% (26)*	*6.4% (7)*	*10.9% (12)*	*17.3% (19)*	*100.0% (110)*
Guido Fawkes	45.0% (382)	12.8% (109)	9.1% (77)	3.7% (31)	29.4% (250)	100% (849)
Guido Fawkes during the 2017 election	*61.7% (253)*	*13.2% (54)*	*2.2% (9)*	*3.9% (16)*	*19.0% (78)*	*100.0% (410)*
Westmonster	24.4% (95)	3.3% (13)	35.0% (136)	14.4% (56)	22.9% (89)	100.0% (389)
Westmonster during the 2017 election	*27.3% (66)*	*5.0% (12)*	*22.7% (55)*	*19.8% (48)*	*25.2% (61)*	*100.0% (242)*
Total	37.3% (1287)	12.9% (445)	12.2% (421)	8.0% (277)	29.6% (1022)	100% (3452)

[a] Isolated 2017 election sample N = 1846.

(broadly reflecting issues such as LGBTQ+, religion, race, and discrimination) were the next two most covered topics, respectively. The remaining topics were diverse in range and grouped together into 'other' topics. This included coverage of parliament, the government, economics, defence, immigration, foreign affairs, education, the NHS, social care, the environment, infrastructure, science and technology, and arts, culture, and sport.

Table 2.3 shows The Canary, Guido Fawkes, and The Skwawkbox were the most party - political centric sites. The Canary and Guido Fawkes also supplied the most coverage of news about the media itself, along with the Conservative Woman. Indeed, just over one in ten articles across all nine sites were mainly focussed on coverage in mainstream media, with Guido Fawkes ("Media Guido") and Conservative Woman ("BBC Watch") having designated online media sections. As the Introduction to the book explored, the identity of new alternative media is often associated with their distinctiveness from mainstream media. But the sheer volume of alternative media coverage dedicated to reporting about professional journalism demonstrates their editorial agenda is largely driven by coverage of mainstream media. For example, it made up a quarter of all news articles on Conservative Woman between 2015 and 2018, and during the 2017 General Election campaign the focus on professional journalism accounted for over four in ten articles. The Canary, meanwhile, covered the media in a fifth of news over four years and it accounted for a quarter of its coverage during the election campaign in 2017.

In terms of which parties were the focus of attention, the two main right-wing and left-wing parties – The Conservatives and Labour – made up 89% of all coverage about party politics. But the reporting of political parties was not entirely determined by whether alternative media were from either the right or left of the political spectrum. For example, while 45.3% of Skwawkbox articles with a party-political focus were from Labour, 54.5% of The Canary's content and 61.8% of Another Angry Voice's coverage focussed more on the Conservative Party. In other words, the reporting of political parties diverged across alternative online political media rather than following a uniform pattern.

To explore the tone of political coverage, every article was assessed according to whether it was either supportive of or critical about parties, after excluding all unclear or neutral items. Once again, a diverse pattern of coverage was identified as opposed to a uniform style of political reporting across alternative media sites. However, the content analysis did reveal that left-leaning sites were the most critical of political parties, especially Another Angry Voice (62.5%), The Canary (56.9%), and Evolve Politics (52.0%). By contrast, right-wing sites such as Breitbart London (17.0%) and Westmonster (25.7%) were the least critical. Very few stories could be described as being neutral in tone across right-wing and left-wing sites. Or, put another way, the agendas of alternative media were highly partisan, in particular on left-wing sites. For example, all stories characterised as positive by The Skwawkbox supported the Labour Party while 95.6% of The

Canary's critical coverage was focussed on the Conservative Party. Alternative right-wing sites, by contrast, did not follow a uniform pattern. While Breitbart London was more critical of the Conservatives than Labour, Westmonster and Conservative Woman were equally critical of the two main parties.

Overall, then, far from there being a shared editorial agenda of hyperpartisan news or agreed set of news values, alternative media sites in the UK exhibited a diverse range of characteristics that did not fit into any uniform categorisation. They can – following Holt et al.'s (2019) relational understanding of alternative media – be understood instead along a continuum, which may include an agenda that has a greater or lesser degree of partisan coverage or focus on attacking mainstream media. Based on this analysis of alternative online political media, typologies of sites in the UK were developed (McDowell-Naylor et al. 2021). They reflected four overlapping areas of editorial focus, which were further supported by a systematic analysis of content: these included political cycle specialists, (left-wing) electoral hyperpartisans, (right-wing) cultural partisans, and vernacular macro-blogs.

Political cycle specialists

Several sites, notably Guido Fawkes and The Skwawkbox, adopted reporting practices akin to professional journalists working at news organisations. Above all, they sought to set and influence the political agenda in real time across their social networks. Rather than reflecting a range of topics, they tended to routinely cover the day-to-day grind of party-political debates, publishing a steady-stream of short articles at speed, and making interventions into topical debates often played out on social media accounts, notably Twitter. These sites can be labelled *political cycle specialists* because they operate within the immediacy of professional news agendas, interacting with party-political debates, with the aim of shaping and reframing media elite opinions.

This can be reflected by the proportion of coverage that contained some form of news about party-political policies (see Table 2.4). Once again, there were editorial differences in focus between sites, with The Skwawkbox and Guido Fawkes, in most years, pursuing a relatively lite agenda of policy news, compared to The Canary and Breitbart, which often focussed on specific issues. Sites described as political cycle specialists, in this respect, were less interested in the machinations of policy debates and more on party-political agendas. For instance, The Skwawkbox obsessively covered the politics of the Labour Party while Guido Fawkes focussed on party politics more generally, such as reporting parliament and developments in legislation. On both sites, the editorial priorities were to break news first or deliver punchy commentary, rather than deep-dive into matters of policy detail. In doing so, there was often an infusion of news and comment, although both sites demarcated coverage that was deemed editorialising (an issue explored in Chapters 5 and 6 in the context of changing production values

TABLE 2.4 The percentage of news including policy information in UK alternative media sites between 2015 and 2018 (frequency in brackets)

Alternative media site	2015	2016	2017	2018	Total
Left-wing sites					
Another Angry Voice	100.0% (4)	50.0% (3)	28.6% (34)	42.9% (3)	32.4% (44)
Evolve Politics	–	54.5% (12)	44.6% (25)	39.1% (9)	45.1% (46)
Novara Media	33.1% (1)	42.9% (3)	60.0% (9)	50.0% (2)	51.7% (15)
The Canary	50.0% (31)	17.1% (18)	27.6% (116)	55.1% (76)	33.2% (241)
The Skwawkbox	–	16.1% (5)	42.4% (89)	3.4% (3)	29.5% (97)
Right-wing sites					
Breitbart	56.3% (76)	26.7% (36)	6.8% (18)	54.8% (51)	28.9% (181)
Conservative Woman	24.2% (8)	47.9% (23)	40.0% (44)	29.3% (22)	36.5% (97)
Guido Fawkes	11.5% (15)	16.9% (23)	9.0% (37)	13.3% (23)	11.5% (98)
Westmonster	–	–	23.6% (57)	49.7% (73)	33.4% (130)
Total	14.2% (135)	13.0% (123)	45.2% (429)	27.6% (262)	100.0% (949)

because of professionalising content and due to operating under external media regulation).

While Guido Fawkes put the editorial views in encircled red text, The Skwawkbox provided an on-screen box separated from 'news' page that focussed on political commentary. Taken together, these editorial features represent political cycle specialists, sites which largely focussed on responding in real-time to the news agenda and influencing live debates.

(Left-wing) Electoral hyperpartisans

The party-political agenda of many alternative media sites were one of their defining characteristics, representing the lion's share of routine coverage. As explored in Chapters Five and Six, the aim of most sites was to have a direct influence on political issues and debates, persuading users to think in a certain way and, during election times, to vote for a particular party consistent with the site's ideological views. The chapter's analysis showed both the production of content and the level of partisanship was enhanced during an election campaign. In other words, alternative political media in the UK were not operating at the margins of debates – which perhaps characterised alternative media in the past – but they strived to directly influence party-political electoral outcomes at key points in the electoral calendar. These sites can be labelled *electoral hyperpartisans*, a second type of category that defined their political ambitions and their impact on mainstream politics.

It was alternative left-wing sites, most strikingly The Canary and Evolve Politics, that best encapsulated a hyperpartisan incursion into electoral politics (c.f. Rae 2021). During the 2017 election campaign, these alternative media sites were far more critical than supportive of parties not consistent with their ideological convictions. They represented, in that sense, Rae's (2021) characterisation of hyperpartisanship, an editorial commitment ramped up during an election campaign. This marked them as somewhat distinctive from sites labelled political cycle specialists, which focussed more on the latest, breaking news about party politics. Sites such as The Canary and Evolve Politics produced not just an abundance of news that was ideologically supportive of their left-wing brand of politics but an uptick of opinion and commentary about party issues during an election campaign, including criticism of their political opponents.

But electoral hyperpartisans were also driven by the ideological agenda of their parties and the characters leading them. After a left-wing leader left the Labour Party in 2019, for example, sites such as The Canary and Evolve Politics did not compromise on their hyperpartisan credentials, but they did re-direct their anger against the new party and new leader who was condemned for following a centrist brand of politics. The hyperpartisan left-wing sites can also be seen as a corrective to partisan mainstream media sites, in particular the UK's tabloid press, which has largely pursued a right-wing agenda and supported Conservative Party leaders over recent elections (Deacon et al. 2019).

(Right-wing) Cultural partisans

While the typologies of new alternative political media has so far focussed on their political and electoral aims, some sites can be defined as *cultural partisans*. They did not have a central editorial focus on the 'humdrum' of party-political coverage driven by partisan interests. Instead, they pursued a more selective editorial agenda of topics that have a cultural bent rather than being in sync with political news cycles. These mainly reflected right-wing issues, such as supporting Brexit and criticising immigration. Sites defined as cultural partisans chose cultural issues they championed which superseded party-political agendas. They were often populist in tone, but not tied down by party-political baggage.

Two right-wing sites, Breitbart London and Westmonster, displayed these characteristics the most fully according to their news agenda, while Conservative Woman delivered more culturally partisan comment and commentary. Between these three sites, they also made up 80% of all immigration articles across the nine sites examined over time. Without the party-political loyalty, right-wing cultural partisans were critical of politicians pursuing policies from either a right-wing or left-wing perspective. Rather than following the political news cycle (political cycle specialists) or the latest party-political shenanigans (electoral hyperpartisans), their editorial focus was firmly rooted in cultural issues that reflected long-term interests and anxieties, which were a central motivation for establishing the alternative media sites. In sticking to an agenda rather than responding to the political cycle or adjusting to the temperature of political debates, cultural partisans ran the risk of being seen as irrelevant to audiences and operating at the margins of media power. Westmonster, for example, was an active and vocal supporter of Brexit, but by 2020 – once the UK had fully committed to exiting the European Union – the relatively new alternative site stopped publishing content.

Vernacular macro-blogs

Many new UK alternative media sites examined were news-heavy, promoting either specific issues, or making real-time interventions in political news cycles using their social media networks. But some sites focussed largely on comment-based articles, notably Another Angry Voice, but also The Skwawkbox and Guido Fawkes (particularly in the early years of the analysis) to a lesser degree. These sites did not pursue an editorially narrow focus, but addressed a range of anxieties and concerns about politics and cultural issues more generally. In doing so, they can be described as *vernacular macro-blogs*, which help characterise their broad, sometimes somewhat eccentric agenda, since they did not conform to a consistent editorial style. The focus on commentary perhaps explained their popularity on social media, which attracted lots of attention with articles shared widely across Facebook and Twitter. When the analysis was carried out, for example, Another Angry Voice had over 300,000 Facebook followers and was based around the personality of Yorkshireman Thomas G. Clarke, while Guido Fawkes described his platform as a "news site with a blog heritage" (cited in McDowell et al. 2022).

Continuities and changes in alternative media (2020–2021)

To assess whether the editorial focus of online political media had changed over time, a follow up study of a random selection of 240 articles was carried out across two different periods (October 2020 and April 2021). However, two sites were excluded from the original analysis (Another Angry Voice and Westmonster) because they no longer produced many articles. This was because the key issues they were championing between 2015 and 2018 – namely Jeremy Corbyn's electoral prospects and Brexit – were no longer high on the political agenda. Instead, Byline Times and UNN – a broadly centre-left site and a right-wing site, respectively – were included in the study because they had grown in prominence and their articles were being shared widely across social media networks. The follow up analysis also included new categories to develop a more nuanced picture of alternative media than the 2015–2018 study.

The analysis began by assessing the balance between news, commentary or analysis, or a hybrid mix of both, or other types of articles. Once again there was a wide divergence in editorial focus across the nine alternative media sites examined. Due to the inclusion of a hybrid category of news and opinion, the follow up study revealed a large majority of articles in two sites – The Skwawkbox and Guido Fawkes – mixed fact-based coverage with editorial commentary and analysis. For both The Canary and Conservative Woman, roughly a quarter of their articles were a mixture of opinion and news. The right-wing site, Breitbart, continued with its agenda of mostly news, while UNN was also predominately driven by fact-based stories. Novara Media stuck overwhelmingly to a limited supply of multimedia-based commentary and analysis, rather than routinely producing news. Finally, Conservative Woman, Guido Fawkes, and Canary included articles beyond news, opinion, or a mixture of both. For Conservative Woman, this was mostly satire, while for Guido Fawkes and The Skwawkbox, this included many announcements and event adverts, among other things. Taken together, the follow-up analysis showed alternative media sites displayed a degree of continuity with their focus on news, while several other sites blended news with editorial opinion and commentary. There were also no fixed patterns of editorial content across both right-wing and left-wing analysis. Or, put another way, the ideological perspectives of alternative media were not a precursor to understanding the format of their articles.

Beyond the style and format of news, the follow-up analysis examined whether the topics driving the news agenda continued or diverged since 2018. Above all, there was a dramatic drop in focus about reporting EU affairs, especially for the right-wing sites, while left-wing sites gave this topic very limited space. Given the political context changed between 2018 and 2020 – after a Conservative Party government with a pro-Brexit leader was elected – it was understandable why this issue slipped down the agenda. Many sites also pivoted to covering social affairs, particularly left-wing sites. These were wide ranging in focus, but broadly related to reporting social inequalities and injustices, such as in crime, politics, and the economy. Articles about party politics remained broadly consistent between 2015 and 2021, but the level of partisanship reduced due to the changing political environment.

To further evidence the diversity of alternative online political sites, there was a higher degree of articles categorised as 'other' issues, which reflected a wider editorial focus beyond the key focus of social affairs and party politics than between 2015 and 2018. Finally, there was a fall in stories about mainstream media. The next chapter is dedicated to exploring the editorial focus on mainstream media, in particular the BBC. The dip in focus about professional journalism could represent a development of their own unique agenda as well as response to the coronavirus pandemic as many people turned to mainstream media to understand the health crisis. Indeed, while Guido Fawkes mentioned COVID in over a third of its articles, the rest of the sites mentioned it in just over half of the stories examined. On Byline Times it made up nearly three-quarters of the articles examined. Many sites made a connection between party politics and ways of handling the pandemic, which were largely centred on the UK government's policy. Byline Times and Novara Media dedicated themselves to in-depth explorations of the pandemic, especially in relation to how the right-wing Conservative's government was dealing with it. While Guido Fawkes largely focussed on the process of policymaking, Breitbart and UNN aligned themselves with sceptics about lockdowns. In focussing so heavily on the pandemic, it meant alternative media did not focus to the same degree on opposing and challenging mainstream media coverage. Since 2021, news about the pandemic has reduced. In doing so, it can be observed that many alternative media sites have resumed their editorial focus on critiquing mainstream media and professional journalism, with the BBC once again the main target.

Understanding alternative media: reflecting and responding to changes in national media and political systems

While alternative media have long been studied, over recent years the fast-changing media and political environment has led to debates about reconceptualising how they are defined and understood. 'New' alternative media have been seen to represent a departure from 'old' media, with different formats, editorial aims, and ideological commitments. But while there has been a renewed scholarly interest in alternative media, the chapter began by arguing that more systematic and rigorous research is needed to assess the new generation of alternative online political media, including any changes in content over time. Most recent research has been qualitative in design and often focussed on the US media and political systems, which is exceptional and does not represent all Western media and political environments (as explored in Chapter 9). While there have been a few cross-national quantitative studies largely focussed on right-wing media, there has been limited comparative analysis of left-wing and right-wing alternative media.

Drawing on a UK-based case study, this chapter examined alternative online political media from right and left perspectives between 2015 and 2021. It assessed their editorial characteristics and whether they had changed over time. In doing so, a diverse range of editorial patterns was identified that could not easily fit into a uniform category of alternative media or a more precise term such as hyperpartisan media (Rae 2021). Nonetheless, four overlapping typologies were developed that helped characterise their content, including their comparative style, format, and editorial aims. The systematic and comparative research demonstrated the different editorial agendas between and within right-wing and left-wing sites, such as the contrasting balance between opinion and news. Over time, this blurred somewhat into a hybrid mix of reporting and commentary, although several sites labelled their coverage as either news or comment. In this sense, alternative online political media cannot be crudely characterised as fixed or static sites but fluid and dynamic, shifting in content, style, and format, and responding to the vicissitudes of national media and political systems.

The changes identified in new alternative online political media were not isolated from mainstream politics or professional journalism but intrinsically tied to their developments. For example, after the 2019 election campaign left-wing alternative online sites began to focus more critically on a new left-wing Labour Party leader because of a perceived shift to the centre-ground of politics. Meanwhile, the right-wing site, Westmonster, which ardently championed Brexit, stopped producing content in 2020 after the UK had formally passed legislation to exit the European Union. In other words, once mainstream party-politics and the political agenda had changed in character, new alternative online political media responded according to their own editorial needs and ambitions. Moreover, similarities were observed in how mainstream media and new alternative online political media operated. For instance, political cycle specialists functioned like many legacy news organisations, producing copy at speed and promoting it heavily across social media accounts to intervene in mainstream media debates. Meanwhile, electoral partisans echoed many of the characteristics of tabloid media by their highly critical and partisan attacks on parties and leaders they opposed in order to achieve specific party-political and parliamentary ambitions.

But more empirical research is needed to understand how the current generation of alternative online political media construct themselves within mainstream media systems, including how they editorially operate across social media platforms, as well as how they convey their alternativeness to professional journalism. The next two chapters address these new lines of inquiry. Chapter 3 analyses how alternative media have been using social media networks to achieve their editorial aims, drawing on the latest scholarship and one of the largest studies to date to examine how alternative media in the UK were using Twitter to communicate their content. Chapter 4 then considers how alternative media portrayed mainstream media and professional journalism.

References

Atton, C. (2002) *Alternative Media*. Thousand Oaks: Sage Publications.

Benkler, Y. Faris, R. Roberts, H. and Zuckerman, E. (2017) 'Study: Breitbart-led right-wing media ecosystem altered broader media agenda', *Columbia Journalism Review*, March 3, https://www.cjr.org/analysis/breitbart-media-trump-harvard-study.php

Couldry, N. and Curran, J. (2003) *Contesting Media Power: Alternative Media in a Networked World*. Lanham and Oxford: Rowan and Littlefield.

Deacon, D. Goode, J. Smith, D. Wring, D. Downey, J. and Vaccari, C. (2019) Report 5: 7 November – 11 December 2019, https://www.lboro.ac.uk/news-events/general-election/report-5/

Downing, J.D.H., Ford, T.V., Gil, G. and Stein, L. (2001) *Radical Media: Rebellious Communication and Social Movements*. Thousand Oaks: SAGE Publications.

Heft, A., Mayerhöffer, E., Reinhardt, S., and Knüpfer, C. (2019) Beyond breitbart: Comparing right-wing digital news infrastructures in six western democracies. *Policy & Internet*, Vol. 12(1): 20–45, https://doi.org/10.1002/poi3.219

Heft, A., Knüpfer, C., Reinhardt, S. and Mayerhöffer, E. (2021) Toward a transnational information ecology on the right? Hyperlink networking among right-wing digital news sites in Europe and the United States. *The International Journal of Press/Politics*, Vol.26(2): 313–519, https://doi.org/10.1177/19401612209636

Holt, K. Figenschou, T.U. and Frischlich, L. (2019) 'Key dimensions of alternative news media', *Digital Journalism*, Vol.7(7): 860–869, https://doi.org/10.1080/21670811.2019.1625715

McDowell-Naylor, D., Cushion, S. and Thomas, R. (2021) 'A typology of alternative online political media in the United Kingdom: A longitudinal content analysis (2015–2018)', *Journalism*, https://doi.org/10.1177/14648849211059585

McDowell-Naylor, D., Cushion, S., Thomas, R. (2022) 'The role of alternative online political media in the 2019 general election'. In: Wring, D., Mortimore, R., Atkinson, S. (eds) *Political Communication in Britain*. Cham: Palgrave Macmillan, https://doi.org/10.1007/978-3-030-81406-9_12

Newman, N., Fletcher, R. Kalogeropoulos, A. and Kleis, R.N. (2019) *Reuters Institute Digital News Report 2019*, http://www.digitalnewsreport.org/survey/2019/overview-key-findings-2019/.

Nygaard, S. (2019) 'The appearance of objectivity: How immigration-critical alternative media report the news', *Journalism Practice*, 13(10): 1147–1163.

Rae, M. (2021) 'Hyperpartisan news: Rethinking the media for populist politics', *New Media & Society*, Vol. 23(5): 875–1338, https://doi.org/10.1177/1461444820910416

Roberts, J. and Wahl-Jorgensen, K. (2021) 'Breitbart's attacks on mainstream media: Victories, victimhood, and vilification', *Affective Politics of Digital Media: Propaganda by Other Means*, edited by M. Boler and E. Davis. London: Routledge.

Schulze, H. (2020) 'Who uses right-wing alternative online media? An exploration of audience characteristics', *Politics and Governance*, Vol. 8(3): 6–18.

Thomas, R. and Cushion, S. (2019) 'Towards an institutional news logic of digital native news media? A case study of buzzfeed's reporting during the 2015 and 2017 UK General Election Campaigns', *Digital Journalism*, Vol. 7(10): 1328–1345, https://doi.org/10.1080/21670811.2019.1661262

Thompson, J. and Hawley, G. (2021) 'Does the Alt-Right still matter? An examination of Alt-Right influence between 2016 and 2018', *Nations and Nationalism*, Vol. 27(4): 1165–1180.

Waterson, J. (2017) 'The rise of the alt-left british media', *Buzzfeed*, May 6, https://www.buzzfeed.com/jimwaterson/the-rise-of-the-alt-left

3
HOW ALTERNATIVE ONLINE POLITICAL MEDIA USE SOCIAL MEDIA

Social media represent an intrinsic part of most Western media environments. From Facebook to Twitter, Instagram to YouTube, WhatsApp to TikTok, they have become popular platforms that allow engagement with other people, sharing messages and pictures, while also accessing information and entertainment. In the US, a survey found seven in ten Americans regularly relied on social media, which has remained broadly stable between 2016 and 2021 (Pew 2021). Across the Western world, young people in particular turn to social media as part of their daily routines, while for older age groups their use is becoming normalised (Pew 2021). But social media are not only used to post pictures and videos or watch and share entertaining clips. Roughly half the population of the US and UK now use social media to access news and current affairs (Ofcom 2021; Pew 2021). Given the growing reliance on social media in the 21st century and their integration into the media landscape, recently launched alternative media in the last decade have been born into the age of social media and developed editorial content under their influence. But, as the previous chapters explored, there have been few systematic studies exploring the editorial character of alternative media over recent years, including how they tailor content and promote their output across social media platforms. When content studies have been carried out, the empirical focus has been almost exclusively on website content rather than anything posted on social media, such as Twitter, Facebook, YouTube, or Instagram.

This chapter will consider the few studies that have examined how alternative media use social media, identifying where more research is needed, such as developing more systematic, comparative, and longitudinal analysis. In doing so, it will also draw on studies examining the output of social media across mainstream news sites, interpreting how professional journalists use sites such as Twitter and

DOI: 10.4324/9781003360865-4

Facebook to post content and interact with other users. These findings will then be compared and contrasted to the main focus of this chapter – an original case study analysis of alternative media in the UK between 2015 and 2021 (Thomas and Cushion 2022). The analysis began by drawing on the first-ever large-scale content analysis of how UK alternative media sites used Twitter. This involved examining 14,807 tweets across nine right-wing and left-wing sites between 2015 and 2018. In order to identify any shifts in social media use after this four-year period, a smaller follow-up study of tweets was examined between 2020 and 2021. The findings will be interpreted in the context of wider international trends of social media use among alternative media. While social media is often invoked broadly, different sites operate with distinctive editorial functions and goals. This chapter primarily focusses on the use of Twitter and, to a lesser extent, Facebook because most research has been conducted using these social media platforms.

The use of social media in alternative and mainstream media

Professional journalism has been transformed by social media. Long-standing conventions and practices have been challenged by sites such as Twitter (Bentivegna and Marchetti 2018; Mellado and Hermida 2021). Since the social networking site was launched in 2008, the platform has been widely used by professional journalists to disseminate news and commentary (Canter 2015; Willnat and Weaver 2018; Molyneux and Mourão 2019). Political journalists, in particular, rely heavily on the site, accelerating the pace of the news cycle as reporters respond to events in near real time to produce newsworthy content (Chadwick 2017; Oschatz et al. 2021). It is a platform that allows journalists to instantly communicate, break news and set the agenda (Canter 2015; Chadwick 2017). Studies have shown journalists reconfiguring their news values to reflect debates played out on social media meaning their newsgathering practices have been in sync with Twitter (Enli and Simonsen 2018; McGregor and Molyneux 2020). Social media also enables interactive opportunities, allowing journalists the potential to directly engage with audiences, most prominently politicians and rival journalists. As journalists have cultivated their own identity over time and attracted a large number of followers on social media, they have used Twitter for their own promotional purposes and developed unique personal brands (Molyneux 2019).

But while Twitter offers the potential for more journalistic engagement with their audiences, research has suggested professional reporters largely follow what has been described as a one-directional "broadcast" approach (Hanusch and Bruns 2017: 40). This involves journalists disseminating their content to a mass of followers, but not developing posts that promote interaction or using the medium to engage with users responding to it. When journalists have engaged on social media, systematic studies of reporters' social media accounts have shown they largely interact with other journalists, politicians, or policy experts (Laor 2022; Lawrence et al. 2014). In other words, social media engagement of professional journalists tends to orbit around media and political elites, rather than ordinary users responding to or commenting upon tweets. Large content analyses of journalists' Twitter accounts have also highlighted an ideological bias and partisanship, with journalists operating in echo chambers and filter bubbles that reinforce their own views and perspectives (Mills et al. 2021). Overall, then, the use of social media has had an impact on mainstream media content, with Twitter widely used by journalists to navigate their way through the news cycle and disseminate news and commentary (Chadwick 2017). But, rather than fully utilise the interactive features of social media, research has shown that often Twitter engagement is largely one-way with journalists tweeting out their content to suit their own marketing and ideological perspectives. In doing so, this limits their correspondence to elites as opposed to 'ordinary' users.

This body of scholarship about the use of social media by professional journalists provides some context to interpreting how alternative media use sites such as Twitter to disseminate their content and engage with audiences. Alternative media sites launched a decade into the 21st century were born and grew up in the age of social media, including the many alternative media sites in the UK examined throughout this book. They can be described as "digital-born organisations" (Nicholls et al. 2018) or "digital media natives" (Hanusch and Bruns 2017; Thomas and Cushion 2019), producing and developing content that is purely designed for audiences to consume and engage with online. Sites such as BuzzFeed and the Huffington Post have been defined as digital media, but also alternative media by audiences (Rauch 2021). But their corporate ownership was at odds with the left-wing ethics of online political media analysed in most chapters of this book – an issue explored in Chapter 9. Bane's (2019) study comparing the use of Twitter among digital-born media and legacy mainstream media discovered important differences in how sources were referenced and quoted in social media. Drawing on a content analysis of over 3,000 articles in 2016 and 2017, the study found The New York Times and The Washington Post used Twitter to quote official sources and for opinion-based comments, whereas BuzzFeed and the Huffington Post drew on social media for fact-finding and to supply additional information and background. The study also revealed that while legacy media quoted official sources in three quarters of its tweets, for digital media it was approximately four in ten tweets. Overall, Bane (2019: 201) concluded that the comparative "data underscore fundamental differences in the way traditional and alternative web-only journalists operate".

But with more limited resources than corporate digital media sites such as BuzzFeed and Huffington Post, many alternative media contributors may have evolved from bloggers or "semi-professional or semi-amateur journalist-activist-experts" (Chadwick 2017: 214) and developed distinctive strategies to promote their content to achieve "viral distribution" (Lasorsa et al. 2012: 20). After all, most alternative media sites do not have the status, profile, and platform to attract large number of readers to their websites, but their social media accounts – including

Twitter – provided them with an opportunity to reach a significant audience if they can post material that will be liked or shared (Conte 2016; Manthorpe 2018; Waterson 2017).

But, as previous chapters have explored, new alternative media have a set of editorially distinctive values that deviate from how mainstream media operate. How they use social media, including Twitter, could diverge from how professional journalists operate given alternative media have long advocated a bottom-up rather than top-down approach to reporting, reflecting the needs and anxieties of ordinary people (Atton 2002; Downing 1984). This has historically been in contrast to commercial media which are seen to operate at a distance, serving the needs of political and media elites ahead of the public. But by relying on large social media companies with a corporate mindset to promote alternative media content, editorially some sites may feel politically compromised. This, as Gehl (2015: 1) has observed,

> leaves alternative media theory in a double-bind: social media allow for people to be producers, certainly more so than traditional media, but they are owned by for-profit firms who can be hostile to alternative ideas, discourses, and organizing—especially when those practices challenge corporate hegemony

In other words, social media have the power to help promote alternative media, creating a more level playing field than what traditional 20th-century gatekeeping allowed.

Of the few studies examining how alternative media have used social media in contrast to mainstream media, the differences appear relatively minor. First off, there have been very few systematic studies that have examined the editorial content of social media produced by new alternative media, including online political media, or even developed a comparative analysis with mainstream media. Of those that have, the focus has tended to be on Twitter and Facebook. So, for example, during the start of the coronavirus pandemic, Boberg et al. (2020) carried out a computational content analysis of German alternative political news media output on Facebook, measuring the reach, interactions, actors, and topics of every post, including whether sites were spreading 'fake news'. In doing so, they discovered that while alternative news media produced content ideologically consistent with their editorial aims and undermined coverage in mainstream media, they did not spread blatant disinformation about the health crisis. Their Facebook posts were ultimately a reflection of their website content. But in terms of the comparative production of content, their reach, and interaction on Facebook, Boberg et al. (2020) found that mainstream media posted three times more articles and received four times more likes per post than alternative media sites. When examining the multiple ways users could engage with Facebook content – including the number of likes, comments, emojis, and shares a post received – mainstream media had a quarter more interactions, on average, per post. However, Boberg et al. (2020: 7) concluded that while their

> analysis showed that even though the mainstream media outlets were dominating the overall information environment on Facebook, single posts by alternative news outlets reached a comparable number of interactions and shares to those published by mainstream outlets, indicating that these might have developed considerable impact in their respective audience group.

The spikes in social media engagement were related to content that the authors described as "pandemic populism" (Boberg et al. 2020: 1), such as sensationalist stories about the coronavirus being a man-made laboratory virus or COVID being like the flu. In other words, alternative media have the potential to reach mass audiences on social media and foster engagement, but this was often driven by populist posts.

Despite new alternative media being born into the social media age, the chapter so far has shown that there has been little research about how they use platforms such as Twitter and Facebook compared to mainstream media. There is, in short, limited evidence about whether alternative media use social media in ways that are distinctive from mainstream media. While research has shown alternative media do not produce the same quantity of social media content as mainstream media, at times their content can reach the same number of users (Boberg et al. 2020; Booth 2017; Waterson 2017). But to date, no study has explored the use of social media across alternative media sites longitudinally or comparatively or developed a detailed analysis of editorial content and interactions with users. This chapter offers an original UK case study of how alternative online political media used Twitter between 2015 and 2021.

The comparative use of Twitter in right-wing and left-wing alternative media sites in the UK (2015–2018)

This chapter draws on a study of social media use in right-wing and left-wing online alternative media, analysing 14,807 tweets on the main Twitter accounts of nine sites between 2015 and 2018 (Thomas et al. 2022). It examines the following periods: 6–25 October 2015, 9–29 October 2016, 30 April–7 June 2017 (the UK general election campaign), and 8–28 October 2018. As previous chapters have explained, this period of analysis was selected in order to track their development since many new sites launched in 2015 or 2016. The different sample dates and length of time in 2017 were due to analysing the whole six-week period during the UK's general election campaign. This represented a critical time when new alternative media sites attracted attention for their coverage and produced content that was often more widely shared than stories produced by mainstream media outlets (Waterson 2017).

Tweets were examined using Twitter's Full Archive Search AP. They were accessed using Twurl to collect JSON files and then subsequently converted into

Excel files that were then examined manually by three researchers. This represented all content produced on Twitter during the sample period, which resulted in analysing 9,284 standard tweets, 634 quote tweets, 1,443 reply tweets, and 3,446 retweets. As well as quantifying the number and each type of tweet, their reach, and interactions were also recorded (as of August 2019). The content analysis of tweets was subject to a robust inter-coder reliability test on 10% of the sample. It found all variables had a high level of reliability (Thomas et al. 2022).

Between 2015 and 2018, the content analysis discovered most alternative online political media social media accounts increased the number of tweets they produced (see Table 3.1). Skwawkbox barely tweeted in 2015 but regularly did in subsequent years. During the general election campaign in 2017, all sites – apart from the Conservative Woman – enhanced their use of Twitter, even after taking into account the longer period of analysis. For example, 89.6% of all tweets over a four-year period were in 2017 on Another Angry Voice's account, while it made up three quarters of their posts on Evolve Politics and Novara Media.

Table 3.2 shows that neither right-wing nor left-wing sites conformed to a uniform pattern in their use of Twitter. For example, while almost all tweets on Breitbart and Conservative Woman were standard tweets – as were nine in ten posts on The Canary's account – only 15.7% and 22.7% were on Another Angry Voice and Skwawkbox, respectively. While several sites heavily retweeted social media content, over half – 57.9% – of tweets produced by Another Angry Voice were quoted replies. The extent to which accounts replied to other users' tweets was also different across left-wing and right-wing sites. Right-wing sites were less likely to engage with users than left-wing sites. Conservative Woman did not reply to any Twitter messages, for instance, while Breitbart did once, and Westmonster

TABLE 3.1 The percentage of tweets produced by alternative media sites in the UK between 2015 and 2018 (frequency in brackets)

	2015	2016	2017	2018	Total
Left-wing sites					
Another Angry Voice	3.5% (17)	2.6% (13)	89.6% (441)	4.3% (21)	100.0% (492)
Evolve Politics	0.1% (1)	7.1% (60)	73.7% (622)	19.1% (161)	100.0% (844)
Novara Media	10.4% (64)	5.2% (32)	74.9% (463)	9.5% (59)	100.0% (618)
The Canary	22.7% (359)	12.4% (197)	33.7% (534)	31.2% (494)	100.0% (1,584)
The Skwawkbox	0.1% (3)	30.9% (913)	50.4% (1,485)	18.6% (547)	100.0% (2,948)
Right-wing sites					
Breitbart	23.1% (460)	18.8% (374)	37.8% (753)	20.4% (407)	100.0% (1,994)
Conservative Woman	5.2% (81)	17.0% (267)	32.2% (505)	45.5% (713)	100.0% (1,566)
Guido Fawkes	18.6% (677)	21.5% (771)	42.9% (1,537)	16.9% (605)	100.0% (3,580)
Westmonster	–	–	66.6% (787)	33.4% (394)	100.0% (1,181)
Total	11.2% (1,652)	17.7% (2,627)	48.1% (7,127)	22.9% (3,401)	100.0% (14,087)

TABLE 3.2 The percentage of the types of tweets produced by alternative media sites in the UK between 2015 and 2018 (frequency in brackets)

	Standard	Retweet	Quote	Reply	Total
Left-wing sites					
Another Angry Voice	15.7% (77)	22.6% (11)	57.9% (285)	3.9% (19)	100.0% (492)
Evolve Politics	37.9% (320)	42.5% (359)	2.3% (19)	17.3% (146)	100.0% (844)
Novara Media	75.3% (453)	20.1% (124)	2.8% (17)	3.9% (24)	100.0% (618)
The Canary	90.0% (1,426)	7.3% (115)	0.3% (4)	2.5% (39)	100.0% (1,584)
The Skwawkbox	22.7% (670)	54.0% (1,592)	4.0% (118)	19.3% (568)	100.0% (2,948)
Right-wing sites					
Breitbart London	99.7% (1,989)	0.2% (4)	–	0.1% (1)	100.0% (1,994)
Conservative Woman	99.4% (1,557)	0.6% (9)	–	–	100.% (1,566)
Guido Fawkes	60.0% (2,147)	16.9% (604)	5.3% (188)	17.9% (641)	100.0% (3,580)
Westmonster	54.6% (645)	44.7% (528)	0.3% (3)	0.4% (5)	100.0% (1,181)
Total	100.0% (9,284)	100.0% (3,446)	100.0% (634)	100.0% (1,443)	100.0% (14,807)

responded to posts on five occasions. By contrast, almost a fifth of all tweets produced by Skwawkbox, Evolve Politics, and Guido Fawkes were replies. Overall, though, replying to tweets – either in quotes or just directly – made up, for most sites, a relatively small proportion of social media content. Most alternative media sites relied largely on standard tweets and retweets.

In order to compare the use of social media content in more detail, the purpose of tweets was interpreted according to the following functions:

- to share content, e.g., links to articles, videos, and images produced by the outlet that is tweeting;
- to share content from other media publications;
- to share opinions, conjectures, speculations, viewpoints, hypotheses, and predictions;
- to share information, e.g., a fact, figure, report, announcement, or event;
- to share hominem, dismissive, inflammatory, sarcastic, insulting content aimed at others; and
- other purposes, including promoting individuals or organisations, appeals for subscribers, and running polls.

Table 3.3 shows a majority of alternative media – six out of nine sites – primarily relied on Twitter to link to their own website content. But three left-wing sites – Another Angry Voice, Skwawkbox, and Evolve Politics – used Twitter for other editorial purposes. For Another Angry Voice, above all, Twitter was used to express their opinions, while Evolve Politics posted content to attack others. Skwawkbox made use of Twitter in perhaps the most editorially diverse way by

TABLE 3.3 The percentage of the purpose of tweets on UK alternative media sites between 2015 and 2018 (frequency in brackets)

Alternative Media site	Link to own	Link other	Opinion	Info sharing	Attack	All other	Total
Left-wing sites							
Another Angry Voice	7.3% (36)	5.7% (28)	57.3% (282)	8.3% (41)	8.1% (40)	13.2% (65)	100.0% (492)
Evolve Politics	20.3% (171)	13.4% (113)	15.8% (133)	11.8% (100)	17.4% (147)	21.3% (180)	100.0% (844)
Novara Media	72.5% (448)	2.9% (18)	2.6% (16)	2.8% (17)	0.2% (1)	19.1% (118)	100.0% (618)
The Canary	84.4% (1,337)	6.8% (107)	4.0% (64)	1.6% (25)	0.1% (2)	3.1% (49)	100.0% (1,584)
The Skwawkbox	21.8% (643)	7.5% (221)	20.6% (608)	13.8% (408)	13.8% (407)	22.5% (661)	100.0% (2,948)
Right-wing sites							
Breitbart	94.6% (1,886)	–	3.0% (59)	2.1% (41)	0.1% (2)	0.3% (6)	100.0% (1,994)
Conservative Woman	95.5% (1495)	0.3% (5)	0.1% (2)	4.0% (63)	–	0.1% (1)	100.0% (1,566)
Guido Fawkes	61.2% (2,191)	3.3% (118)	6.9% (248)	11.5% (410)	2.9% (105)	14.2% (508)	100.0% (3,580)
Westmonster	82.3% (973)	0.1% (1)	11.8% (139)	3.4% (40)	0.3% (4)	2.0% (24)	100.0% (1,181)
Total	62.0% (9,180)	4.1% (611)	10.5% (1,551)	7.7% (1,145)	4.8% (708)	10.9% (1,612)	100.0% (14,807)

not only linking to its own material, but other media publications too, as well as sharing information, attacking users, offering opinions, and for more idiosyncratic purposes.

But despite there being, once again, a lack of uniformity across the social media accounts of alternative media, most sites conformed to a fairly standard approach of linking to their own content. As explored earlier in the chapter, this broadly reflects the way mainstream news media accounts have historically used Twitter, promoting their own articles and limiting their engagement with users.

The final part of the content analysis study examined the tone of tweets. It first assessed whether alternative media sites were conventionally partisan by largely criticising political parties opposite to their perspectives (e.g., right-wing sites being negative about the Labour Party and left-wing sites being negative about the Conservative Party). While these parties do not represent the full ideological perspective of political debates, they reflect the vast majority of tweets expressing a political sentiment by alternative media. Analysing the tone of their tweets can therefore provide an insight into how they cover politics, which – as Chapter 2 explored – have been described as "hyperpartisan" (Rae 2021: 875).

Unsurprisingly, Table 3.4 shows right-wing sites were more negative than positive about a left-wing party, while left-wing sites were more negative than positive about a right-wing party. In that sense, the use of social media was broadly consistent with the ideological position of each site. However, that interpretation alone does not fully reflect the political tone of social media use among all alternative media sites. For example, while right-wing sites were rarely positive about the Labour Party, they were, at times, highly critical of the Conservatives. A majority of tweets by Conservative Woman – 57.8% – were critical of the UK's main right-wing party. To a lesser degree, other right-wing sites' support for the Conservatives was more tentative than left-wing sites were for Labour. This reflects the political context, which shaped the tonal support of parties. As the previous chapters acknowledged, throughout this period of time, the Labour Party had a left-wing leader, Jeremy Corbyn, who was ideologically aligned with many new left alternative political sites. The Conservative Party, by contrast, had a more centrist leader who did not support Brexit, which many more partisan right-wing sites championed, especially Conservative Woman and Westmonster. This largely explained their criticism of the party on social media.

Given many new alternative media sites defined their identity by an opposition to mainstream media, the final part of the analysis examined the tone towards professional journalism on social media. Table 3.5 reveals every sentiment expressed when a tweet referred to the mainstream media (or via a specific journalist), a media organisation, or more generic references, such as 'the UK media'.

The majority of tweets about mainstream media – 59.1% – were neither positively nor negatively portrayed. But this still meant that well over a third of tweets – 37.9% – were critical, in some way, of professional journalism. Once again, there

TABLE 3.4 The percentage of the political tone of tweets on UK alternative media sites between 2015 and 2018 (frequency in brackets)

Alternative media sites	Party focus	Positive	Negative	Neutral	Unclear	Total
Left-wing sites						
Another Angry Voice	Labour	56.7% (38)	6.0% (4)	32.8% (22)	4.5% (3)	100.0% (67)
Another Angry Voice	Conservative	–	87.7% (157)	10.6% (19)	1.7% (3)	100.% (179)
Evolve Politics	Labour	68.7% (180)	5.7% (15)	23.7% (62)	1.9% (5)	100.0% (262)
Evolve Politics	Conservative	0.2% (1)	91.5% (399)	8.0% (35)	0.2% (1)	100.0% (436)
Novara Media	Labour	25.4% (18)	5.6% (4)	62.0% (44)	7.0% (5)	100.0% (71)
Novara Media	Conservative	4.7% (3)	82.8% (53)	9.4% (6)	3.1% (2)	100.0% (64)
The Canary	Labour	42.6% (115)	10.0% (27)	46.3% (125)	1.1% (3)	100.0% (270)
The Canary	Conservative		87.9% (589)	11.0% (74)	1.0% (7)	100.0% (670)
The Skwawkbox	Labour	52.3% (626)	18.8% (225)	26.9% (322)	1.9% (23)	100.0% (1,196)
The Skwawkbox	Conservative	0.1% (1)	85.4% (920)	12.9% (139)	1.5% (17)	100.0% (1,077)
Right-wing sites						
Breitbart London	Labour	–	60.3% (38)	31.7% (20)	7.9% (5)	100.0% (63)
Breitbart London	Conservative	1.9% (4)	34.1% (72)	60.1% (127)	3.8% (8)	100.0% (211)
Conservative Woman	Labour	–	82.9% (116)	10.7% (15)	6.4% (9)	100.0% (140)
Conservative Woman	Conservative	19.0% (40)	57.8% (121)	19.0% (40)	4.3% (9)	100.0% (210)
Guido Fawkes	Labour	0.8% (9)	58.7% (680)	39.8% (461)	0.8% (9)	100.0% (1,159)
Guido Fawkes	Conservative	4.3% (40)	27.3% (254)	66.7% (619)	1.6% (15)	100.0% (928)
Westmonster	Labour	1.8% (3)	68.6% (116)	28.4% (48)	1.2% (2)	100.0% (169)
Westmonster	Conservative	11.4% (54)	40.8% (194)	46.7% (222)	1.1% (5)	100.0% (475)
Total	Labour	29.1% (989)	36.1% (1,225)	32.9% (1,119)	1.9% (64)	100.0% (3,397)
Total	Conservative	3.4% (143)	64.9% (2,759)	30.1% (1,281)	1.6% (67)	100.0% (4,250)

TABLE 3.5 Percentage of tweets referencing mainstream media on UK alternative media sites between 2015 and 2018 (frequency in brackets)

Alternative media sites	Positive	Negative	Neutral	Unclear	Total
Left-wing sites					
Another Angry Voice	3.2% (2)	72.6% (45)	22.6% (14)	1.6% (1)	100.0% (62)
Evolve Politics	4.9% (13)	35.2% (94)	59.9% (160)	–	100.0% (267)
Novara Media	5.6% (3)	44.4% (24)	46.3% (25)	3.7% (2)	100.0% (54)
The Canary	5.6% (21)	59.3% (224)	32.8% (124)	2.4% (9)	100.0% (378)
The Skwawkbox	5.2% (41)	36.6% (290)	56.3% (446)	1.9% (15)	100.0% (792)
Right-wing sites					
Breitbart London	–	40.3% (31)	57.1% (44)	2.6% (2)	100.0% (77)
Conservative Woman	2.2% (6)	48.6% (135)	47.1% (131)	2.2% (6)	100.0% (278)
Guido Fawkes	5.5 (27)	22.4% (110)	71.1% (349)	1.0% (5)	100.0% (491)
Westmonster	1.5% (1)	46.3% (31)	50.7% (34)	1.5% (1)	100.0% (67)
Total	2.0% (114)	37.9% (984)	59.1% (1,327)	1.1% (41)	100.0% (2,466)

was some variation in the degree of hostility towards mainstream media, with left-wing sites generally more critical than right-wing sites. Above all, Another Angry Voice and The Canary stood out with 72.6% and 59.3%, respectively, including negative tweets about professional journalism. Table 3.5 also revealed there was very little positive sentiment towards mainstream media when alternative media tweeted on social media.

How the changing political environment shapes social media content (2020–2021)

In order to explore whether UK alternative media had changed their social media use over time, a follow-up study was carried out in three periods in April 2020 and April and October 2021. A random sample of 50 tweets from eight left-wing and right-wing alternative sites' main accounts was selected, which amounted to analysing an additional 2,400 social media posts in total. As the previous chapter explained, the sample for the follow-up study of alternative online political media sites was revised because of a lack of editorial content by some sites after 2020 (e.g. Another Angry Voice and Westmonster) while new outlets had become more prominent (e.g., a left-wing site, Byline Times and a right-wing site, Unity News Network). While Byline Times has been classified as a left-wing site, it does not pursue a partisan party-centric agenda but tends to select stories focussed on liberal issues.

The analysis of Twitter throughout 2020 and 2021 found alternative media sites followed broadly the same pattern of social media use as they did from 2015 to

TABLE 3.6 The percentage of types of tweets posted by UK alternative media sites in 2020 and 2021

Alternative media site	Standard tweet	Quote tweet	Reply tweet	Total
Left-wing sites				
Byline Times	69.3% (104)	1.3% (2)	29.3% (44)	100.0% (150)
Novara Media	86.0% (129)	6.0% (9)	8.0% (12)	100.0% (150)
The Canary	96.7% (145)	1.3% (2)	2.0% (3)	100.0% (150)
The Skwawkbox	74.7% (112)	14.7% (22)	10.7% (16)	100.0% (150)
Unity News Network	93.0% (140)	2% (3)	4.7% (7)	100.0% (150)
Right-wing sites				
Breitbart London	100.0% (150)	–	–	100.0% (150)
Conservative Woman	98.7% (148)	0.7% (1)	0.7% (1)	100.0% (150)
Guido Fawkes	72.7% (109)	6.7% (10)	20.7% (31)	100.0% (150)
Unity News Network	93.0% (140)	2% (3)	4.7% (7)	100.0% (150)
Total	86.4% (1,037)	4.1% (49)	9.5% (114)	100.0% (1,200)

2018. But there was more uniformity with standard tweets making up the vast majority of social media content (see Table 3.6). The Skwawkbox and, to a lesser degree, Novara and Guido Fawkes used quote tweets in their social media content. Byline times stood out for replying to other users – representing 29.3% of tweets – followed by Guido Fawkes at 20.7%.

In order to explore the level of interaction on social media content produced by new alternative media sites, metrics including retweets, likes, and quote replies were examined. Two salient themes emerged. First, most of the time, social media interactions on alternative media accounts were low. They often attracted tens of engagements rather than 100s or even 1,000s of interactions. Second, some sites produced content that went viral, most consistently Novara Media and Guido Fawkes. For example, in April 2020 Guido Fawkes posted a quote tweet about a BBC documentary favouring left-wing politics: "We looked into the interviewees on #Panorama last night. Every single one of them was a pro-Labour activist before the pandemic. Every single one. It was a party political broadcast on behalf of the Labour Party". It had 11,949 interactions, 6,755 likes, and 3,442 replies. More broadly, Guido Fawkes's reliance on quote tweets garnered attention by provocatively raising questions or engaging with users in order to generate responses.

In terms of the purpose of tweets, consistent with the 2015 to 2018 analysis the majority of tweets across all sites focussed on promoting articles from their websites (see Table 3.7). This made up 78.1% of all tweets, with only two left-wing sites – the Skwawkbox and Byline Times – slight outliers with just over half of all tweets linking to their articles. As they did between 2015 and 2018, Skwawkbox often linked to other media content, shared information, and promoted other individuals and organisations. Meanwhile, Byline Times often tweeted appeals for support and also promoted activities of others rather than their own content. The

TABLE 3.7 The percentage of the purpose of tweets on UK alternative media sites between 2020 and 2021 (frequency in brackets)

Alternative media site	Link to own content	Link to other content	Opinion	Info sharing	Promotion	Appeal for support	Addressing followers	Attack	Other	Total
Left-wing sites										
Byline Times	52.7% (79)	2.7% (4)	1.3% (2)	0.7% (1)	2.7% (4)	15.3% (23)	–	–	24.7% (37)	100.0% (150)
Novara Media	75.3% (113)	1.3% (2)	0.7% (1)	4.0% (6)	14.7% (22)	0.7% (1)	–	–	3.3% (5)	100.0% (150)
The Canary	93.3% (140)	–	3.3% (5)	1.3% (2)	–	–	1.3% (2)	–	0.7% (1)	100.0% (150)
The Skwawkbox	58.7% (88)	8.0% (12)	11.3% (17)	5.3% (8)	3.3% (5)	–	–	–	13.3% (20)	100.0% (150)
Right-wing sites										
Breitbart London	100.0% (150)	–	–	–	–	–	–	–	–	100.0% (150)
Conservative Woman	98.87% (148)	–	0.7% (1)	0.7% (1)	–	–	–	–	–	100.0% (150)
Guido Fawkes	70.7% (106)	–	8.0% (12)	6.0% (9)	1.3% (2)	0.7% (1)	–	2.0% (3)	11.3% (17)	100.0% (150)
Unity News Network	75.3% (113)	1.3% (2)	3.3% (5)	4.0% (6)	8.7% (13)	3.3% (5)	1.3% (2)	–	2.7% (4)	100.0% (150)
Total	78.1% (937)	1.7% (20)	3.6% (43)	2.8% (33)	3.8% (46)	2.5% (30)	0.3% (4)	0.3% (3)	7.0% (84)	100% (1,200)

site's tweets early on in April 2020 often lacked any real editorial direction with user interactions and often amounted to little more than saying 'thanks' or updating followers that their site was still under development. By October 2021 they began to tweet more conventionally, mostly to promote their own website material.

Another contrast to prevailing trends, in 2020 and 2021, there were almost no tweets attacking other users, with just three identified across the entire sample. This suggests alternative media have become less volatile on social media over time, and more standardised or even professionalised in their use of Twitter. This observation is explored further in Chapters 5 and 6 in interviews with editors and contributors.

In order to explore whether the degree of partisanship had been enhanced or not since 2018, every tweet was examined to assess whether it featured no criticism or it expressed some criticism towards either the main right-wing party, The Conservatives, or the main left-wing party, or general references to "the establishment" or politicians in general (see Table 3.8).

Across both right and left-wing sites, direct criticism of political parties on social media fell between 2018 and 2021. A large majority of tweets – in fact almost all of them for right-wing sites – did not feature criticism of Labour, Conservatives, or general references to politicians or the political class. It can also be observed that – unlike between 2015 and 2018 – many of the criticisms towards parties were not left-wing sites opposing the main right-wing party or right-wing sites opposing the main left-wing party. Put simply, the degree of partisanship on social media significantly reduced between 2018 and 2021. Two

TABLE 3.8 The percentage degree of partisanship in tweets produced by UK alternative media between 2020 and 2021 (frequency in brackets)

Alternative media site	None	Labour	Conservative Party	General critical reference	Total
Left-wing sites					
Byline Times	84.0% (126)	–	16.0% (24)	–	100.0% (150)
Novara Media	75.3% (113)	12.0% (18)	12.0% (18)	0.7% (1)	100.0% (150)
The Canary	74.7% (112)	4.0% (6)	21.3% (32)	–	100.0% (150)
The Skwawkbox	66.0% (99)	12.7% (19)	21.3% (32)	–	100.0% (150)
Right-wing sites					100.0% (150)
Breitbart London	96.0% (144)	2.0% (3)	2.0% (3)	–	100.0% (150)
Conservative Woman	93.3% (140)	0.7% (1)	6.0% (9)	–	100.0% (150)
Guido Fawkes	76.0% (114)	17.3% (26)	5.3% (8)	1.3% (2)	100.0% (150)
Unity Network	95.3% (143)	0.7% (1)	4.0% (6)	–	100.0% (150)
Total	82.6% (991)	6.2% (74)	11.0% (132)	0.3% (3)	100.0% (1,200)

reasons could explain this. First, as Chapter 2 acknowledged, the UK's political environment changed in this period. A more centrist figure, Kier Starmer, was now leading the Labour Party rather than Jeremy Corbyn, who was ideologically aligned with many left-wing sites. This meant left-wing sites were focussed more on opposing his party agenda than between 2015 and 2018, and less centred on criticising the Conservatives. Similarly, after the 2019 general election, the right-wing government finally passed legislation to exit the European Union. This meant Brexit was not high on the agenda, perhaps explaining the relatively limited focus on the Conservative Party on right-wing sites. Put in broader terms, the changing political context had reshaped the use of Twitter by alternative media. But there was a second reason why social media content may have changed over time. As explored in the following two chapters, alternative media sites have become increasingly professionalised in their editorial processes. It may follow that their focus was on promoting articles from websites – in the form of standard tweets as the study found – rather than tweeting ideological attacks on political parties.

Finally, the follow-up study assessed whether criticism of mainstream media was as prominent on alternative media social media accounts as it was between 2015 and 2018. Overall, a drop in criticism towards mainstream media was identified. With the exception of Unity News Network (which was not part of the 2015 and 2018 study), approximately 95% of tweets did not contain any criticism towards mainstream media. Of the few that did, most related to generalised criticism towards the mainstream media rather than specific organisations. When they were directed to specific outlets, above all it was the BBC that was singled out for its questionable journalistic standards. As discussed in the previous chapter, the fall in coverage towards mainstream media was influenced by the heavy focus on the pandemic, which dominated the editorial agenda during the follow-up analysis. Post-pandemic many alternative media sites have re-focussed their attention on mainstream media and professional journalism.

Towards a mainstreaming of social media use in alternative media

Just as social media have become an intrinsic part of how mainstream news and professional journalists routinely operate, this chapter has shown how alternative media have embraced sites such as Twitter, regularly tweeting out their editorial content. Given most alternative media were born in the age of social media, they appear to have adapted their editorial practices to promote content and enhance their influence in mainstream political debates. But there have been few systematic studies examining how social media has been used by alternative media over recent years or how they compare with the practices of mainstream media. Of the few studies exploring social media use, the focus has been on website content rather than output posted on social media platforms, such as Twitter, Facebook, YouTube, or Instagram.

This chapter drew on an original UK case study of how new alternative media sites used Twitter between 2015 and 2021. On the face of it, it showed there was little conformity in how alternative media used social media. By sheer quantity alone, sites such as Another Angry Voice tweeted just 492 times between 2015 and 2018, whereas Guido Fawkes did so seven times more with 3,580 posts on Twitter over four years. Moreover, while standard tweets accounted for 99% of social behaviour on Breitbart and Conservative Woman, for Another Angry Voice it made up less than a fifth of posts. More generally, there were contrasting levels of partisanship and criticism of mainstream media displayed on social media. But by 2020 and 2021, most alternative media sites followed a relatively uniform pattern of social media use. They almost exclusively used standard tweets linked to their own website content, had limited engagement with other users, and were less hostile towards political parties and mainstream media. When professional journalism was tweeted about, above all, the BBC bore the brunt of most criticism.

The chapter argued that the homogeneity of social content was partly a response to the changing political environment given the shifting ideological directions of the main left-wing and right-wing parties. But, as the later chapters consider in more depth, the more uniform approach to social media may also be a reflection of many sites becoming professionalised. After all, over recent years there appears to be a shared editorial logic shaping how most alternative media sites used social media. The outliers, at least in the initial analysis between 2015 and 2018, were Another Angry Voice, The Skwawkbox, and Guido Fawkes. But, as explored in Chapters Five and Six, these sites are largely reliant on individuals than a larger editorial team to develop their content, including in the use of Twitter. The Skwawkbox, for example, is run by Steve Walker and Another Angry Voice by Thomas G. Clark, while Guido Fawkes is closely associated with journalist Paul Staines. In other words, individuals rather than editorial teams may not be as susceptible to replicating the same practices as mainstream media because they exercise more control and autonomy.

More broadly, it can be observed that the editorial direction of alternative media on social media was aligned with how mainstream news organisations have used Twitter. The organising models and frameworks of legacy media, which have broadly been labelled "social media logics" (van Dijck and Poell 2013), "Twitter logics" (Olausson 2017), or even the "broadcast model" (Liang et al. 2019), echo many of the practices of alternative media. By adopting a traditional, one-directional "broadcast" approach in Twitter use (Hanusch and Bruns 2017: 40), alternative online media sites have broadly replicated many of the same practices and conventions of social media use as mainstream media (see Holcomb and Mitchell 2011). Or, put another way, their social media use today is not particularly 'alternative' to mainstream media accounts. This contrasts with claims that the use of new technologies among alternative media represents "rebellious" (Harlow and Harp 2013:42) or "innovative" (Lee 2005: 12) practices on Twitter given they reproduce rather than deviate from how legacy news editorially function. The acceptance of traditional journalistic norms by new alternative media challenges any claims there are clear editorial boundaries between mainstream and alternative journalism (Nygaard 2019). In other words, since some alternative media sites used Twitter in broadly the same way as legacy news outlets, the lines between what is considered 'alternative' and 'mainstream' media appear to be blurring. This arguably represents a mainstreaming of alternative media, a shift towards professionalised practices and standards of professional journalism.

Chapters 5 and 6 explore the professionalisation of alternative media by considering the routine production of content, including the use of social media. But first the next chapter considers how alternative media portray mainstream media and critique professional journalists, which represents a central part of their editorial agenda.

References

Atton, C. (2002) *Alternative Media*. Thousand Oaks: Sage Publications.

Bane, K.C. (2019) 'Tweeting the agenda', *Journalism Practice*, Vol. 13(2): 191–205, https://doi.org/10.1080/17512786.2017.1413587

Bentivegna, S. and Marchetti, R. (2018) 'Journalists at a crossroads: Are traditional norms and practices challenged by twitter?', *Journalism*, Vol. 19(2): 270–290, https://doi.org/10.1177/1464884917716594

Boberg, S., Quandt, T., Schatto-Eckrodt, T. and Frischlich, L. (2020) 'Pandemic populism: Facebook pages of alternative news media and the corona crisis: A computational content analysis', *arXiv preprint arXiv:2004.02566*.

Booth, R. (2017) 'DIY political websites: New force shaping the general election debate', *The Guardian*, 1st June, https://www.theguardian.com/politics/2017/jun/01/diy-political-websites-new-force-shaping-general-election-debate-canary

Canter, L. (2015) 'Personalised tweeting', *Digital Journalism*, Vol. 3(6): 888–907, https://doi.org/10.1080/21670811.2014.973148

Chadwick, A. (2017) *The Hybrid Media System: Politics and Power*. Oxford: Oxford University Press.

Conte, M.L. (2016) 'How a pro-corbyn viral website with a pay-per-click business model is taking over social media', *BuzzFeed News*, https://www.buzzfeed.com/marieleconte/the-rise-of-the-canary

Downing, J. (1984) *Radical Media: The Political Experience of Alternative Communication*. Boston: South End Press.

Enli, G. and Simonsen, C.A. (2018) '"Social media logic" meets professional norms: twitter hashtags usage by journalists and politicians', *Information, Communication and Society*, Vol. 21 (8): 1081–1096, https://doi.org/10.1080/1369118X.2017.1301515

Gehl, R.W. (2015) 'The case for alternative social media', *Social Media + Society*, Vo.1(2), https://doi.org/10.1177/2056305115604338

Hanusch, F., and Bruns, A. (2017) 'Journalistic Branding on Twitter', *Digital Journalism*, Vol. 5 (1): 26–43, https://doi.org/10.1080/21670811.2016.1152161

Harlow, S. and Harp, D. (2013) 'Alternative media in a digital era: Comparing news and information use among activists in the United States and Latin America', *Comunicacion y Sociedad*, Vol. 26: 25–51.

Holcomb, J. and Mitchell, A. (2011) 'How mainstream media outlets use twitter', Pew Research Center, https://www.pewresearch.org/journalism/2011/11/14/how-mainstream-media-outletsuse-twitter/

Laor, T. (2022) 'Twitter as a clique: Journalists' patterns of Twitter use in Israel', *Online Information Review*, Vol. 46(1): 40–58, https://doi.org/10.1108/OIR-07-2020-0324

Lasorsa, D.L., Lewis, S.C. and Holton, A.E. (2012) 'Normalizing twitter', *Journalism Studies*, Vol. 13 (1): 19–36, https://doi.org/10.1080/1461670X.2011.571825

Lawrence, R.G. Molyneux, L. Coddington, M. and Holton, A. (2014) 'Tweeting conventions', *Journalism Studies*, Vol.15(6): 789–806, https://doi.org/10.1080/1461670X.2013.836378

Lee, T. (2005) *Online Media and Civil Society in the "New" Singapore.* Murdoch, WA: Murdoch University. Asia Research Centre, Murdoch University.

Liang, H., Fung, I.C.-H., Tse, Z.T.H., Yin, J., Chan, C.-H., Pechta, L.E., Smith, B.J., et al. (2019) 'How did ebola information spread on twitter: Broadcasting or viral spreading?', *BMC Public Health*, https://doi.org/10.1186/s12889-019-6747-8.

Manthorpe, R. (2018) 'The UK's left is scrambling to adapt to Facebook's algorithm change', 20th March. *Wired UK*.

McGregor, S.C. and Molyneux, L. (2020) 'Twitter's influence on news judgment: An experiment among journalists', *Journalism*, Vol. 21(5): 597–613, https://doi.org/10.1177/1464884918802975

Mellado, C. and Hermida, A. (2021) 'The Promoter, Celebrity, and Joker Roles in Journalists' Social Media Performance', *Social Media + Society*, 7(1), https://doi.org/10.117/2056305121990643

Mills, T. Mullan, K. and Fooks, G. (2021) 'Impartiality on platforms: The politics of BBC journalists' twitter networks', *Journalism Studies*, Vol. 22(1): 22–41, https://doi.org/10.1080/1461670X.2020.1852099

Molyneux, L. (2019) 'A personalized self-image: Gender and branding practices among journalists', *Social Media + Society*, Vol. 5: 3, https://doi.org/10.1177/2056305119872950

Molyneux, L. and Mourão, R.R. (2019) 'Political journalists' normalization of twitter', *Journalism Studies*, Vol. 20(2): 248–266, https://doi.org/10.1080/1461670X.2017.1370978

Nicholls, T., Shabbir, N., Graves, L. and Nielsen, R.K. (2018) 'Coming of age: Developments in DigitalBorn news media in Europe', *Reuters Institute 11*, https://reutersinstitute.politics.ox.ac.uk/sites/default/files/2018-12/Nicholls_Developments_of_Digital_News_Media_FINAL_0.pdf

Nygaard, S. (2019) The appearance of objectivity: How immigration-critical alternative media report the news. *Journalism Practice*, Vol. 13(10): 1147–1163.

Ofcom (2021) *News Consumption in the UK: 2021.* London: Ofcom, https://www.ofcom.org.uk/__data/assets/pdf_file/0025/222478/news-consumption-in-the-uk-overview-of-findings-2021.pdf

Olausson, U. (2017) 'The reinvented journalist', *Digital Journalism*, Vol. 5(1): 61–81, https://doi.org/10.1080/21670811.2016.1146082

Oschatz, C., Stier, S. and Maier, J. (2021) 'Twitter in the news: An analysis of embedded tweets in political news coverage', *Digital Journalism*, 1–20, https://doi.org/10.1080/21670811.2021.1912624

Pew (2021) 'Social media use in 2021', *Pew Research Center*, 7 April, https://www.pewresearch.org/internet/2021/04/07/social-media-use-in-2021/ #

Rae, M. (2021) 'Hyperpartisan news: Rethinking the media for populist politics', *New Media & Society*, Vol. 23(5): 875–1338, https://doi.org/10.1177/1461444820910416

Rauch, J. (2021) *Resisting the News: Engaged Audiences, Alternative Media, and Popular Critique of Journalism*. New York: Routledge

Thomas, R. and Cushion, S. (2019) 'Towards an institutional news logic of digital native news media? A case study of buzzfeed's reporting during the 2015 and 2017 UK General Election Campaigns', *Digital Journalism*, Vol. 7 (10): 1328-1345, http://dx.doi.org/10.1080/21670811.2019.1661262

Thomas, R. McDowell-Naylor, D. and Cushion, S. (2022) 'Understanding 'good' and 'bad' twitter practices in alternative media: An analysis of online political media in the UK (2015–2018)', *Journalism Practice*, https://doi.org/10.1080/17512786.2022.2050469

van Dijck, J. and Poell, T. (2013) 'Understanding social media logic', *Media and Communication*, Vol 1: 2–14, https://doi.org/10.12924/mac2013.01010002

Waterson, J. (2017) 'The rise of the alt-left British media', *BuzzFeed*, May 6, https://www.buzzfeed. com/jimwaterson/the-rise-of-the-alt-left

Willnat, L. and Weaver, D.H. (2018) 'Social media and U.S. journalists', *Digital Journalism*, Vol.6(7): 889–909, https://doi.org/10.1080/21670811.2018.1495570

4
ATTACKING MAINSTREAM MEDIA

The role media systems play in shaping how professional journalism is critiqued

Alternative media have historically been driven by covering issues often marginalised or ignored by professional journalists (Downing 1984). Over time, this editorial goal has become central to the DNA of many alternative media sites, adopting a media watchdog role that monitors and corrects the portrayal of politics in mainstream media. Holt et al.'s (2019) conceptualisation of alternative media is defined, in part, by a self-perceived opposition to mainstream media. This represents, in their words, "opposing the overall tendency of public discourse emanating from what is perceived as the dominant mainstream media in a given system" (Holt et al. 2019: 862). This is self-evident from what alternative media editors claim publicly or put on their websites, which ultimately aim to correct the biases of mainstream media and challenge their hegemonic perspective.

The US left-wing website, Daily Kos, for example, has stated its journalism centres on "the people, places, and issues currently underreported by national media" (Daily Kos 2022[1]), while the editor of a right-wing alternative media site, The Tennessee Star, has said: "If you want to have political influence, you need to be planting a flag and competing with the left-leaning mainstream media in the Ohios, in the Pennsylvanias, in the Colorados, in the North Carolinas in some states" (cited in Waldow 2018). In the UK, The Canary's (2022) website points out that "a handful of powerful moguls control our mainstream media. As such, its coverage is largely conservative. But we have created a truly independent and viable alternative". Evolve Politics (2022) boldly claims to be "100% independent – meaning that, unlike the vast proportion of mainstream media outlets, we have no wealthy financial backers supporting us, and no political or corporate ties influencing our output", while the right-wing site, Conservative Woman, states on its website:

DOI: 10.4324/9781003360865-5

Left-liberal thinking dominates the news media (most worryingly the licence fee-funded BBC) … destroying independent and critical thought in the attempt to control how we speak and think … Six years ago, few would have thought that an independent and unashamedly social conservative website would have any traction. The Conservative Woman has confounded this assumption, and our challenge to the virtue-signalling, intolerant and self-interested elites has been widely welcomed.[2]

While different sites have contrasting editorial aims around the world, there remains a shared agenda – irrespective of their left-wing and right-wing political agendas – to challenge the hegemony of mainstream media and correct their perceived ideologically driven biases.

Given the diversity of alternative media sites across and within different countries, their portrayal of professional journalism, including which news organisations they centre their agenda on, can reveal why they question and attack the value of their mainstream media systems. As Chapter 2 and Chapter 3 revealed, alternative media pay a lot of attention to mainstream media. But the portrayal of mainstream media and interpretation of professional journalism in routine alternative media content has not been subject to much systematic analysis. Holt (2019), for example, relied on interviews with editors of right-wing sites in Sweden to explore their perceptions of mainstream media reporters. He found they were deeply suspicious of their values and judgements, framing coverage in ways that reinforced their own ideological agendas. But more evidence is needed to consider how mainstream media have portrayed and critiqued professional journalism.

This chapter first examines the few studies that have explored the representation of mainstream media in alternative media sites, including whether coverage is different across partisan sources. It then draws on the most extensive study produced to date, which examined 3,352 articles in order to quantify the degree of coverage about mainstream media across nine UK alternative media sites between 2015 and 2021 and assess the nature of how professional journalism was critiqued (Cushion et al. 2021). The chapter then carries out a qualitative analysis of two left-wing sites, The Canary and Evolve Politics, developing typologies of how their reporting attacked mainstream media and delegitimised professional journalism (Cushion 2020, 2022). The wider relevance of the findings helps explain why alternative media focus their editorial attention on mainstream media. Above all, the chapter argues that it is important to first understand national media systems in order to then interpret and explain the nature of alternative media criticism towards professional journalism

The portrayal of mainstream media in alternative media: a cross-national perspective

There have been few systematic content analysis studies that have examined how alternative media portray mainstream media or professional journalism more generally. Of the studies that have examined coverage in alternative media sites, most have been qualitative in design and focussed on mainly right-wing rather than left-wing alternative media sites (Figenschou and Ihlebæk 2019; Holt 2019; Roberts and Wahl-Jorgensen 2020).

Mayerhöffer (2021) undertook a qualitative content analysis of websites and articles of five right-wing alternative sites in Denmark and found a difference between how they presented themselves in contrast to mainstream media. She discovered that "Rather than mimicking legacy news outlets, all of the sites included in the study present themselves as being distinct from and in opposition to established MSM" (Mayerhöffer 2021: 133). But this positioning was limited to the websites rather than specific articles, which, in her words, "mainly function as a supplement to the existing legacy news infrastructure and display limited capacity and/or ambition to challenge legacy media as news providers to the larger public". Mayerhöffer suggested that this complicity is partly a result of the somewhat right-wing agenda of much of Denmark's legacy media environment (Mayerhöffer 2021, 133). The role played by national media systems shaping alternative media coverage of professional journalism is a common theme explored throughout this chapter.

Figenschou and Ihlebæk's (2019) qualitative textual analysis of far-right sites in Norway represents the most detailed study of how alternative media represent mainstream media to date. Drawing on a sample of 600 articles, they developed a typology of five categories that demonstrated how alternative media sites conveyed journalistic legitimacy and authority. First, alternative media sites selectively criticised stories from mainstream media and suggested they reflected bias generally among professional journalists. Second, they supplied their own expert knowledge on issues including international news or in the use of statistics, questioning the expertise of mainstream media journalists. Third, alternative media sites personalised reporting, drawing on their own experiences to question claims in mainstream coverage and cast themselves as victims. Fourth, ordinary people's views were regularly featured in coverage, in contrast to mainstream media often alienating their perspectives. Finally, alternative media sites re-interpreted mainstream media coverage and alleged ideological bias by, for example, interrogating the transcripts of mainstream media coverage, such as interviews, and suggesting their views were editorially driven. Overall, Figenschou and Ihlebæk's study (2019: 1236) concluded that "to capture the complexities of far-right media criticism (as well as other forms of contemporary interest-based, non-elite critique), it is useful to identify the multiple communications strategies deployed to gain authority as a media critic" (Figenschou and Ihlebæk 2019: 1236).

The communication strategies of alternative media were examined in a study about the US right-wing media site, Breitbart, which analysed 213 media-related articles about criticism of mainstream media (Roberts and Wahl-Jorgensen 2020). They identified three ways mainstream media were delegitimatised. First, Breitbart regularly declared so-called 'victories' in its journalism or in Trump's decision-making, which were achieved despite the corporate and political influences of mainstream media, such as appointing a right-wing judge to the supreme court. Second, Breitbart selected stories that suggested the values and sensibilities of patriotic Americans were being undermined, championing itself as a watchdog upholding traditional, conservative values in contrast to the liberal media. Third, the journalistic authority of mainstream media was challenged by directly attacking reporters and – following Trump's lead – labelling their journalism 'fake news'.

Overall, the few studies examining how alternative media portray professional journalism and provide a corrective to mainstream media have largely focussed on right-wing sites rather than left-wing counterparts. But right-wing sites may 'correct' professional journalism differently from left-wing sites within a media system but also cross-nationally depending on the characteristics of national mainstream media. After all, alternative media should be viewed as a relational concept, responding to and interacting within the ideological parameters set out by mainstream media in national contexts.

The (changing) editorial focus on mainstream media and professional journalism

This chapter now draws on a content analysis study that developed an original approach to understanding how professional journalism was critiqued in alternative media (Cushion et al. 2021). It develops four new lines of inquiry. First, it goes beyond qualitative studies to provide the most systematic quantitative examination to date about the degree and nature of how mainstream media are represented in alternative media. Second, it compares and contrasts any differences in how right-wing and left-wing alternative media sites represent legacy media. Third, it examines reporting over time to assess whether the editorial focus on professional journalists was a stable part of the coverage. Fourth, it considers the degree of hostility towards mainstream media in the context of the UK's national media system, which has a powerful right-wing partisan press but also a dominant broadcasting ecology required to be impartial, with many people relying on the BBC for their news and analysis (Cushion 2015).

The study began by examining left-wing and right-wing alternative media between 2015 and 2018, which represented a period when many sites were first launched (see Introduction chapter). This included a more substantial analysis over six weeks (rather than three weeks for the other years) in 2017 during the UK general election campaign. In doing so, it assessed the extent of editorial attention paid to mainstream media from when many sites first started and empirically charts whether they have enhanced their agenda about professional media over time. It draws on an analysis of 3,452 articles over four years, which then isolated every substantive story that critiqued mainstream media. This generated 665 articles in total which were made up of stories including general references to the media (e.g., MSM), to media organisations (e.g., the BBC or The Sun), or to specific journalists.

The analysis discovered that a fifth of all alternative media articles – 19.3% – over four years related to mainstream media. This broadly rose over time, with 16.6% of articles related to mainstream media in 2016, 18.9% in 2016, and 22.7% in 2017, before dropping to 12.3% in 2018. Perhaps most striking was that almost a quarter of alternative media coverage was dedicated to critiquing mainstream media during the 2017 general election period. In 2015, left-wing and right-wing sites included a critique of mainstream media in roughly the same amount of coverage (see Table 4.1).

But over time the difference between left-wing and right-wing alternative media agendas grew starker, with the former far more likely to critique legacy media than the latter sites, especially in 2016 and 2017, when they supplied approximately three to four more articles than right-wing sites about professional journalism. Indeed, the focus on mainstream media fell over time, but there were significant differences in editorial emphasis between sites across the political spectrum (see Table 4.2).

Above all, Another Angry Voice was most editorially focussed on mainstream media, with close to half of all its articles – 45.6% – critiquing legacy media and professional journalists. For example, it featured headlines such as:

Are the Daily Mail deliberately ridiculing their own readers? (20 October 2016)

Don't let the mainstream media con you into believing the Tories aren't ideological extremists. (28 May 2017)

Why do the mainstream press let the Tories get away with systematically abusing disabled people? (29 May 2017)

Of the right-wing alternative media sites, The Conservative Woman focussed most heavily on mainstream media, making up almost three in ten of its articles – 28.9% overall – between 2015 and 2018. Headlines included:

The BBC stacks the deck against grammar schools – no surprise there. (27 May 2017)

The Telegraph Wimmin's section – a fact-free zone. (12 October 2016)

By comparison, other right-wing sites included far fewer media critiques – between three to five times less – including Breitbart, Guido Fawkes, and Westmonster.

The content analysis also examined whether alternative media coverage of mainstream media either praised or criticised professional journalism. To analyse coverage in a more nuanced way, the tone of articles about mainstream media was classified as either overt or implied criticism or overt or implied praise. As Table 4.3 reveals, 92.4% were critical in tone, with 81.6% overtly critical of mainstream media.

TABLE 4.1 The percentage of UK right-wing and left-wing alternative media articles that include a critique of mainstream media (frequency in brackets)

	2015		2016		2017		2018		Total
	Yes	No	Yes	No	Yes	No	Yes	No	
Left-wing sites	18.6% (13)	81.4% (57)	36.8% (63)	63.2% (108)	38.1% (313)	61.9% (508)	21.9% (57)	78.1% (203)	100.0% (1322)
Right-wing sites	16.1% (48)	83.9% (250)	9.4% (30)	90.6% (289)	10.3% (106)	89.7% (919)	7.2% (35)	92.8% (453)	100.0% (2130)
Total	1.8% (61)	8.9% (307)	2.7% (93)	11.5% (397)	12.1% (419)	41.3% (1427)	2.7% (92)	19.0% (656)	100.0% (3452)

TABLE 4.2 The percentage of UK alternative media articles that include a critique of mainstream media (N in brackets)

	Yes	No	Total
Left-wing sites			
Another Angry Voice	45.6% (62)	54.4% (74)	100% (136)
Evolve Politics	29.4% (30)	70.6% (72)	100% (102)
Novara Media	20.7% (6)	79.3% (23)	100% (29)
The Canary	33.3% (242)	66.7% (484)	100% (726)
The Skwawkbox	32.2% (106)	67.8% (223)	100% (329)
Right-wing sites			
Breitbart	8.3% (52)	91.7% (574)	100% (626)
Guido Fawkes	8.1% (68)	91.9% (781)	100% (849)
The Conservative Woman	28.9% (76)	71.1% (190)	100% (266)
Westmonster	5.4% (21)	94.6% (368)	100% (389)
Total	18.3% (633)	80.8% (2,789)	100% (3,452)

TABLE 4.3 The percentage of articles with different types of tone towards mainstream media in UK alternative media articles (frequency in brackets)

	Overt criticism	Implied criticism	Overt praise	Implied praise	Total
Left-wing sites					
Another Angry Voice	89.6% (1,380)	5.2% (8)	2.6% (4)	2.6% (4)	100.0% (154)
Evolve Politics	68.4% (26)	21.1% (8)	5.3% (2)	2.6% (1)	100.0% (38)
Novara Media	85.7% (6)	–	–	14.3% (1)	100.0% (7)
The Canary	83.8% (537)	9.8% (63)	2.2% (14)	4.3% (27)	100.0% (641)
The Skwawkbox	72.3% (167)	13.8% (32)	13.4% (31)	0.4% (1)	100.0% (231)
Right-wing sites					
Breitbart	78.7% (85)	21.3% (23)	–	–	100.0% (108)
Guido Fawkes	70.2% (59)	16.7% (14)	10.7% (9)	2.4% (2)	100.0% (84)
The Conservative Woman	89.4% (143)	3.8% (6)	2.5% (4)	4.4% (7)	100.0% (160)
Westmonster	77.8% (14)	16.7% (3)	5.6% (1)	–	100.0% (18)
Total	81.5% (1,175)	10.9% (157)	4.6% (66)	3.0% (43)	100.0% (1,441)

A high degree of overt criticism towards mainstream media was on display across both left-wing and right-wing alternative media sites. On the left, Another Angry Voice, Novara Media, and The Canary supplied the most overt opposition to professional journalism, while for right-wing sites, The Conservative Woman was the most hostile. This was reflected in criticism directed at both specific news outlets or the media more generally such as:

The vicious anti-Corbyn bias of the mainstream media. (Another Angry Voice, 27 May 2017) mainstream media bias (The Canary, 7 May 2020)

notoriously Conservative boot-licking newspaper [The Telegraph]. (Evolve Politics, 24 October 2020)

The Conservative Woman often directly alleged that the BBC was biased or that specific reporters had a party-political agenda (The Conservative Woman, 30 May 2017). The nature of criticism did not meaningfully change over time across both right-wing and left-wing sites. In sum, not only did alternative media report on mainstream media more prominently over time, when they did it was mostly highly critical of professional journalism.

In order to further understand how mainstream media was being critiqued, the content analysis study specifically assessed if the editorial focus was directed at an individual journalist or editor, a publication or outlet, a media leader or owner, or if it was a more general reference to mainstream media or alternative media. As Table 4.4 reveals, the object of abuse was focussed on specific outlets, most notably in right-wing alternative media. Right-wing sites also directed criticism at specific journalists more than left-wing sites.

Roughly a third of left-wing alternative media sites centred their editorial focus on generalised references to the media, compared to just 7.6% on right-wing sites. Examples included:

13 questions mainstream media should be asking about Salman Abedi. (Another Angry Voice, 29 May 2017)

A filmmaker has accused the mainstream media of 'disgusting' bullying of Jeremy Corbyn. (The Canary, 3/6/17)

TABLE 4.4 The percentage of references to critiques of mainstream media in UK alternative media sites (frequency in brackets)

	IJ	IEIC	P/O	L/O	GRMSM	GRAM	Total
Left-wing sites							
Another Angry Voice	6.5% (10)	–	37.0% (57)	9.1% (14)	45.5% (70)	1.9% (3)	100.0% (154)
Evolve Politics	10.5% (4)	–	47.4% (18)	–	42.1% (16)	–	100.0% (38)
Novara Media	–	–	42.9% (3)	–	42.9% (3)	14.3% (1)	100.0% (7)
The Canary	15.1% (97)	0.5% (3)	47.0% (303)	7.5% (48)	29.3% (189)	0.6% (4)	100.0% (644)
The Skwawkbox	20.7% (48)	0.4% (1)	37.9% (88)	3.4% (8)	35.3% (82)	2.2% (5)	100.0% (232)
Right-wing sites							
Breitbart	26.6% (29)	0.9% (1)	58.7% (64)	0.9% (1)	12.8% (14)	–	100.0% (109)
Guido Fawkes	24.4% (21)	1.2% (1)	67.4% (58)	3.5% (3)	2.3% (2)	1.2% (1)	100.0% (86)
The Conservative Woman	29.3% (49)	2.4% (4)	61.1% (102)	0.6% (1)	6.6% (11)	–	100.0% (167)
Westmonster	11.1% (2)	16.7% (3)	55.6% (10)	5.6% (1)	11.1% (2)	–	100.0% (18)
Total	17.9% (260)	0.9% (13)	48.3% (703)	5.2% (76)	26.7% (389)	1.0% (14)	100.0% (1455)

NB: IJ – Individual Journalist; IEIC – Individual Editor in Chief; P/O – Publication/Outlet; L/O – Leader/Ownership; GRMSM – General reference to MSM; GRAM – General reference to Alt Media.

When a specific outlet was critiqued, every reference to them was classified according to whether it was directed at either the BBC, other broadcasters, right-wing newspapers and magazines, left-wing newspapers and magazines, alternative right-wing media, alternative left-wing media, and other media (see Table 4.5). Above all, the BBC received the most criticism – especially during the 2017 general election campaign – and over time it grew more hostile (see Table 4.6).

Hostility towards the BBC was more on display in all of the right-wing alternative media sites, whereas there were different degrees of focus on left-wing sites. Of the right-wing sites, The Conservative Woman was the most unrelenting and vociferous critic of the BBC. It featured headlines including:

BBC Election Watch: "Impartial" BBC website loads dice against Tories. (15 May 2017)

David Keighley's BBC Election Watch: Past it Paxman left Corbyn in the clear. (30 May 2017)

Three quarters of all Conservative Woman articles critiquing the mainstream media were directed at the BBC.

Finally, the content analysis study identified why mainstream media was being critiqued. This included five categories: not being factually accurate; breaching rules on impartiality or displaying bias; not producing quality journalism; omitting stories from the news agenda; for the culture and regulation of news; or another type of criticism. As Table 4.7 reveals, almost half of all references to mainstream media related to a perceived bias or lack of impartiality in mainstream media, such as The Canary item headlined: "A BBC editor has spelled out why the broadcaster's bias is justified, and it's utterly outrageous" (14 October 2016).

The heavy editorial focus journalistic on bias or infringements of impartiality were criticisms directed across right-wing and left-wing sites. However, they were more prominent on left-wing sites, especially during the 2017 general election campaign. The final part of the chapter qualitatively explores how left-wing alternative media attacked mainstream media and delegitimated professional journalism.

Six ways alternative media delegitimise mainstream media

Since mainstream media was critiqued more in left-wing than right-wing alternative media sites, this chapter now focusses on exploring two sites in more depth and detail. Based on a five-year study of 1,284 articles in The Canary articles and Evolve Politics, every story that criticised mainstream media was examined more

TABLE 4.5 Percentage of references to mainstream media in UK alternative media articles with a critique of specific media outlets (frequency in brackets)

	BBC	OB	RWNM	LWNM	RAM	LAM	Other	Total
Left-wing sites								
Another Angry Voice	7.4% (5)	2.9% (2)	76.5% (52)	2.9% (2)	/	1.5% (1)	8.8% (6)	100.0% (68)
Evolve Politics	18.2% (4)	13.6% (3)	27.3% (6)	27.3% (6)	/	/	13.6% (3)	100.0% (22)
Novara Media	33.3% (1)		33.3% (1)	33.3% (1)	/	/		100.0% (3)
The Canary	33.0% (146)	8.6% (38)	35.3% (156)	12.4% (55)	0.5% (2)	-	10.2% (45)	100.0% (442)
The Skwawkbox	43.0% (55)	5.5% (7)	14.1% (18)	15.6% (20)	4.7% (6)	10.9% (14)	6.3% (8)	100.0% (128)
Right-wing sites								
Breitbart	37.9% (36)	14.7% (14)	16.8% (16)	18.9% (18)	1.1% (1)	/	10.5% (10)	100.0% (95)
Guido Fawkes	27.7% (26)	5.3% (5)	22.3% (21)	20.2% (19)	/	14.9% (14)	9.6% (9)	100.0% (94)
The Conservative Woman	74.2% (115)	2.6% (4)	9.0% (14)	7.1% (11)	1.9% (3)	0.6% (1)	4.5% (7)	100.0% (155)
Westmonster	43.8% (7)	25.0% (4)	12.5% (2)	/	/	/	18.8% (3)	100.0% (16)
Total	38.6% (395)	7.5% (77)	28.0% (286)	12.9% (132)	1.2% (12)	2.9% (30)	8.9% (91)	100.0% (1023)

NB: BBC – BBC; OB – other broadcasters; RWNM – Right-wing newspapers or magazines; LWNM – Left-wing newspapers or magazines; RAM – Right Alt Media; LAM – Left Alt Media

TABLE 4.6 Percentage of references to the BBC in UK alternative media sites expressing either overt or implicit criticism (frequency in brackets)

Year	Right-wing sites	Left-wing sites	Percentage
2015	92.9% (13)	7.1% (1)	3.8% (14)
2016	52.0% (26)	48.0% (24)	13.6% (50)
2017	40.2% (103)	59.8% (153)	69.4% (256)
2018	65.3% (32)	34.7% (17)	13.3% (49)
Total	47.2% (174)	52.8% (195)	100.0% (369)

TABLE 4.7 Percentage of topics about references to mainstream media in UK alternative media sites (frequency in brackets)

	FA	I/B	Q	CO	C+R	Other	Total
Left-wing sites							
Another Angry Voice	5.8% (9)	61.7% (95)	15.6% (24)	9.1% (14)	3.9% (6)	3.9% (6)	100.0% (154)
Evolve Politics	15.8% (6)	36.8% (14)	28.9% (11)	10.5% (4)	–	7.9% (3)	100.0% (38)
Novara Media	–	71.4% (5)	–	–	28.6% (2)	–	100.0% (7)
The Canary	14.6% (94)	52.3% (337)	13.2% (85)	13.0% (84)	0.8% (5)	6.1% (39)	100.0% (644)
The Skwawkbox	21.1% (49)	37.9% (88)	22.0% (51)	12.5% (29)	–	6.5% (15)	100.0% (232)
Right-wing sites							
Breitbart	14.7% (16)	50.5% (55)	8.3% (9)	6.4% (7)	15.6% (17)	4.6% (5)	100.0% (109)
Guido Fawkes	22.1% (19)	23.3% (20)	34.9% (30)	7.0% (6)	–	12.8% (11)	100.0% (86)
The Conservative Woman	3.6% (6)	59.6% (99)	12.7% (21)	6.6% (11)	12.7% (21)	4.8% (8)	100.0% (166)
Westmonster	5.6% (1)	61.1% (11)	5.6% (1)	–	22.2% (4)	5.6% (1)	100.0% (18)
Total	13.7% (200)	49.8% (724)	16.0% (232)	10.7% (155)	3.8% (55)	6.1% (88)	100.0% (1454)

NB: FA – Factual Accuracy; IB – Impartiality/Bias; Q- Quality- CO – Coverage Omissions; C+R – Culture and Regulations; Other – Other.

closely (Cushion 2022). This amounted to 158 articles in total (Cushion 2020). In doing so, six ways alternative left-wing media delegitimatised mainstream media were identified.

First, and above all, both sites focussed much of their criticism towards an alleged political bias in mainstream media reporting. As already acknowledged, the BBC was often at the centre of this focus, with its political editor, Laura Kuennssberg, frequently singled out for criticism. This was directed not only at what was reported, but in what was excluded from coverage. The language and framing of stories were closely analysed. At times, criticism was highly nuanced, considering language choice, editing, and visual imagery, which were used to demonstrate political bias and breaches of broadcasters' impartiality.

Second, both left-wing alternative media sites often drew on the views of a high-profile professional journalist or a left-wing public figure to undermine the authority of mainstream media. By deferring this judgement to an outside authoritative voice, the criticism of professional journalism was portrayed as being independent of either The Canary or Evolve Politics.

Third, left-wing alternative media sites used 'hard' evidence from official bodies and academic sources to legitimise their criticism of mainstream media. One Canary story, for example, was headlined: "Now we have evidence, everyone can see the real reason it looks like Corbyn didn't back Remain". The story was informed by three academic studies that were used to contest the allegation that the Labour leader, Jeremy Corbyn, was not an active campaigner during the referendum to remain or leave the EU (10 October 2016). The Canary claimed this amounted to "hard evidence of mainstream media bias during the EU referendum". Other official reports, such as an EU Council of Europe review and (10 October 2016) and a UK Ofcom study (24 October 2019), were also used to critique professional journalism.

Fourth, rather than selecting isolated stories and issues, another tactic used by left-wing alternative media sites was to critique the structural conditions of the media. This was evidenced by critiquing the conventions, practices, and values of the mainstream media generally. For example, one Evolve Politics story was a general attack of mainstream media coverage of a report by the Intergovernmental Panel on Climate Change (IPCC) (8 October 2018). Its critique centred on the downmarket values of professional journalism:

> with a tabloid media intent on delusion, on reflecting a world to its readership that has no cares nor qualms, save reality TV gossip, that isn't standing with its toes curled around the lip of the precipice, how is change to come?

Likewise, a Canary story entitled: "After last night, the BBC's impartiality guidelines aren't worth the paper they're written on" (9 October 2018), delegitimised journalism according to external rules about media regulation. By singling out specific stories and editorial misjudgements, they were used to highlight systemic issues within the larger media system.

Fifth, sloppy or inaccurate instances of journalism were often the object of focus on The Canary and Evolve Politics. Opinion writers, for example, were criticised, with passages of newspaper articles isolated and broadcast programming graphically reproduced online and subject to intense scrutiny. A Canary story, for instance, focussed on the racist language of a Sunday Times columnist and pointed out there had been complaints to IPSO, the main UK press regulator (23 October 2018). By drawing on selective textual evidence from mainstream media and prominently displaying it within coverage, the legitimacy of professional journalism was undermined by sustained analysis and considered to be indicative of legacy reporting more generally.

Sixth, and finally, mainstream media was subjected to criticism because of media ownership and political partisanship influencing professional journalists. This took the form of systemic critiques of commercial marketisation and concentration of media ownership. For instance, Rupert Murdoch was referenced by both sites for influencing the political coverage of his right-wing newspapers and diminishing the prospect of a left-wing Labour Party ever gaining power.

Overall, both left-wing alternative media sites sought to delegitimise professional journalism by isolating specific stories or selected quotes from mainstream media, and scrutinising them with references to authoritative sources, including academic sources. Of course, making extensive use of elite, institutional actors has long been part of how mainstream media legitimise their own journalism (Fishman 1980). But interestingly, the contrasting difference between the agendas of alternative media and mainstream media is that professional journalism in the UK does not routinely hold itself up to criticism of coverage. Moreover, communication scholars rarely inform mainstream media reporting (Bennett and Kidd 2017).

Why the wider media system shapes alternative media criticism of professional journalism

Overall, this chapter revealed the full extent and nature of alternative media criticism towards mainstream media. This critique was more prominent in left-wing than right-wing sites, with hostility towards professional journalism generally increasing over time. This was most apparent during the 2017 general election campaign when attacks on the BBC, in particular, dominated the agenda of many alternative media sites. Above all, a perceived media bias or lack of impartiality in broadcast news was central to the critique of mainstream media. The chapter then qualitatively explored how two left-wing sites delegitimised professional journalism. This was carried out by close surveillance of mainstream media reporting, challenging editorial judgements with hard evidence, and drawing on official bodies and academic evidence to support their claims.

The quantitative analysis in this chapter represented the first study to document a rise in mainstream media criticism in alternative media over time. But it also drew attention to the editorial focus on the BBC and, amongst left-wing sites, right-wing newspapers and magazines. The chapter argued this represented the distinctive role national media systems play in understanding the nature of alternative media criticism towards mainstream media and professional journalism. The UK's unique hybrid system of a dominant public service broadcaster and right-wing partisan press contrasts with many other media systems around the world (Curran 2011). In the US, for example, Rauch (2021) found left-wing alternative media audiences were largely supportive of American Public Broadcasting System due to its impartial approach to reporting. Moreover, she discovered their criticism of professional journalism was directed at America's highly commercialised media environment, which was seen to compromise high standards of reporting. The same pattern was revealed in a Scandinavian-based study of right-wing alternative media coverage. Nygaard's (2019) study of 90 immigration articles in Swedish, Danish, and Norwegian right-wing alternative media sites suggested that the ideological parameters of mainstream political and media debates moderated coverage. In her words, "alternative media outlets seem to a certain extent to adapt to the prevailing political consensus and mainstream media discourses in which they coexist" (Nygaard 2019, 1160). In short, the editorial agenda of alternative media criticism towards professional journalism is shaped by the national characteristics of mainstream media.

From another perspective, this chapter showed that the more people encounter alternative media, the more likely they are to be exposed to criticism of mainstream media and professional journalism. Since most people rely on mainstream media for news about politics and public affairs, their critical portrayal in alternative media could be undermining their journalistic authority and role as an information source. Needless to say, the cause and effect between alternative media coverage consumption and how people respond to attacks of mainstream media cannot be assumed. The final three chapters of the book explore the body of evidence exploring the relationship between high levels of alternative media use and users' understanding of mainstream media and politics more generally. But first the following two chapters examine the production practices of alternative media sites, including their editorial aims to challenge mainstream media perspectives and critique professional journalism. In doing so, they shed light on how alternative media sites seek to correct professional reporting and how distinctive their ownership practices and editorial conventions are from mainstream media production.

Notes

1 This quote was taken from Daily Kos's website, https://m.dailykos.com/
2 The quotes were taken from the websites of The Canary (https://www.thecanary.co/about/), Evolve Politics (https://evolvepolitics.com/about/) and Conservative Women (https://www.conservativewoman.co.uk/our-mission/).

References

Bennett, L. and Kidd, J. (2017) 'Myths about media studies: The construction of media studies education in the British press', *Continuum*, Vol. 31(2): 163–176, https://doi.org/10.1080/10304312.2016.1265096
Curran, J. (2011) *Media and Democracy*. London: Routledge. ISBN 978-0-415-31707-8
Cushion, S. (2022) 'UK alternative left media and their criticism of mainstream news: Analysing the Canary and Evolve politics', *Journalism Practice*, Vol. 16(8): 1695–1714. https://doi.org/10.1080/17512786.2021.1882875

Cushion, S. (2020) 'Six ways alt-left media legitimatize their criticism of mainstream media: An analysis of The Canary and Evolve Politics (2015–19)', *Journal of Alternative and Community Media*, Vol. 5(2): 153–171, https://doi.org/10.1386/joacm _00081_1

Cushion, S. (2015) 'Journalism and current affairs' in M. Conboy and J. Steel (eds.) *The Routledge Companion to British Media History*. London: Routledge, pp. 504–513.

Cushion, S. McDowell-Naylor, D. and Thomas, R. (2021) 'Why national media systems matter: A longitudinal analysis of how UK left-wing and right-wing alternative media critique mainstream media (2015–2018)', *Journalism Studies*, Vol. 22(5): 633–652, https://doi.org/10.1080/1461670X.2021.1893795

Downing, J. (1984) *Radical Media: The Political Experience of Alternative Communication*. Boston, MA: South End Press.

Figenschou, T. U. and Ihlebæk, K. A. (2019) 'Challenging journalistic authority', *Journalism Studies*, Vol. 20(9): 1221–1237, https://doi.org/10.1080/1461670X.2018.1500868

Fishman, M. (1980) *Manufacturing the News*. Austin: University of Texas Press.

Holt, K. (2019). *Right-Wing Alternative Media*. Abingdon: Routledge.

Holt, K. Figenschou, T.U. and Frischlich, L. (2019) 'Key dimensions of alternative news media', *Digital Journalism*, Vol. 7(7): 860–869, https://doi.org/10.1080/21670811.2019 .1625715

Mayerhöffer, E. (2021) 'How do Danish right-wing alternative media position themselves against the mainstream? Advancing the study of alternative media structure and content', *Journalism Studies*, Vol. 22(2): 119–136 https://doi.org/10.1080/1461670X .2020.1814846

Nygaard, S. (2019). The appearance of objectivity: How immigration-critical alternative media report the news. *Journalism Practice*, Vol. 13(10): 1147–1163.

Rauch, J. (2021) *Resisting the News: Engaged Audiences, Alternative Media, and Popular Critique of Journalism*. New York: Routledge.

Roberts, J. and Wahl-Jorgensen, K. (2020) 'Breitbart's attacks on mainstream media: Victories, victimhood, and vilification' in M. Boler and E. Davis (eds.) *Affective Politics of Digital Media: Propaganda by Other Means*. London: Routledge.

Waldow, J. (2018) 'Inside the business model of a "baby Breitbart"', *CNN Business*, 4 May, https://money.cnn.com/2018/05/04/media/reliable-sources-tennessee-star-steve-gill/ index.html

5

THE PROFESSIONALISATION OF ALTERNATIVE POLITICAL MEDIA PRODUCTION

Where once alternative media struggled with the costs of producing print or analogue content for audiences to readily consume, the new digital landscape over recent decades has enabled them to produce affordable content with global online and social media reach. But, as this chapter and the following one will explore, few academic studies have comprehensively explored the production processes of alternative political media, examined the main actors who create content, and, importantly, questioned their editorial choices and motivations. Some empirical studies – as Chapter 1 briefly explored – have examined the production of a *particular* site, such as Indymedia in the US (Pickard 2006). These single case studies of alternative media sites have, in different ways, painted a similar picture of production processes and editorial aims. For example, Farinosi and Treré (2014) explored the motivations of people producing information after an Italian earthquake in 2009. They found a desire to be distinctive from Italian mainstream media by giving a localised perspective and bringing together communities in the aftermath of the earthquake. But achieving these goals was mitigated by structural issues, such as limited funding to a lack of journalistic skills. Likewise, Heikka and Carayannis (2019) examined how citizens responded to public school closings in Chicago by initiating media production independent of news organisations in order to challenge the local government's decision.

But this *singular* focus has been on the mission of a site within a national political and media context, rather than examining a broader range of alternative media production practices from both right-wing and left-wing perspectives. As Chapter 1 highlighted, there has been a scarcity of studies interviewing alternative media practitioners, or observing their practices and conventions. This chapter explores the motivations and practices of alternative media actors by drawing on 40 interviews

DOI: 10.4324/9781003360865-6

with editors and contributors. First, however, it sets some context by considering the few studies that have examined alternative media sites from a production perspective in recent years. Above all, they signal the need for more production research given the fast-changing editorial practices and organisational structures of alternative media and the development of new technologies and platforms of dissemination.

Interpreting the hybridity of alternative media production

Historically, scholars have contrasted the production of alternative media distinctively from mainstream media. As Chapter 1 explored, mainstream media have conventionally been seen as producing content via a top-down model according to shared professional norms and formalised editorial training, such as reporting objectively or impartially (Ford 2011). Scholars have often emphasised alternative media sites adopting practices and conventions viewed as bottom up, with citizens or local community members encouraging deliberation and participation in order to achieve specific political goals (Atton 2002; Downing et al. 2001; Rodríguez 2001). Many accounts of alternative media in the latter decades of the 20th century and the early 21st century centred on citizens becoming producers and pursuing activist causes that promoted a more radical agenda than the mainstream media. At this point in time, technology was fast changing, enabling the public to produce content that could be produced and shared globally. This meant, as was often provocatively claimed at the start of the 21st century, that anyone could be a journalist if they had access to the Internet (Schofield 2008).

But alternative media around the world have been subject to fierce criticism for lacking the professional skills and commercial experience to produce content that is of sufficient quality, influence, and long-term sustainability. Viewed from this perspective, the production of alternative media sites has often been portrayed as amateurish and short-lived, too centred on opposing mainstream media and politics rather than developing a journalistic infrastructure to permanently challenge the status quo. A group of British researchers, all partners of Comedia (1984), forcefully made this argument in the 1980s. They believed the failure of alternative media in Britain was due to

> the absence of a clear conception of target audiences and of marketing strategies to reach new audiences; the failure to develop necessary skills in the areas of administration and financial planning; and the commitment to an inflexible model of collectivity as the solution to all organizational problems. Our argument is that these failures derive from the "blind spots" in the libertarian political perspective which has dominated this sector over the last ten years.
> *(Comedia 1984: 95)*

In the decades that followed, the few production studies about alternative media similarly found that the failure to develop commercially sustainable content hampered the ability to attract large audiences and fulfil the political goals of not all but many sites (Khiabany 2000). Of course, many alternative media sites – particularly from the left – have not had the luxury of rich donors or corporate sponsors enabling them to produce ideologically driven content some mainstream sites have long enjoyed (as explored in Chapter 9). In the UK, for example, the partisan press has been financially supported by rich owners with clear political agendas. Meanwhile, in the US, broadcast media have become increasingly partisan over recent decades because a Republican President softened the regulation of rules about impartiality in the 1980s, allowing politically driven owners, notably Rupert Murdoch, to help reshape the nature of mainstream journalism (Cushion 2012b). In the online and social media age, Chapter 9 explores how right-wing partisan media have enhanced their influence in the US by sustained funding from corporate owners with political motives.

In the 21st century, mainstream journalists have also sought to deviate from conventional norms and develop what might be defined as alternative media. In other words, the traditional view of alternative media producers operating outside the 'mainstream' has been challenged (Sandoval and Fuchs 2010). In this broader conception of alternative media outlined in the opening chapters of this book (Holt et al. 2019), the production of alternative media has not exclusively been driven by political activists but by new media actors with professionalised editorial training and experience of working in commercially sustainable content. Over recent years seasoned journalists, even senior editors, working for legacy news organisations have moved to new digital start-up news companies that may be considered more alternative to mainstream media. For example, the BBC's Director of News between 2015 and 2019, James Harding, quit his role to start a new slow news service entitled Tortoise Media (Bell 2018).

A blurring of lines between the production of alternative and mainstream media was well articulated by Kenix's (2011) conceptualisation of a converging spectrum of media – a point developed further in the next chapter. She suggested organisational and editorial practices should be understood and interpreted within their media context to assess the characteristics of how far a site should be classified as being mainstream and alternative. As Chapters 7 and 8 will also explore, research with audiences has revealed that the distinction between alternative and mainstream is far more fluid than how scholars have historically interpreted them (Rauch 2021). All of this makes understanding the production processes of alternative media highly challenging, particularly in light of how new digital media and technologies have changed the news landscape. But, as previously explained, there have been few studies examining the production of alternative media across sites, such as engaging with editorial staff about their content and organisational practices, including, for instance, how far their structures intersect with or operate distinctively from mainstream media (Atkinson et al. 2019). When research into production processes has been investigated, the focus has often been on single case studies of a particular alternative media site, rather than a broader examination of practices across competing alternative media or between right-wing and left-wing sites.

Over recent years, a few comparative studies have shed empirical light on new and important ways alternative media self-identify, including their editorial and ideological principles. Ozgul and Veneti (2022), for example, carried out interviews with editorial staff across a range of alternative media sites in Turkey and Greece. They demonstrated their contrasting aims and practices across nations as well as between organisations. This was due to the resources available at different sites as larger organisations operated like mainstream media outlets including holding daily editorial meetings. But those working on smaller sites acted more independently and autonomously. In analysing Turkish and Greek alternative media sites, Ozgul and Veneti (2022) observed an editorial intersection with mainstream media conventions and practices. In their words:

> alternative professional media outlets in Turkey differentiate themselves from mainstream media outlets through their producers and news content, rather than organisational structures, which reflect many of the characteristics of mainstream media. Instead these journalists struggle to change the mainstream media from within and so, like their Greek counterparts, they seek to do this via alternative professional media. While creating alternative content, they maintain the traditional news production routines that they used to operate within.
> *(Ozgul and Veneti 2022: 1317)*

In both countries, especially among Greek journalists, they considered themselves to be professional journalists rather than alternative media activists. Indeed, according to interviewees, "activism is perceived to be an undermining factor in their professional practices" (Ozgul and Veneti 2022: 1317). But, interestingly, the study found different editorial principles in how Turkish and Greek journalists sought to achieve their shared goals of producing alternative news to the mainstream media agenda. For example, while Greek journalists challenged the normative ideal of reporting impartially, Turkish journalists embraced the practice as a way of legitimising their coverage and challenging disinformation in the wider-media environment.

From a Latin American perspective, Harlow (2022) carried out focus groups with 18 journalists from independent, digital native sites that could be considered alternative media, in order to explore how they were conceived as being distinctive from mainstream media. Three overriding themes were uncovered, which included innovation, participation, and stances. By innovation, the importance of financial and editorial independence was stressed, including striving for sustainability. Participation related to ensuring their production processes directly engaged with readers and sources to shape content, while stances meant offering an alternative perspective to mainstream media. However, like Turkish and Greek alternative media producers, Harlow (2022: 1337) found Latin American "respondents didn't consider themselves activists or alternative media producers", even though they self-consciously selected stories and issues mainstream media do not cover and rejected the need to be objective to carry out their journalism. Overall, she argued that the findings show that these Latin American journalists are professionals – rather than amateurs – but they did not "fit neatly into alternative or mainstream categorisations" (Harlow 2022: 1338). In her view, "these digital-native sites offer an alternative to mainstream media that has evolved beyond the partisan role of the media of times past, requiring an updated understanding of 'alternative'" (Harlow 2022: 1338).

Taken together, recent studies with alternative media producers have suggested the need to move beyond focussing on their activist goals in order to better understand their editorial practices and organisational structures. While this can include their distinction from mainstream media, the overlap between alternative media and professional journalism over recent years suggests more empirical research is needed to understand new reporting practices, funding streams, and editorial pressures. It is only by engaging with producers of alternative media can their editorial aims and decision making be interpreted more effectively.

This chapter now turns to a UK production case study of right-wing and left-wing alternative media sites, drawing on interviews with editors and contributors about their content, how this relates to the mainstream media and the wider environment including the role played by social media. The analysis of the organisational structure of alternative media in the UK was informed by 40 interviews, conducted primarily through Zoom between November 2020 and April 2021. They typically lasted between 30 and 60 minutes and followed a broadly similar set of questions. Some interviewees asked for their names not to be mentioned, while others were happy to be on the record.[1] The main aim of the interviews was to understand alternative media production first-hand from the contributors and editors, and to critically assess their decisions and processes. In doing so, their insights can be interpreted in light of studies from other national contexts, and across different media and political systems. The focus was largely on the political economy of alternative media, with a view to interpreting how their institutional processes influenced the production of news. The findings of the interviews reflected four overarching themes. It showed how right-wing and left-wing alternative media sites organised their (1) structures, including financial decision making; (2) editorial practices, including story production; (3) as well as their reporting conventions; and all of which point towards (4) a professionalisation of journalism.

Production processes of alternative media

Organisational structures

The interviews helped explain the organisational structures that shape the inner workings of alternative media sites. Taken together, they unravel how sites have been developed and structured, including how they fund content and manage their finances.

The interviews with editors and contributors across both right-wing and left-wing alternative media sites revealed a large disparity in the resources available to fund the production of content. Matt Turner, an ex-editor of Evolve Politics, acknowledged that when the site launched

> it wasn't a full time job for anybody. It was something which people did in their spare time but that's why I kind of liked it really. There was nobody out there trying to make a name for themselves ... it was just a really broad range of people who come from all of these walks of life, especially in the public sector who wanted to write about their field.

In exploring their financial budgets, the interviews showed that most alternative media sites had limited resources, especially left-wing sites. Indeed, with the exception of Brietbart, only a few of the sites could be described as well funded. This was evidenced by the variation in staff size between sites, ranging from Novara's highly developed multi-media team, to Skwawkbox's solo production. The following responses demonstrated the disparity in resources shaping routine production:

> I'm a one man operation and I'm a cast of thousands because people who like what I do and believe I handle information in a good way, whether they're normal Labour Party members in a local area somewhere or MPs would come to me with information because I've built up a lot of trust. ... Well, people chip in if they want to help cover the costs and so on but it's not a commercial entity in that sense. I'm not trying to gain advertising revenue or anything like that. I actually pay extra to stop there being any ads on the site from the hosting provider as well.
>
> *(Steve Walker, editor of the Skwawkbox)*

> The organisation currently is run by the business strategy group, which is the head of articles, the head of audio, the head of video, the head of operations, and two other people, because at the moment they're within the operations where they don't have a line manager, so they're kind of at the top of their specific remit. So a lot of my time actually goes on helping to run the organisation.
> *(Senior editor of a left-wing alternative media site)*

Some interviewees explained that their editorial teams were growing, whereas others stated their intention was to maintain the same level of staff recruitment. It was also revealed that many new hires were becoming increasingly specialised, as sites developed longer-term strategic planning. Many sites explained they did not have a central physical hub – like a newsroom based in central London – but relied on a network of contributors around the UK. Nancy Mendoza, who helped launch

The Canary, explained how the site rapidly grew in reach between 2015 and 2017, employing more contributors from different communities, and shifting its funding streams from advertisers to readers:

> We've built from £500 to a business that is turning over getting on for about £250,000 a year. We're employing now 19 people, mostly part-time … and those people have all the benefits of being employed, holiday pay, sick pay, pension and all that stuff. We've got about three freelancers that we employ as well and then a bunch of regular contributors. So we've kind of gone from this very kind of homemade thing to something that is much more formal and looks much more traditional, but we've done all sorts in between … we've gone from basically all funding coming from advertising to then we had quite a long period of time where we were about 80% funded by advertising and about 20% by readers and, in the last couple of years, that has shifted again and we're now 95% funded by readers.

The limitations of exclusively relying on advertising were mentioned by several contributors, leading to a degree of uncertainty and instability about future strategies.

A key theme when discussing organisational structures was how alternative online sites sought to improve their financial income in order to ensure long-term survival. This was not something ignored or sidelined by respondents as past critiques of alternative media have suggested (Comedia 1984). Several interviewees explained they were on a financial journey – transitioning towards a subscriber-based model. In particular, respondents stressed if they moved in this direction it would bring greater stability and editorial independence. As a senior editor of a left-wing site put it:

> We have thousands of people giving us money and I think the average sum every month is less than a tenner … We believe that obviously the financial underpinning of a media organisation necessarily impacts its editorial and political output and so that's why we consider ourselves independent … we've got a sustainable revenue model, we've got a large team.

Editors of other alternative media sites also mentioned new initiatives to develop subscription model funding, but their income revenue and editorial team was comparatively limited.

In terms of explaining how they spent the revenue generated or where staff used their time and resources, most respondents suggested that much of it revolved around their websites, including developing content and promoting it across social media networks. The editor of a right-wing site described its relatively small-scale operations and dependence on a small self-taught team:

we've got contributors who contribute on an ad hoc basis …We update the website as well with the articles, we have to do it … We've learnt how to put on a website, learnt how to stream, learnt how to put a show together. So it's all been learned on the job, so to speak.

Since almost all alternative media sites did not have a centralised newsroom – like most mainstream media organisations – many used what might be described as 'virtual newsrooms', with editorial meeting conducted through various online platforms. One multi-media left-wing site was able to make its whole editorial operation remote if required. A senior editor explained its routine editorial processes run as follows:

We have team meetings on Mondays, the whole team is generally on Slack and so people will be like we should cover this, I've seen this, but we have specific commissioning meetings on Monday morning, and then Thursday afternoon. So if news events have happened over the weekend, or on Thursday, they will normally be raised and we will cover them, we'll decide to cover them in those meetings.

With a far smaller editorial team, scale of production, and budget, Ian Middleton, an excontributor to Evolve Politics, revealed that its newsroom was, in effect "basically a chatroom. It's a sort of secret, members only group, or whatever it was, on Facebook". In short, most alternative media sites made use of new cost-effective digital tools and platforms to manage communication between staff and take editorial decisions. This point is developed in the next section, which examines organisational practices.

Organisational practices

The interviews revealed the contrasting organisational features of alternative media sites, considering more closely the individual and collective behaviour of the production process. Taken together, they explain how routine production decisions determine each site's editorial practices.

As the previous section explored, the interviews showed how alternative media sites were incorporating a number of traditional organisational and professional workplace features, such as daily meetings. Several respondents discussed their news-making practices in detail, including some common features around pitching articles and meetings to discuss what should be on the news agenda, not unlike their mainstream media counterparts. The difference between alternative and mainstream media was that these discussions were almost exclusively online, rather than in a centralised London-based studio. For example, several interviewees explained there were copy editor shifts in the mornings and afternoons, a routine process where ideas were shared and articles pitched to editors. In other words, the production process largely resembled how mainstream media operate, but was carried out virtually rather than in person. In fact, over recent years it is not uncommon for mainstream media to operate virtually. For example, research has shown BBC teams across the devolved nations of the UK hold regular remote meetings to contribute to centralised editorial meetings (Cushion 2019). This has been exacerbated post-pandemic as sites such as Zoom and Microsoft Teams have made it easier for large organisations to subscribe to software that seamlessly connects colleagues aurally and visually.

But there were differences in how alternative media editorially selected stories compared to professional journalists. Several interviewees highlighted how mainstream media stories would be monitored before daily editorial meetings in order for them to be repackaged and redeveloped for their own sites. An ex-contributor to a right-wing alternative media site explained this process:

> So each morning at around about 9 o'clock roughly, there would be an editorial call. … they'd be maybe about an hour long, and I wasn't but everybody would be expected to pitch maybe five stories, each of which … [the editor] … might then say, three of those go with. As I say, those stories would often be sourced from an existing news story elsewhere that you would then pull together, and you would always have to credit that news story. You couldn't take someone else's story. If you look, there is always actually a link to The Mail or The Telegraph, where they reported the first part and then you might move on and contact some people in the story.

Drawing on mainstream media sources to develop a new story was a recurrent theme in the production process among many alternative media sites. An ex-contributor to a right-wing site revealed that one key objective

> was to keep up with just the news cycle. So we would start our days by reading everyone else's, all the Daily Mail, probably not the Mirror so much but The Guardian, Telegraph, Times and just seeing what was out there. We would make a list of stories that we wanted to write about and we would just send the links, the Mail has written about it, I think it would be good for our audience or The Guardian has written this, I think we should rewrite it for our audience. So a lot of the time was taking what was going on and, especially with The Guardian's stuff, just giving the alternate view on the facts on the ground. So there was a lot of that going on.

Similarly, Ian Middleton, ex-contributor to Evolve Politics, revealed that:

> People would throw ideas up for articles. A lot of the stuff was screen scraped, gleaned from other sites, which again I began to find a bit uncomfortable because we were kind of regurgitating, and I can't remember what the correct

term for that is now, we were sort of rewriting stuff that had come up in The Guardian or other news platforms. Giving it a different slant, in some cases, but I don't think, the way the whole platform was set up, that it had really much scope for having its own reporters per se.

Many individuals also explained the editorial processes by which they acquired original material, such as Steve Walker, the editor of Skwawkbox, relied upon building a traditional network of sources:

I built up good relations with lots of Labour politicians over lots of years. Those kind of connections then have borne fruit that I never intended them to bear really. You wouldn't expect me to comment on sources really, I don't think but let's just say that the media's assumptions do a disservice to the level of connections that I've built up and the amount of work I've done in making sure that I have lots and lots of channels open to get information from people that trust me to handle it properly.

As well as rewriting mainstream media stories, Ian Middleton, ex-contributor to Evolve Politics, revealed that he and colleagues drew on social media networks or their own private contacts to generate fresh stories:

The other thing that we were trying to do was also find original stories, which was a lot harder to do as I was at home, they were in the office, so a lot of it was done through things like Twitter, Facebook and word of mouth contacts, that kind of thing. One of the guys, Chris, who was based in Canada, he came in a bit later, was amazing at getting interviews with people. I don't know how he did it but he would find all sorts of really interesting characters and then go and interview them, and also politicians. He was really good at phoning the politicians' offices and asking for an interview.

This account of the sourcing practices of alternative media is not that dissimilar too many mainstream journalists – building up networks of contacts, often quite specialised political contacts, and working hard to maintain their trust. With far fewer resources, the challenge for many alternative media sites was finding the time to identify and preserve these relationships as well as working from home. After all, many institutional sources sit in offices that limit formal communications whereas professional journalists share the same physical space, which can often informally generate new contacts and more effectively manage and maintain source interactions.

Editorial functions

The interviews revealed specific ways in which editorial processes worked across different alternative media sites. Above all, many of the editorial functions carried out replicated the newsgathering patterns of professional journalists. A senior editor of a left-wing site outlined its rigorous standards in news reporting:

> Our various editors have networks of sources in various ways, but then the thing is that when things come to being a story, then they're going to go through the editorial framing. So they will be assigned an editor from our articles team and if there is anything in it that needs some oversight, then I have an articles editor involved in that, and our editorial strategy group will be involved in that. Sources are treated in-line with our editorial standards code, so there is a kind of governance structure.

Several interviewees across different sites described the relatively streamlined production Process, with morning Zoom meeting reflecting on what stories to select and monitoring other news outlets. Some contributors pointed out that the pitching process was akin to their experiences of writing for mainstream media publications.

However, there were important differences between alternative media production and professional journalism, such as the balance between independent reporting and relying on secondary sources, in particular, mainstream media for stories. As already explored, several interviewees explained how much of their newsgathering was driven by finding 'hidden leads' in mainstream media articles that could be repackaged and rewritten according to their ideological objectives. This was well articulated by contributors at both right-wing and left-wing alternative media sites. Indeed, it was striking how similar their approach was to re-calibrating professional journalism, as one ex-contributor to a right-wing site explained:

> On the pitching front, what … [a right-wing alternative media site] aimed to do wasn't necessarily to produce a huge quantity of original news material, although there were bits of that and I will get on to that, but it was to look at the way that the news might be reported elsewhere and find … hidden leads. It might be paragraph 12 in a 15 paragraph news story in a newspaper, which has the actual kernel of something that he would then want us to run with and find out more; the buried lead.

Meanwhile, an ex-contributor to a left-wing site openly acknowledged how they would draw on professional journalism to re-frame the issue according to their ideological agenda. They revealed the site

> would take something in a mainstream article and use that as an angle to kind of expose some sort of issue or problem within … I suppose they tried to read between the lines in the news report in that way … I know a lot of the

mainstream media sort of slammed them for being fake news or whatever, but actually they were pretty hot on fact checking and stuff like that. Basic facts had to be linked back and the editing process was quite rigorous, and I had written for mainstream outlets and sometimes their editing process isn't that rigorous, so kudos to them there.

Almost all interviewees recognised the value and importance of high-quality editing and explained the rigour of their own editorial processes. John Ranson, ex-editor at The Canary, said that "At its peak, The Canary had a five gate editorial process with pieces being checked by the writer, the editor and a copy editor before publication and the chief sub-editor and the editor-in-chief after publication". Likewise, an editor of a left-wing site explained the time, effort, and attention to detail behind the production process:

Day-to-day I run the news site and once-a-month I also edit the print edition, which is a different set of skills ... So day-to-day I edit the news site. So I will review people's work, edit it myself, proof it, edit it, copy edit it, and get it ready for publication and publish it.

Several contributors across different sites mentioned there were expectations placed on them to produce several stories a day but through a robust editorial process.

Many interviewees working for different sites explained how stories were editorially selected and on what basis, such as making it newsworthy for the site, and ensuring it was in line with a particular ideological perspective. Some editors stressed the importance of being distinctive from mainstream media and offering audiences a new perspective that would appeal to their political interests. Some right-wing contributors suggested that their work was edited very lightly, whereas several left-wing contributors reported heavy editing, including adding more sensational language. A few interviewees revealed how they followed specific editorial processes about their formatting and stylistic approaches to writing news. For example, The Canary used software to help modulate the level and depth of written English to make the content simpler and more akin to tabloid language in order to offer its audiences clarity of expression. Steve Topple, contributor at The Canary, explained its production process in detail:

The software we work off is WordPress and you've got a plug-in called Yoast which gives you various readability scores and allows you, as a writer, to very much focus on making your writing as accessible as possible. Kerry-Anne and the other founder's idea was always that The Canary was going to be a left-wing tabloid, if you like, so we wouldn't tread on the areas that Novara do where it's very heavy, very academic. The point was to be accessible to everyone. It's kind of the notion that a university educated person is the only person who can really read university level literature, but if you take it down to the reading age of a 12 year old, everyone can read that. So accessibility has always been central to what we do, and that does drill down into the most basic things like active and passive voice, sentence length, syllable count.

Alternative media sites, from this perspective, can be viewed as quite sophisticated in design, strategically developing their production processes to appeal not just to left-leaning or right-leaning audiences but segments of audiences within a particular ideological position. This point is developed in the next section.

Professionalisation

Taken together, a consistent overarching theme to emerge from all the interviews was the increasing professionalisation of the production process. This term was even used on occasions by editors and contributors as a way of signalling a site's long-term sustainability, and driven by the experiences many had when working in professional journalism or aspiring to operate like mainstream media. Rather than being distinctive from the editorial practices of legacy media, there was an admission that alternative media sites should replicate some of their conventions to professionalise content.

A senior editor of a left-wing site admitted "I would like us to be more of a prestige better resourced more professional organisation than a lot of people out there, and I think already Politico or Vice – Vice not so much now – but BuzzFeed until last year, they were doing a lot more heavyweight journalism than legacy outlets". The editor went on to view professionalisation through the lens of mainstream norms, such as having a reporter within Westminster. Meanwhile, another senior editor of a left-wing outlet, acknowledged that the editorial team had long been discussing the need to develop a more professional site:

It's like anything that starts out as a passion project, ultimately you end up having a conversation internally about what sustainability looks like and with that what professionalization looks like. We've kind of had those conversations internally for about a good year or so because when you start out, you're just doing it because of the thing itself, and thinking about the cool content you can do, etc. and you don't really think about the bigger picture.

Another aspect of professionalisation was the development of individual skills by recruiting new staff to lead editorial practices and help train other contributors. This was well articulated by Steve Topple, a contributor to The Canary, who explained how the site changed after its standards of journalism had been questioned:

a lot of criticism that's levelled at independent left media is it blurs those lines between opinion and news. So we have rigid structures in place now to ensure that those lines aren't blurred. It's been a constant work-in-progress ... That [developing a style] was a big learning curve for all of us, because we were just used to getting on a keyboard and typing out what was in our heads ... I suppose it is, in some respects, a guerrilla warfare in terms of the fact that we're using new methods and up-to-date technology, and new ways of working against the corporate press which, in many respects, are still trying to catch up with that.

This tacit acknowledgement that alternative media needed to modernise to keep up with the pace of mainstream media demonstrates the commitment many sites had to professionalise production by enhancing editorial standards.

Needless to say, the purpose of professionalisation, according to some interviewees, was somewhat contentious. On the one hand, it was viewed through the prism of survival and longevity. But, on the other hand, it conveyed a faint sense of 'selling out' to mainstream norms and values. A strong recognition, particularly from left-wing alternative media sites, was a defence of their own newsgathering practices and ownership standards (a point developed in Chapter 9). Several left-wing sites, for example, have signed up to Impress, an independent media regulator, to oversee their content and assess if any editorial rules have been broken. When considering the standards of his own website, Steve Walker, editor of the Skwawkbox, explicitly pointed this out:

I'm a regulated news publication in that sense, so if people don't like what I publish, they've got a complaints avenue to pursue that's outside of my control. From a narrative point of view, it's better to use that kind of language rather than playing into the hands of people who just want to dismiss.

In other words, by signing up with a media regulator, which is also responsible for overseeing a wide range of mainstream media publications, many alternative left-wing sites wanted external legitimacy and recognition of their professional journalistic standards.

Beyond activism: the professionalisation of alternative media

Alternative media have long been studied through the prism of their activist aspirations. While their ideological pursuit of political issues remains a key part of their editorial identity, recent studies have shown the need to move beyond just focussing on their activist goals in order to better understand their editorial practices and organisational structures. As the previous chapters showed, the agendas of alternative media are driven by opposition to mainstream media and professional journalism. But while their output is distinctive from mainstream media, in recent years there appears to be convergence between the production of alternative media and professional journalism along with how audiences view them (Atkinson et al. 2019; Holt et al. 2019; Kenix 2011; Rauch 2014). But more empirical research is needed to understand new reporting practices, funding streams, and editorial pressures. The growing international scholarship of alternative media has demonstrated their increasing hybridity, challenging long-standing binary oppositional definitions between mainstream media and alternative media (Atkinson et al. 2019; Harlow 2023; Rae 2021). Moreover, as previous chapters identified, there is a need to consider alternative media within their broader national media and political environments in order to help understand how they position their journalism. Within a Greek or Turkish context, for instance, alternative media reporting impartially was interpreted either as an unnecessary or essential practice. This was in response to the broader characteristics of their respective national media and political environments (Ozgul and Veneti 2022).

More research with producers of alternative media is needed in order to interpret and understand their editorial aims and decision making. This chapter drew on a UK based-case study of editors and contributors of right-wing and left-wing alternative media sites to explore their production values and processes, including their relationship with mainstream media and use of journalistic practices and conventions. Needless to say, it found that, with perhaps the exception of Breitbart News, most sites were not well resourced, and operated with a limited editorial team (or, in the case of Skwawkbox, a "one man operation") and income revenue. But all alternative media sites made use of new cost-effective digital tools and platforms to help manage their production processes and editorial decision making. Notwithstanding the differences in resources between mainstream and alternative media, there was considerable overlap in their organisational practices. For example, the way editors and contributors of alternative news sites undertook their news gathering or source practices closely resembled how professional journalists operated. From building up networks of contacts, including specialised political contacts, to maintaining relationships and engendering trust, their daily editorial processes were not distinctive from mainstream media. Several interviewees explained they had previously worked for sites that could be characterised as mainstream media, perhaps signalling the continuum between what might be considered 'alternative' or 'mainstream' media production is not that distant. Of course, with finite resources, alternative media sites struggle to gather news because many work from home and lack routine institutional connections, such as having a permanent reporter in Westminster. Novara Media, according to one editor, wanted to enhance the site's professionalisation by recruiting someone to be a constant source covering Westminster-based politics. The next chapter explores how one left-wing site – Evolve Politics – obtained a Westminster lobby pass in order to gain more legitimacy even though it was a temporary measure.

More broadly, understanding the production processes of alternative media from the perspective of editors and contributors revealed how they developed often sophisticated editorial strategies that aligned with the work of professional journalists. Far from sites being dogmatically ideological or solely focussed on activist goals, several interviewees explained they had rigorous editorial policies to safeguard reporting standards. Frustrated that their journalism was being derided as disinformation or being labelled 'fake news', some left-wing sites had signed up to a media regulator, Impress, in order for their content to gain greater journalistic legitimacy and professionalisation. At the same time, all interviewees openly acknowledged their right or left-leaning editorial positions, rejecting the need for a neutral or objective approach. In pursuing their ideological goals and serving their readers, some interviewees explained how they went beyond just appealing to crude right-wing or left-wing perspectives, but instead addressed audiences with nuanced ideological positions and editorial practices, such as The Canary's left-wing tabloid approach. In doing so, they were not cynically creating news through an activist lens, but producing distinctive content through a professionalised process that was aligned with their editorial and ideological goals.

Consistent with recent production studies of alternative media, this UK case study of sites has demonstrated the need to understand the editorial practices of alternative media sites beyond their political activism. In the new digital landscape, many alternative media sites were following editorial norms, conventions, and standards long practised by professional journalists in mainstream media, but producing distinctively ideologically driven content.

The next chapter further explores the intersection between alternative and mainstream media production processes. In doing so, it explores how alternative media editors and contributors define political journalism, develop their own agenda, correct mainstream media, and disseminate their content across social media networks.

Note

1 Of the 40 interviews conducted who did not want anonymity, the following participants agreed to be on record to discuss their views about alternative media: Steve Walker from The Skwawkbox; Ian Middleton and Matt Turner from Evolve Politics; Nancy Mendoza, John Ranson, and Steve Topple from The Canary; Gary McQuiggin, Michael Walker, and Jack Barraclough from Novara Media; Jack Peat, Tim Coles, and Gavin Esler from the London Economic; Peter Jukes and Sam Bright from Byline Times; Deb Cridland from Dorset Eye; Conrad Bower from the Manchester Meteor; and Calvin Robinson from Breitbart, Westmonster, and Conservative Woman. Due to word-length limitations, not everyone was directly quoted in the book. But, taken together, all the interviews – on and off the record – helpfully informed the context, background, and analysis of alternative media throughout the book. The role and status of interviewees may have changed since the book was published.

References

Atkinson, J. D, Kenix, L.J. and Andersson, L. (2019) *Alternative Media Meets. Mainstream Politics: Activist Nation Rising.* Lanham: Lexington Books

Atton, C. (2002) *Alternative Media*. London: Sage

Bell, E. (2018) 'Can James Harding's Tortoise be more than a rich person's club?', *The Guardian*, 22 October, https://www.theguardian.com/commentisfree/2018/oct/22/james-harding-tortoise-rich-persons-club-journalism-problems

Comedia (1984) 'The alternative press: The development of underdevelopment', *Media, Culture & Society*, Vol. 6(2), 95–102. https://doi.org/10.1177/016344378400600202

Cushion, S. (2019) *The Range and Depth of BBC News and Current Affairs: A Content Analysis*. London: Ofcom.

Cushion, S. (2012b) *Television Journalism*. London: Sage.

Downing, J.D.H., Ford, T.V., Gil, G. and Stein, L. (2001). *Radical Media: Rebellious Communication and Social Movements*. Thousand Oaks: SAGE Publications.

Farinosi, M. and Treré, E. (2014) 'Challenging mainstream media, documenting real life and sharing with the community: An analysis of the motivations for producing citizen journalism in a post-disaster city', *Global Media and Communication*, Vol. 10(1): 73–92, https://doi.org/10.1177/1742766513513192

Harlow, S. (2022) 'A new people's press? Understanding digital-native news sites in Latin America as alternative media', *Digital Journalism*, Vol. 10(8): 1322–1341, https://doi.org/10.1080/21670811.2021.1907204

Harlow, S. (2023) *Digital-Native News and the Remaking of Latin American Mainstream and Alternative Journalism*. London: Routledge. https://doi.org/10.4324/9781003152477

Heikka, T. and Carayannis, E. G. (2019) 'Three stages of innovation in participatory journalism—co-initiating, co-sensing, and co-creating news in the Chicago school cuts case', Journal of the Knowledge Economy, Vol. 10(2), 437–464, https//doi.org/10.1007/s13132-017-0466-0

Holt, K. Figenschou, T.U. and Frischlich, L. (2019) 'Key Dimensions of Alternative News Media, Digital Journalism, Vol.7(7): 860–869, https://doi.org/10.1080/21670811.2019.1625715

Kenix, L.J. (2011) *Alternative and Mainstream Media: The Converging Spectrum*. London: Bloomsbury Publishing

Khiabany, G. (2000) 'Red Pepper: A new model for the alternative press?', *Media, Culture & Society*, Vol. 22(4): 447–463, https://doi.org/10.1177/016344300022004005

Ozgul, A.B. and Veneti, A. (2022) 'The different organizational structures of alternative media: Through the perspective of alternative media journalists in Turkey and Greece', *Digital Journalism*, Vol. 10(8): 1302–1321. https://doi.org/10.1080/21670811.2021.1943482

Pickard, V. (2006) 'United yet autonomous: Indymedia and the struggle to sustain a radical democratic network', *Media, Culture & Society, Vol. 28(3):* 315–336. https://doi.org/10.1177/0163443706061685

Rae, M. (2021) 'Hyperpartisan News: Rethinking the Media for Populist Politics', *New Media & Society*, Vol. 23 (5): 1117–1132, https://doi.org/10.1177/1461444820910416

Rauch, J. (2014) 'Exploring the alternative–mainstream dialectic: What "alternative media" means to a hybrid audience', *Communication, Culture & Critique*, Vol. 8 (1): 124–143.

Rauch, J. (2021) *Resisting the News: Engaged Audiences, Alternative Media, and Popular Critique of Journalism*. New York: Routledge.

Rodríguez, C. (2001) *Fissures in the Mediascape: An International Study of Citizens' Media*. Cresskill: The Hampton Press.

Sandoval, M. and Fuchs, C. (2010) 'Towards a critical theory of alternative media', *Telematics and Informatics*, Vol. 27: 141–150. https://doi.org/10.1016/j.tele.2009.06.011

Schofield, J. (2008) 'iReport: Now anyone can be a journalist', *The Guardian*, 2, 2 June, https://www.theguardian.com/technology/2008/jun/02/ireport

6

THE INFLUENCE OF MAINSTREAM MEDIA ON ALTERNATIVE MEDIA PRODUCTION

This chapter considers the intersection between alternative and mainstream media production, interpreting the continuities and differences in how political news is conceptualised and operationalised by editors and contributors of alternative media. It charts how, over the last decade or so, the production practices of alternative media have been conceptualised by a continuum that swings between what is defined as 'alternative' and 'mainstream' (Harcup 2013; Kenix 2011), acknowledging the overlap that many scholars resisted in the early years of alternative media studies. This hybridity is how alternative media have gradually been understood and interpreted in the 21st century (Atton 2004), recognising the diverse formats and stylistic approaches of sites in the digital age.

Against this backdrop, this chapter explores how the producers of alternative media view their relationship with mainstream media and professional journalism. It does so by drawing on interviews with 40 editors and contributors that examined their editorial judgements and specific journalistic practices. The chapter moves beyond a focus on single case studies of production processes – which is often how alternative media have been examined in the past (see Chapter 1) – by scrutinising the motivations of both right-wing and left-wing alternative media sites from the UK. It builds on the findings of the previous chapter, which demonstrated that many sites had become more professionalised in their approach, reflecting a convergence with how mainstream newsrooms operate. The chapter develops this analysis further by exploring how alternative media editors and contributors interpret political journalism and their editorial agenda, as well as understanding how they carry out specific practices, such as correcting the media and using social media to disseminate content and influence political debates. But it first begins by setting some context to how scholars have understood the production of alternative media in comparison with mainstream media.

DOI: 10.4324/9781003360865-7

Interpreting the continuum between mainstream and alternative media

With some caveats (e.g., Harcup 2013), much of the research about the production of alternative media has emphasised their distinction from mainstream media, including their reporting practices, their funding streams, and, perhaps above, their activist goals. But, as the previous chapter acknowledged, when conceptualising alternative media through a largest activist prism it can narrowly and misleadingly characterise their production characteristics. Lievrouw's book (2011), *Alternative and Activist New Media*, attempted to categorise alternative media distinctly by developing genres that distinguished between their content and function. For example, participatory journalism, mediated mobilisation, and common knowledge. While participatory journalism was defined as innovative newsgathering techniques, mediated mobilisation was a site where people could find out how activist plans and issues. Commons knowledge, meanwhile, related to the shared discussion and deliberation of debates, which audiences could always access and contribute. These production processes were often centred on specific social and political issues.

Engaging with Lievrouw's (2011) conceptualisation of alternative media, Atkinson's book (2017), *Journey Into Social Activism*, agreed these categorises were largely designed for the production of activist media. He offered the following definition of alternative media:

> Alternative media refers to news that is produced by activists. Such media is different from mainstream media as the content is either critical of dominant power structures, produced in ways that are different from mainstream media, or interpreted by the audience to be alternative from the mainstream media. Activist media are used by activist to draw attention to an issue, promote a cause, or reframe an issue.
>
> *(Atkinson 2017: 45–46)*

But, as the previous chapter concluded, the production of alternative media is not that dissimilar to mainstream media processes and conventions. While it found some differences between the motivations of alternative and mainstream media production, there was also overlap in the organisational structures and editorial strategies of professional journalism. This intersplicing of alternative and mainstream media conventions has been recognised by some scholars as hybrid practices of alternative media, blurring the boundaries between the production of activism media and professional journalism. As Atton observed (2006: 16):

> Hybridity can also been found in the form and content for alternative media reporting. It can be argued that, far from alternative media establishing ways of doing journalism that are radical to the extent that they mark dramatic ruptures

from existing practices of journalism, their work may draw from existing forms (such as tabloid journalism) and methods (such as investigative journalism).

The previous chapter, for example, revealed that The Canary drew on tabloid practices to make its journalism politically accessible to readers in ways that were less highbrow than left-wing competitors, such as Novara Media. In other words, alternative media journalism was not driven purely by activist goals, but mainstream journalistic practices (e.g., tabloid) that could enhance a site's reach and influence.

The focus on activism and alternative media has often meant studies examining the production of alternative media have been quite narrowly classified, excluding many sites that may not have conventionally been interpreted as alternatives to mainstream media (e.g., Downing 1984). Kenix's (2011) book, *Alternative and Mainstream Media: The Converging Spectrum*, challenged the conventional orthodoxy of much alternative media scholarship. Rather than accept the binary distinctions scholars have previously used to differentiate mainstream media from alternative media, she believed there was a converging spectrum of editorial characteristics that demonstrated a significant overlap between all forms of media. Her argument is worth quoting at length:

> traditionally conceptualized mainstream and alternative media now draw so heavily from practices historically thought to be the purview of the other that it is increasingly difficult to ascertain any clear demarcations of difference. Most individual media can no longer be compartmentalized within each categorical nuance of what has traditionally been conceived as alternative or as mainstream. This relatively recent shift in media is not only a change in the linguistic assessment of a category for organizational purposes. This shift represents a convergence in the media spectrum, which has traditionally been conceptualized as sections of mutually exclusive domains for alternative and mainstream media to occupy separately.
>
> *(Kenix 2011: 4)*

Kenix's analysis was based exclusively on examining the content of either mainstream or alternative media, and unpacking practices that have been conventionally defined as representing either alternative or mainstream journalism. For example, she found the practice of citizen journalism – once a defining characteristic of alternative media – to be on display as much on CNN and BBC as it was in alternative media blogs. Meanwhile, her content analysis of what blogs labelled alternative media concluded they "critiqued mainstream content with mainstream ideology and normative practices found in mainstream journalism" (Kenix 2011: 119). However, Kenix's (2011) analysis relied solely on textual analysis to observe any differences between alternative and mainstream media. The editorial choices and motivations of alternative media producers to either conform to or deviate from mainstream media were not assessed.

As Chapter 1 explored, Harcup (2013) carried out a qualitative survey with journalists who had worked for both alternative and mainstream media outlets in the UK. Reinforcing Kenix's perspective, he found many contributors did not subscribe to any clear-cut distinctions between what might be defined as 'mainstream' journalism or 'alternative' media production. He found they drew freely on the editorial practices of professional journalists. A more distinctive difference was found in the autonomy of alternative media producers, since they felt they were more involved in news selection and decision making, pursuing stories that had a public or ideological purpose. Like Kenix, Harcup (2013: 115) used the term "continuum" to reflect the shifting of shared practices between alternative and mainstream journalism, while acknowledging that differences remained including their relative degree of power and influence.

The shifting parameters of alternative and mainstream media was recognised in Atkinson et al.'s (2019) edited book *Alternative Media Meets Mainstream Politics: Activist Nation*. Taken together, the chapters demonstrated that contemporary alternative media should not be placed on the margins of mainstream media because across different contexts, they can, at times, play an influential role in setting the mainstream media and political agenda. In other words, the power dynamics of alternative and mainstream media have changed over recent years. Some national media environments – notably in the US – have produced alternative media sites that more fully intersect with mainstream media and professional journalism than other Western nations (a point explored in Chapter 9). Reflecting on this shifting media ecology, Rauch (2021: 3) argued that "The goal of placing all media into categories, alternative and mainstream, disregards the ways in which these interdependent genres resemble, influence, interact, and compete with each other".

But while there has been a growing number of empirical studies examining the characteristics of alternative media (see Chapters 2, 3, and 4) and how audiences interpret them (see Chapters 7 and 8), there has been limited research from the producers of alternative media, asking editors and contributors directly about their editorial choices and relationship with professional journalism. The aim of this chapter is to explore the increasing professionalisation of alternative media first-hand by drawing on 40 interviews with different right-wing and left-wing alternative media sites from the UK conducted primarily on Zoom between November 2020 and April 2021. The interviews, on average, lasted between 30 and 60 minutes, with a researcher following the same set of semi-structured questions. Some interviewees asked for their names not be mentioned, while others were conducted on the record (see Footnote 4 in Chapter 5). This chapter focusses on the inner workings of alternative media outlets from the perspective of their editors and contributors, providing new insights into their production processes, in particular understanding their relationship with mainstream media and professional journalism.

The findings of the interviews will be split into four salient themes. Each reveals how editorial staff conceptualise their approach (1) generally to political journalism, (2) in specific editorial practices, (3) in how they correct mainstream media, and (4) in how they use social media to promote their ideological goals.

The relationship between alternative media and mainstream media production

Political journalism

The interviews explored first-hand with editors and contributors how they understood and interpreted the role of political journalism, their editorial practices, and ultimately how they viewed themselves working for an alternative media site in contrast to mainstream media.

Above all, there was universal acknowledgement among respondents that their approach to producing content was politically driven, with most providing a relatively clear articulation of the issues or political ideology they were pursuing. Ex-editor of the left-wing Canary, John Ranson, for example, described the site as

> Progressive in that our ethos and content reflected broadly left-wing politics and social liberalism. As an organisation The Canary sits in the continuum that includes the Occupy movement, the anti-austerity movement and the surge of support for Labour under Jeremy Corbyn. However The Canary was "independent" in that it wasn't part of any political party or body and had no big money owner or funder calling the shots. "Campaigning journalism" to us meant not only informing our readers but also seeking to empower them to take meaningful steps to improve their bit of the world. Many stories would include either a call to action of some sort or, for example, further reading or resources.

Similarly, Calvin Robinson, a contributor to Breitbart, Westmonster, and Conservative Woman, explained that:

> It's all about the cause for me. So the issues that I'm working on are the cultural wars, fighting against these hard left ideologies such as critical race theory, identity politics and when there is an issue that I want to discuss, to be honest these days mostly the media outlets contact me. But back in the beginning of my writing, I used to just, if I had an idea I would pitch it to an outlet that I thought maybe might be interested in hearing my perspective and then took it from there really.

In this account, a contributor was able to produce ideological content across three major UK right-wing sites, but according to their different formats and styles (as Chapters 2 and 3 revealed).

Among some respondents, there was an awareness of how the issues they were championing conflicted with traditional normative approaches of delivering 'professional' or 'objective' journalism. In many cases, this was defended, even justified, because in their view *all* journalism had some kind of ideological agenda beneath the surface. This was well articulated by a senior editor of a left-wing site:

> Our journalism is always committed. That might sound like you're saying you're independent but you're also saying you're politically committed, are those not at odds with each other? Our view is it's possible to create objective journalism, and you should create objective journalism, there is an objective truth but everybody has political commitments and in order to furnish the reader or the listener or the viewer with as much information as possible, it's important to say I'm producing this, I'm trying to do it as an objective professional. However, at the same time, I want you to know I'm a socialist.

In further defending why an impartial approach to political journalism was rejected, several contributors pointed out they were providing political pluralism to the media system through either their left-wing or right-wing alternative media political agendas that the mainstream media did not cover.

But neither left-wing nor right-wing contributors ever hid or disguised the fact that their alternative media sites were politically motivated. Yet, at the same time, they rigidly held the view that what they did was journalism, despite their open political opinions and what others might think of them. Michael Walker, contributing editor at Novara Media, acknowledged that he

> used to think of myself as an activist first and a journalist second, so journalism was kind of a wing of my activism. Whereas now I very much think of myself as a journalist first … I think that's actually quite important for having a decent product.

Likewise, some contributors to right-wing sites revealed they enjoyed not being solely partisan and were able to exercise their own autonomy by criticising specific policy decisions from across the ideological spectrum. In this sense, contributors of alternative media were conveying a degree of journalistic independence, with a thirst for scrutiny being applied to political parties on the left and right as well across a range of ideological issues. There was no partisan motivation to be blindly faithful to a particular party or leader. A similar position was espoused by one left-wing editor: "We are independent, we're not aligned to any political party … we want to expose injustice and corruption and distorting aspects of society, and have factual reporting again, and investigation … The mission is, let's rebuild independent journalism".

In explaining their approach to journalism, several interviewees mentioned their background as a key influence in the production of alternative media. For example, many on the left had activist backgrounds (especially for staff at Novara Media), while some on the right have emerged from professional or semi-professional backgrounds in politics. In doing so, this was viewed as a motivating reason for the production of content because alternative media sites allowed them to articulate unspoken or marginalised voices in society. Steve Topple, a contributor to The Canary, explained that his background and experience informed his journalism:

> Coming from an activist background, a journalist background, and coming from a poor background and living in a poor background now, I just have people I know, whether it be disabled people, people living with mental health issues, whether it be housing activists, whether it be climate change activists, whether it be fracking activists.

Similarly, an ex-contributor to a right-wing site put it succinctly, stating they "wanted to give a voice to people who felt that they had no voice".

Taken together, on both sides of the political spectrum, contributors and editors of alternative media defined themselves as political journalists, but with activist goals. Or, put differently, their rejection of the objectivity norm did not undermine their legitimacy as independent journalists. While several contributors revealed their backgrounds in party politics and campaigning, they put their journalism ahead of activism.

Editorial coverage and agenda

Both editors and contributors were reflexive about their site's agenda, championing the stories that motivated them and acknowledging aspects of journalism that could be approved and topics that could be reported more effectively. Overall, there was a clear ideological difference in the stories editors and contributors pursued across right-wing and left-wing sites. Broadly speaking, right-wing interviewees focussed on coverage of Brexit as a key area of focus and importance for their outlets, while left-wing interviewees tended to focus on how they covered the then left-wing Labour leader, Jeremy Corbyn. This editorial focus was evidenced by the systematic content analysis drawn upon in Chapters 3 and 4.

Many interviewees discussed their plans to develop and expand their journalism in order to keep up with the new political environment – especially since both Brexit and Corbyn's leadership had receded as major issues. Indeed, conversations about coverage were as much about the content they currently provided as they were about the output they aspired to cover. Many interviewees expressed aspirations to grow and expand their content across multiple issues. Some contributors to Novara Media, for example, were particularly self-critical of the site's coverage of

Corbyn and stressed they were exploring ways of diversifying the news agenda and creating more audiovisual and multimedia output. One interviewee admitted that "we [Novara Media] have maybe in the past got stuck a bit in a loop of examining the Labour Party, and looking at what went wrong with Corbyn and the election, in a slightly unconstructive way". Interestingly, they went on to say that there was a

> specific idea [of] getting a lobby pass and being a Westminster correspond- ent is something that we're discussing now. I'm not necessary convinced that they should do more stuff like that rather than ... I think there are plenty of things like that that a political correspondent could pick up that are beyond Westminster.

Similarly, Matt Turner, a former co-editor of Evolve Politics, said his site was one of the first recently launched alternative media outlets to obtain a lobby pass in order to gain credibility and enhance its journalistic legitimacy after receiving criticism from mainstream media. Reflecting on his experiences, Turner revealed that

> The Number 10 briefings were interesting and I was just kind of taking it all in. It's something which is completely foreign to me. I never felt at home there, let's put it that way. Even when I was in, I felt like an outsider.

Turner further revealed he could not name any specific Evolve Politics stories that were generated from attending a government briefing at Number 10 Downing Street – perhaps illustrating the difficulty of offering an alternative agenda when reporting with a pack of mainstream journalists. Turner went on to say that

> when it comes to a lot of under-reported issues, I think we did quite well and that's what we did want to focus on instead of the broad topics that the kind of mainstream were already discussing. Incessantly every day people were saying I'm sick of Brexit, I'm sick of hearing it on the news.

The Canary also developed its coverage beyond the party politics of Corbyn or Brexit because readers had moved on. According to John Ranson, an ex-editor,

> I think The Canary has achieved a good range of coverage. For example, I'm immensely proud of the body of work regarding environmental issues. There's also been some very good reporting on a number of knotty international situa- tions, especially Venezuela.

Indeed, several left-wing editors and contributors signalled that their intention was to provide more factual reporting on, broadly speaking, home affairs and economics (a hard news agenda) under what can be defined as reportage (see Chapters 2 and 3). Conversely, more contributors and editors across right-wing outlets often referenced issues related broadly to the 'culture war', that is, coverage that explored social and cultural stories, many of which were covered from a perceived biased perspective in mainstream media. Calvin Robinson, a contributor to Breitbart, Westmonster, and Conservative Woman, revealed that he

> used to write a lot about the indoctrination going on in schools. So I'd write about what I saw in education, I was an Assistant Principal and I saw it all over the place and I wanted to make people aware of what was going on ... these days often I'm writing more about critical race theory and I suppose it's very much linked because in education, that's still being shovelled down the throats of our young people.

Culture and politics, in this sense, intersected far more editorially in right-wing than left-leaning alternative media sites. It drove the agendas of right-wing sites, whereas most left-wing sites were more closely aligned to following party political news cycles (see Chapter 2).

Another interesting acknowledgement from both right-wing and left-wing sites was that their agendas were guided by mainstream media coverage. This was tied to the fact that they were taking their 'hidden leads' from mainstream media stories (see Chapter 5), which they repackaged to suit their editorial agenda. In doing so, this meant they often relied on commentary rather than primary reporting because it was less time consuming and costly to produce. For example, Michael Walker, a contributing editor to Novara Media, openly admitted that:

> In a way most of what we cover is sourced from the mainstream media. So I'll read the Financial Times a lot, I'll read The Times a lot, not really the comment section but just the news section and then it'll often be on the show we've found an interesting story in the FT that we think probably deserves a bit more coverage than it's getting on the TV news. So, in a way, I feel like I have quite a collegiate relationship with lots of the media.

From another perspective, Steve Walker, editor of The Skwawkbox, revealed much of his site's coverage was driven in reaction to how Labour's left-wing leader was portrayed by mainstream media and then rebutting it with facts: "In the Corbyn era, it was very much the media would be claiming one thing and I would be finding out the facts and releasing the different narrative". Walker went on to reveal that The Skwawkbox was "definitely a niche or kind of specialist site .... I'm not interested in covering the kind of stories you might find as filler in a typical newspaper or site or whatever. So that's not ... 1) I don't have the time to do it and 2) I don't want to dilute the actual core information that's on there".

The intersection between mainstream and alternative media agendas was a central part of how many interviewees explained their own editorial agenda. As explored in the previous chapter and developed further below, correcting media narratives drove the agenda of left-wing and right-wing alternative media sites.

Media correctives

The interviews revealed how editors and contributors of alternative media sites navigated their relationship with mainstream media. Above all, they showed how all sites – from right and left perspectives – believed a central part of their role was to provide a corrective to the mainstream media, challenging and re-telling stories to more accurately reflect what they considered to be 'the facts'.

Despite the clear antagonism between mainstream media and alternative media sites – as demonstrated by Chapters 2 and 4 – many of the interviewees did not simply dismiss or devalue the work of professional journalism. Many respondents stated they regularly consumed mainstream media for reasons other than critiquing it. Instead, some editors and contributors explained how their sites had a complicated mutual relationship with mainstream media, drawing on their news agendas but also correcting them in the process. As Matt Turner, a former editor of Evolve Politics, put it: "we'd never attack them [mainstream media] for the sake of it. There was always rationale, data or at the very least some kind of questionable editorialising on the mainstream's part involved in what was right". In exploring the complicated relationship between alternative and mainstream media, several interviewees described a somewhat fractious interdependence, such as being invited onto mainstream media broadcasters, and the ways in which they engaged with producers, who often pigeonholed them to suit a narrative. For example, some interviewees from left-wing sites complained about being professional journalists stereotyping them as unapologetic left-wing Corbyn fans, devoid of any common sense or critical reasoning. Moreover, many interviewees either directly stated or alluded to the fact that the shortcomings of the mainstream media were, in effect, the very reason that they exist as alternative outlets. For instance, an ex-contributor to a right-wing site, stated: "We were very clear that our mission … was to bring balance actually because we felt very strongly that there was definitely a left-wing bias within the mainstream media". Several interviewees from both right-wing and left-wing sites described their intense scepticism towards mainstream media – reinforcing the content analysis findings in Chapters 2 and 4 in how they reported professional journalism. But, as the qualitative textual analysis revealed, their critiques were not always simplistically articulated. On occasions, there was quite sophisticated understanding of mainstream media practices, deconstructing journalistic language, and how news agendas were shaped by regulation or ownership. An editor of a left-wing site, for example, believed

that large aspects of the mainstream media in Britain are seriously compromised. They have relationships with people in positions of power that are way too close and they're following a mission by proprietors who have a lot of money and influence as well, and it's often their proprietor's interests that are being advanced rather than public interest, necessarily.

An oft-repeated criticism from respondents was that mainstream media were 'out of touch' with the public. While they were labelled 'mainstream' media, several respondents believed they represented a narrow (liberal) viewpoint that was far from a reflection of mainstream public opinion. Some interviewees claimed their alternative media sites represented the most common views and were more in step with public opinion. Calvin Robinson, contributor to Breitbart, Westmonster, and Conservative Woman, conveyed this perspective:

> I think mainstream media is alternative quite often and that's why sometimes we have to step around it until they pick up an issue, because I think there's very much a liberal perspective from mainstream media and I don't think that is the same with the rest of the country … I really don't think of myself as an alternative. I think of myself as on the side of the everyman and it's just that the mainstream media voice or the liberal voice is the loudest, and it's the silent majority that need sometimes to have their voice expressed.

Several interviewees from left-wing sites developed their critiques of professional journalists by making reference to the structural constraints they worked under, such as following a commercial logic ahead of pursuing stories in the 'public interest'. In the case of the BBC, its financial reliance on the government of the day was viewed by some interviewees from left-wing sites as undermining the public service broadcaster's political independence. But, above all, left-wing editors and contributors often criticised and attacked BBC journalism for editorial misjudgements and breaches of impartiality – a critique routinely found in their coverage (see Chapters 2, 3, and 4). From a right-wing perspective, the critique of the BBC often focussed on a so-called 'group think', which was largely a result – according to interviewees – of the recruitment of editorial staff from a 'liberal' background. Calvin Robinson, a contributor to Breitbart, Westmonster, and Conservative Woman, for example, explained that:

> The problem I had with the BBC is that it's so narrow minded. There's a massive group thing, not just at the BBC but in mainstream media, where there is an approved narrative which everyone subscribes to, which wouldn't always be a problem but the issue there is that if you don't subscribe to it, you are perceived as bad or evil and, therefore, they are free to attack you. So it's like the so-called anti-racists that will racially attack you and they don't see the irony behind that.

This structural critique of professional journalism was a motivation for many editors and contributors to correct mainstream media coverage, especially BBC News because of its self-proclaimed commitment towards impartiality.

The importance of social media

Taken together, the interviews with editors and contributors from a range of alternative media sites collectively revealed how they wanted to overcome the power of mainstream media in order to challenge their perspectives and influence people's understanding of the world. In doing so, respondents pointedly made reference to the strategic importance of social media to reach audiences and convey their agenda.

Almost all interviewees believed that without social media their alternative media sites would have far fewer users. Social media was seen to significantly enhance their audience reach across a range of networks, but there were many obstacles to effectively disseminating their editorial output. Several editors and contributors stressed the need to come up with creative strategies to share content in ways that appealed to users and would gain traction online. In other words, there was an editorial consciousness of asking what would play well on social media in order to reach target audiences. One left-wing senior editor acknowledged that:

> I think it [social media] is good for us, for our editors to have a good following online … It's useful for us because often conversations about stories will kind of happen in real-time and places like Twitter are useful for our editors to either be engaged in those, or be observant of them.

That said, several contributors voiced their discontent with how social media operated, from the personal hostility they faced to the opaque way in which it can successfully lead to clicks and audience growth. For instance, an ex-contributor to a left-wing site described the strategy designed to attract audiences:

> The way it kind of works inside is they would schedule stories in the best slots on social media that were going to get the best hits. So some writers had already kind of cracked it and knew how to pick headlines. That was the worst part of the job, I think, picking a headline, because I could never get the right headline to get people to click on it.

Several interviewees raised concerns about following a social media logic because it could undermine the quality of political debates. Calvin Robinson, contributor to Breitbart, Westmonster, and Conservative Woman, was vociferous in his criticism of social media. He said bluntly that:

> Social media is toxic, it's the devil's work, it really is, it's the devil's playground. I think it was a mistake but it is a tool that we have to use to publicise our work and to get it out there and build traction, to get the message across.

A more precise concern raised by several interviewees was working out how social media platforms operated, in particular how their algorithms worked, in order to be able to understand when an article was widely shared or ignored. For example, Nancy Mendoza, who helped launch The Canary, revealed that in the early years of the site's development "we've had to do all sorts of things to try and game the Facebook algorithm. 2017, 80% of the traffic was coming from social and of that, 92% was from Facebook. … Yes, we are reliant on social media". Among some respondents, there was a wide range of professional experience gained from working with social media, such as Jack Peat, editor of the London Economic, who explained the complexities of understanding algorithms and ensuring articles would gain traction online:

> with Facebook … you had to have at least one point of differentiation to stand a chance, and two or three if you wanted to do well. So really, as a content package, there's three things that go into Facebook: it's the title, which needs to be something different; the image needs to mixed up, which is why often you'll see images where they're split images, or they could even be cartoon images, and you'll get a lot of these images that have at least one point of differentiation; and then the content itself also has to be different.

Changes to how social media algorithms worked were frequently highlighted as a negative issue by editors and contributors that had serious strategic implications for alternative media sites. Some of them believed it was an intentional attempt by social media companies to limit their reach. There were also some differences between interviewees about whether media criticism was a driver of traffic. But there was broad agreement that news cycles and timing played a part in alternative media content being shared widely online, rather than simply dumping content onto social media sites. Moreover, how you engaged varied according to different social media sites and their prevailing logics. For instance, Steve Topple, contributor to The Canary, challenged the notion that social media is

> predominantly a driver of traffic. In our experience, there's no guarantees on that at all. What we've learned over the years is that there is no rhyme or reason to what drives our traffic. It's very much depending on how tuned in you are, as a writer, to the news cycle, but also tuned into what the discussions are on social media, especially Twitter, because Twitter always tends to pre-empt Facebook in terms of what's been talked about. Twitter comes first and then it dribbles down slowly to Facebook.

From a different perspective, social media was viewed as an important place for sourcing stories or keeping up with events as they occur in real time. Steve Walker, editor of The Skwawkbox, articulated this position well:

> I think Twitter is more interest driven. So people who want to find out about a particular topic or follow a particular person, whether that's a celebrity or a politician or whatever. So people talk about the Twitter echo-chamber. I think it

probably applies more to Twitter than to Facebook in that sense because I think there's this broader use of Facebook as a genuinely social media in that sense rather than an information source, that allows some of the information to bleed across those boundaries into other people's awareness if you do it right.

As the opening part of this chapter explored, using Twitter as an information source to monitor public opinion and engagement, or to keep up with the news cycle, replicates how many mainstream media journalists operate. In other words, the use of social media by alternative media sites broadly follows the logic of professional journalism.

Developing professional production practices to challenge mainstream media power

This chapter has shed new empirical light on how the production of alternative media intersects with professional journalism. Informed by 40 interviews with editors and contributors from a range of left-wing and right-wing alternative media sites in the UK, it revealed that they were relatively open about their politicised approach to media production. But several interviewees viewed themselves as political journalists first, with activist goals, which they believed did not undermine their role as independent journalists. This was evidenced by the different ideological agendas pursued across right-wing and left-wing sites. Brexit, for example, was central to right-wing sites, while for left-wing sites there was a heavy focus on the then left-wing Labour leader, Jeremy Corbyn, and how he and his policies were, in their view, unfairly portrayed by mainstream media.

Indeed, most editors and contributors of alternative media openly acknowledged that a central part of their agenda was correcting mainstream media by challenging and reframing their coverage in order to more accurately reflect what they consider to be 'the facts'. Across both right-wing and left-wing sites, acting as a corrective to mainstream media was interpreted by interviewees as addressing ideological biases within the media system as a whole. For example, contributors to sites across the political spectrum claimed to be acting in ways that rectified biases within the BBC's coverage and explained numerous media production techniques used to reach audiences. These included reframing existing stories in the media and the use of provocative headlines. The use of sensational or provocative headlines was justified by editors and contributors as not reflecting their own preferred forms of journalism but as a consequence of wider influences, such as the structural forces of mainstream media and the role played by social media platforms. For instance, there was an actuate awareness of how social media algorithms worked in ways that often undermined a site's reach and influence. This was fully appreciated by editors and contributors of alternative media because they often referenced how they used social media to challenge the power of mainstream media. The strategic importance of social media being able to reach people and to convey an alternative media site's agenda was viewed by many respondents as central to them being able to influence their readers' understanding of the world distinctively from mainstream media.

Academic studies have begun to recognise the shared practices between alternative and mainstream media, even though the world of professional journalism wields far greater collective power and influence. Scholars have interpreted this as a shifting continuum (Harcup 2013; Kenix 2011), with alternative media sites embracing to different degrees the production and editorial traits of professional journalism. But there has been little scholarship examining how, from the voices of producers, alternative media sites editorially decide their agenda, select stories and sources, frame coverage and distribute content to audiences online and across different social media platforms. This chapter's analysis – informed by insights from 40 editors and contributors of alternative media sites – has demonstrated that it is becoming increasingly difficult to separate what constitutes 'mainstream' and 'alternative' media production processes.

Alternative media sites today draw on the practices and conventions of mainstream media, with many editors and contributors now self-identifying as a journalist rather than an activist. As the book has so far revealed, most alternative media sites have become increasingly sophisticated in their production of content by adapting to the digital media environment, drawing on new sophisticated technological tools, and extending their reach online and across new social media networks. In doing so, they have become more professionalised in their approach, representing a mainstreaming of alternative media production. Rather than being produced distinctly from mainstream media – as academic studies have historically emphasised (see Chapter 1) – they have become ever more entwined with the values and practices of how professional journalists operate, developing ways of producing sustainable media that meets the ideological aims and objectives of their sites. As the chapter showed, while activism still fuels the motivations of editors and contributors of alternative media, there was a drive to produce content through new professionalised structures and processes enabled by the new digital media environment.

The next chapter moves beyond the production of alternative media to the users who engage with them across both right-wing and left-wing sites. As alternative media sites have evolved into the new digital media environment, it considers who engages with them and their wider relationship with mainstream media and politics.

References

Atkinson, J.D. (2017) *Journey into Social Activism: Qualitative Approaches.* New York: Fordham University Press.

Atkinson, J.D, Kenix, L.J. and Andersson, L. (2019) *Alternative Media Meets. Mainstream Politics: Activist Nation Rising.* Lanham: Lexington Books.

Atton, C. (2004) *An Alternative Internet. Edinburgh n Alternative Internet.* Edinburgh: Edinburgh University Press.

Atton, C. (2006) 'Ethical issues in alternative journalism' in Keeble, R. (ed.) *Communication Ethics Today*. Leicester: Troubador Publishing.

Downing, J. (1984) *Radical Media: The Political Experience of Alternative Communication*. Boston, MA: South End Press.

Harcup, T. (2013) *Alternative Journalism, Alternative Voices*. London: Routledge.

Kenix, L.J. (2011) *Alternative and Mainstream Media: The Converging Spectrum*. London: Bloomsbury Publishing.

Lievrouw, L. (2011) *Alternative and Activist New Media*. Cambridge: Polity Press.

Rauch, J. (2021) *Resisting the News: Engaged Audiences, Alternative Media, and Popular Critique of Journalism*. New York: Routledge.

7

WHO USES ALTERNATIVE MEDIA AND WHY?

Who are alternative media users, and why do they choose to go beyond mainstream media to access news and information? That is the question this chapter and the following one will explore. On the face of it, identifying alternative media users might seem a relatively easy task. After all, opinions are regularly sought about mainstream media by pollsters and researchers. But since alternative media are not widely used sources like the BBC or The New York Times, finding audiences who regularly access their online sites and social media networks is far from straightforward. It can take considerable time and resources to locate users and then persuade them to share their understanding and perspectives of alternative media sites (Rauch 2021).

Without hearing first-hand from people who regularly access alternative media content, misleading stereotypes can develop about the character and motivation of alternative media users. As the Introduction to the book explored, when alternative media have been discussed in popular discourse, they have tended to be associated with debates about the rise of disinformation, public disaffection from mainstream media, or hostility towards professional journalists. Perhaps most bleakly, when people turn to alternative media it has been used to represent a dystopian future of political media engagement, fostering ideological echo chambers and filter bubbles that confirm rather than challenge users' pre-existing biases. In doing so, alternative media users can often be cast as highly partisan activists, with their media consumption habits driven exclusively by narrow ideological interests. This can pejoratively frame them as irrationally partisan, abandoning reliable mainstream media sources for dodgy websites full of lies and conspiracy theories. And yet, as this chapter and the following one will explore, alternative media users cannot be easily or narrowly caricatured. They can exhibit contradictory

DOI: 10.4324/9781003360865-8

characteristics, and their engagement with and attitudes towards alternative and mainstream media need to be understood in the wider media and political systems they routinely inhabit.

But, as Chapter 1 explained, academic studies of alternative media audiences have historically been limited in size and scope. This chapter will explore the most recent body of scholarship about the relationship between audiences and alternative media, while the following chapter will explore their relationship in more depth with mainstream media. Over very recent years, a few large-scale national and cross-national studies have helped paint a broad picture of alternative media users. But this chapter will argue that more qualitative research is needed to better understand the complexity and fluidity of alternative media users. In doing so, it will draw on an original UK-based study of 2,741 respondents about why people use and understand alternative media. It was designed to identify alternative media users, which then led to a follow-up survey with a targeted subset of 303 regular *self-defined* alternative media users. They were isolated and examined more closely, including exploring their demographic characteristics, their specific democratic needs, and motivations as alternative media users in the context of the national media and political system they inhabit.

Identifying and characterising alternative media users

As Chapter 1 explored, leading academics in the field have long observed that studies exploring alternative media users have been few and far between (Downing 2003; Rauch 2021). When they have been researched, the focus has often been on single case studies of a particular media form or political issue, such as a new political blog or activist cause (Harcup 2013; Atkinson 2010). As the digital media landscape has diversified over the last decade or so, scholars have begun to pay greater attention to new formats of alternative media. A methodological hurdle when studying alternative media users has always been to define what constitutes alternative media – and, importantly, what does not. As Rauch (2021) recently observed, how scholars view alternative media can be different from the public's understanding of them. In other words, there needs to be an inclusive and shared understanding of alternative media to allow researchers to accurately interrogate how people feel about them.

Drawing on focus group interviews in Turkey, Demir's (2023) research showed there was no fixed definition or interpretation of alternative media among university students. Moreover, the research revealed striking differences between how scholars' and audiences' interpreted alternative media. For example, unlike much academic theorising, respondents did not give significant weight to alternative media being small in scale, or not being commercially incentivised, or not having a horizontal type of working environment. Nor did many of the respondents understand alternative media as being driven by citizens or a community-based organisation in pursuit of some kind of activist goal. In fact, the opinions of professional journalists were valued and not dismissed by some respondents. But there were some broad areas of agreement, which moved respondents to a shared understanding of what constitutes alternative media. They associated alternative media as sites operated mainly on the internet and across social media networks, and their editorial approach was perceived as being oppositional or critical. They often understood alternative media in the context of mainstream media not fulfilling their role. Taken together, the conclusion of the study struck at the heart of academic scholarship because it "highlighted various aspects of the concept of alternative media, and how these aspects differed among interviewees and in relation to leading academic theories" (Demir 2023: 53).

Steppat et al.'s (2020) cross-national surveys from Denmark, Italy, Poland, Switzerland, and the US also established that what the public constitutes as alternative media can vary between countries. They found, for instance, that nations such as Italy and Poland had more respondents who felt mainstream media was considered more alternative than self-proclaimed alternative media. Meanwhile, in the US there was a relatively high number of respondents who blurred the lines between what is conventionally defined as mainstream and alternative media. Steppat et al.'s (2020) analysis led them to conclude that the boundaries of alternative and mainstream media were fuzzier among respondents in nations with fragmented information environments and partisan media systems. Put differently, in Italy, Poland, and, to a lesser extent, the US, many people associated some professional mainstream media with what might be termed alternative media. In their words, "political information environments characterized by enhanced media fragmentation and polarization contribute to further convergence between alternative and mainstream media" (Steppat et al. 2020: 15).

Klawier et al.'s (2021) survey of German internet users further demonstrated the challenges associated with agreeing on a shared definition of alternative media. While over four in ten respondents – 43% – stated they used alternative media, just 5% could namecheck an alternative media site when asked in the survey. As Chapter 1 explored, Klawier et al.'s (2021) study highlighted the importance of not broadly classifying alternative media and assuming a shared understanding between audiences and researchers studying them. This also points to the limitations of survey research, which can rely on sometimes crude, quantitative measures to understand complex, human behaviours. It is qualitative research that can arguably better enlighten researchers about the blurred boundaries between how users differentiate (if at all they do) mainstream and alternative media, and more broadly their motivations for seeking news and information.

This point was partly acknowledged by the Reuters global survey in 2018. Kalogeropoulos and Newman (2018) extrapolated representative data of news consumption and examined alternative and partisan media use in depth across ten nations. With the exception of Breitbart in the US, which was used mainly by those over 35, they found no significant differences in people using alternative media from specific age groups. In Germany, however, many right-wing sites were consumed by men under 35, and across people from a range of household incomes. They asked users of alternative media to self-identify their political views and, broadly speaking, they reflected the ideological agenda of the sites being consumed. For example, the Another Angry Voice blog and The Canary website were mainly left-leaning users, whereas Breitbart UK were right-leaning users. Likewise, in the US, Breitbart, The Daily Caller, and InfoWars all had right-leaning audiences, whereas Occupy Democrats was made up of left-wing users. In Sweden, Fria Tider, Nyheter Idag, and Ledarsidorna were all broadly right-wing audiences as was the far-right Unzensuriert (Uncensored) site in Austria while Kontrast.at was made up of more left-wing than right-wing users.

The one shared characteristic of right-wing alternative media users identified in their study was low trust in mainstream news. For instance, 13% of Breitbart users trusted news compared to over a third of survey respondents in the nationally representative US survey. Likewise, users of the right-wing sites, Unzensuriert in Austria and Fria Tider and Nyheter Idag in Sweden, mistrusted news more than all survey respondents. But they also found some users in left-wing partisan sites – including Occupy Democrats in the US – invested more trust than the national average. To explore the motivations of alternative media users more qualitatively, they asked what their main motivation was for using the site. The resounding response was a lack of trust in mainstream media, most strikingly among US respondents. German and Austrian users were motivated by finding alternative views on the issue of immigration, with particular frustration aimed at news reporting by public service broadcasters. Overall, Kalogeropoulos and Newman (2018) concluded that

> alternative or partisan websites in a number of countries show a more diverse profile than expected, although they tend to be predominately male. Most users of these sites have low trust in the news and in mainstream media outlets in particular, which they think fail to tell the truth on issues like Europe and immigration.

Since publishing their analysis, a more detailed qualitative analysis of alternative media audiences has emerged. This has added further evidence that alternative media users represent a range of profiles as opposed to reflecting a narrow group of partisan actors. Rather than living in so-called echo chambers, fuelled by ideological anger, recent studies have challenged conventional wisdom and suggested they use alternative media for a wide range of reasons.

Schwarzenengger's (2022) interviews with 35 alternative media users in Germany revealed the complexity behind their consumption practices and beliefs. He developed a typology of five different types of users. First, the awakened warrior user, which represented those who wanted to wake up much of the public as they believed they were asleep to the propaganda shaping mainstream media.

They were heavy consumers of alternative media and highly sceptical of professional journalists. Second, the critical curator user, which included those seeking out oppositional content that diversified their news diet. They used alternative media to complement rather than replace their use of mainstream media. Third, the completist user defined as heavily consuming *all* media content – alternative and mainstream – who were searching for the fullest possible picture of news and information. They were a rare breed, according to Schwarzenegger (2022), and distinctive from users seeking critical and oppositional content. Fourth, the reconnaissance user, which represented audiences motivated by correcting disinformation. They used alternative media, notably right-wing sites, to understand where 'fake news' might emanate from. Far from exclusively using alternative media to satisfy their ideological impulses, they used all forms of news to help them navigate 'the truth'. Fifth, a community seeker user who was viewed as someone sharing content and participating in debates with like-minded audiences. Not wanting to feel ridiculed for their beliefs and scepticism towards mainstream media, they were seen to find comfort in forging relationships with other alternative media users in order to form a community of social acceptance. Taken together, the typology acknowledged the complexity and fluidity of alternative media use. While some users strongly identified with alternative media, others were selective or casually connected with them. Contrary to stereotyping, they were not hostile to mainstream media. Some used legacy news media in tandem with alternative media for their news diet, while others did so but remained deeply hostile towards professional journalists.

Similarly, Noppari et al.'s (2019) interviews with 24 users of populist Finnish websites identified three profiles. First, system sceptics, who mistrusted not just mainstream media, but society more broadly, and turned to alternative media for social acceptance reasons. Second, agenda critics, who were highly opinionated users who relied largely on alternative media because they believed mainstream media and professional journalists were driven by political and ideological motives. Third, casually discontent audience members, who were not necessarily driven by political interests, but disapproved of journalistic standards of mainstream media, and used alternative media to find more accurate and reliable news and information. The study concluded that the "user profiles we have presented in this article highlight vastly different motivations for Finnish users engaging with populist counter-media websites" (Noppari et al. 2019: 33). In other words, there was not one but multiple explanations for how and why people turned to alternative media for news and information. Overall, Nappari et al. (2019: 33) argued that "instead of simply attributing the proliferation of partisan online media content to post-truth or insufficient media literacy, multiple developments, including technological-, cultural-, social-, political- and individual-level phenomena, should be examined".

Taken together, these studies demonstrate the complexity and fluidity of alternative media users and help explain why they turn to news and information sources beyond mainstream media. They challenge simplistic stereotypes of alternative media users, which paint them as purely partisan activists, devoid of any media literacy skills. But there remains a need to deepen our knowledge of alternative media users. An original UK-based case study of alternative media users is now drawn upon to explore how often they access different sites, what motivates their use, and what agenda they wanted addressed.

To what extent have people heard or accessed alternative media sites?

The UK-based survey of alternative media audiences began by identifying regular users of specific sites. This was not a straightforward task or something that could easily be achieved by carrying out a representative survey. As one of the most comprehensive annual global news consumption studies revealed (Newman et al. 2018), UK alternative media sites were regularly used by just 1–2% of the UK population (see Table 7.1). Or, put in raw terms, approximately 20–40 people out of a nationally representative survey of 2,117 in 2018 stated they used one of the alternative media sites in the last week. But awareness of alternative media sites, such as Breitbart (19%) and The Canary (16%), was relatively high.

Since most representative samples are typically made up of approximately 1,000 respondents it could mean regular users (defined by using it weekly) of alternative media make up as little as 10–20 people in a survey. In other words, representative opinion polls have limited value when attempting to identify a large group of alternative media users.

To capture a much larger group of alternative media users, and to explore their use and understanding of different sites, a targeted two-phase survey was developed. This process began by using Prolific, an online recruitment company, to identify alternative media users. The sample, in this sense, was self-selecting, consisting of people living in the UK who were asked to complete a general survey about their media consumption habits and level of political engagement. It

TABLE 7.1 The percentage of UK public who had heard of alternative online news sites and used them in 2018

Site	Heard of	Used in last week
Breitbart	19%	2%
The Canary	16%	2%
Another Angry Voice	9%	2%
Westmonster	6%	2%
The Skwawkbox	7%	1%
Evolve Politics	5%	1%
Wings Over Scotland	4%	1%

Source: Reuters 2018 Digital News Study (Newman et al.2018).

generated 2,751 responses. From here, respondents could then be identified as alternative media users or not. To do so, participants were asked a series of questions to establish their knowledge and use of alternative media, as well as their wider views of mainstream media and politics.

Of the 2,751 participants who completed the survey, 34.6% were aged between 18 and 29, 45.2% between 30 and 49, and 20.2% aged 50 or over. Two people did not reveal their age. In terms of gender, 61.5% identified as female, 37.6% as male, 0.8% as binary while five people did not answer the question. In terms of education, 29.1% had qualifications up to secondary school, 32.6% at college level (typically A Levels taken between the ages of 16 and 18), 21.5% had an undergraduate degree, while 3.5% had some kind of a graduate degree. 1.8% indicated they had another type of qualification, while 0.3% preferred not to say. Finally, 11.2% of respondents indicated they did not have any formal qualifications. Participants overwhelmingly identified as English, Welsh, Scottish, Northern Irish, or British (85.1% in total), followed by a small number of other ethnicities, such as Indian (2.4%), other White (1.7%), and African (1.6%). Although the sample was not representative of the UK public, it did include a mix of ages (predominantly under 50), gender (although more female than male), a range of educational levels, and overwhelmingly participants who identified as being either English, Welsh, Scottish, Northern Irish, or British.

The survey then asked if they had any knowledge of specific alternative media sites. By namechecking sites, the question avoided asking respondents generally about alternative media use in an abstract way. As previous research has established (Demir 2023; Klawier et al. 2021; Rauch 2021), discussing alternative media in isolation can lead to misinterpretation about what constitutes alternative media. Table 7.2 shows that most respondents – as expected – had not heard of any

TABLE 7.2 The percentage of public knowledge about alternative media sites in the UK (frequency in brackets)

Site	I have heard of this site	I have not heard of this site	Total
Left-wing sites			
Another Angry Voice	16.1% (444)	83.9% (2,307)	100% (2,751)
Byline Times	11.1% (304)	89.0% (2,447)	100% (2,751)
Evolve Politics	12.5% (345)	87.5% (2,406)	100% (2,751)
Novara Media	11.9% (313)	88.6% (2,438)	100% (2,751)
The Skwawkbox	11.3% (310)	88.7% (2,441)	100% (2,751)
The Canary	23.2% (639)	76.8% (2,112)	100% (2,751)
The London Economic	38.8% (1,066)	61.3% (1,685)	100% (2,751)
Right-wing sites			
Breitbart	30.5% (840)	69.5% (1,911)	100% (2,751)
Conservative Woman	12.8% (351)	87.2% (2,400)	100% (2,751)
Guido Fawkes	33.8% (929)	66.2% (1,822)	100% (2,751)

of the alternative media sites. Overall, more than half indicated they had heard of at least one outlet, although roughly a third said they had not. Approximately 2% of respondents claimed to know all sites, while about 5% stated they were aware of the majority of the outlets. To widen the sample of alternative media sites, The London Economic and Byline Times were included in the survey because they had become prominent left-wing sources, while other alternative media sites examined in previous chapters may have fallen from the public's radar because they were producing fewer articles than in previous years (see Chapters 2 and 3). While Byline Times does not adopt a partisan, left-wing approach to reporting politics, it does tend to cover more liberal than conservative issues. There were no prominent right-wing alternative sites to add to the sample at the time of administering the survey, perhaps because the UK's mainstream press remains a dominant online news source for right-wing issues (Media Reform Coalition 2021).

But there was, relatively speaking, wide recognition of some alternative media sites, including 38.8% who had heard of London Economic, 33.8% for Guido Fawkes, 30.5% for Breitbart News, and 23.2% for The Canary. Between 11.3% and 16.4%, meanwhile, had heard of The Skwawkbox, Another Angry Voice, Evolve Politics, Novara Media, Byline Times, and Conservative Woman. In other words, a reasonably large minority of people in the UK were aware of both left-wing and right-wing alternative media sites.

The survey then explored the self-identification of alternative media users. Asked to respond to the question, "Do you consider yourself someone who closely followed alternative/independent media?" 41.1% strongly agreed they did, while 34.2% agreed. Just 6.4% disagreed and 1.9% strongly disagreed, leaving 16.7% who said they were neutral on the statement. In short, three quarters of respondents identified as someone who followed alternative media, even though many respondents had not heard of many of the specific UK alternative media sites. When asked further about whether they were satisfied with the content of alternative/independent media, a large majority (73.9%) indicated they were neutral, suggesting they did not have an opinion one way or the other. Just 6.3% agreed they were satisfied with alternative media content, with 2.9% strongly agreeing. By contrast, 15.0% disagreed they were satisfied with the content, while 1.8% strongly disagreed. This suggests, overall, that most respondents did not regularly encounter alternative media sites to the extent that they formed a judgement about their quality or significance.

To explore more closely respondents' engagement with specific sites, they were asked how regularly, if at all, they had accessed them either through the website or indirectly via social media networks. In terms of usage, Table 7.3 shows few respondents regularly accessed sites frequently. The vast majority (87% or more) indicated they never or rarely used any of the sites.

However, over one in ten respondents – 10.3% – used London Economic one to three times a month, while 6.0% and 3.9% did so for Guido Fawkes and The Canary, respectively. Weekly or daily use of alternative media sites was generally

TABLE 7.3 The percentage of the public using alternative media sites in the UK (frequency in brackets)

Site	Never or very rarely	1–3 times a month	1–3 times a week	Daily	Total
Left-wing sites					
Another Angry Voice	94.7% (2,605)	3.9% (107)	1.1% (29)	0.36% (10)	100% (2,751)
Byline Times	96.3% (2,649)	2.2% (60)	1.3% (36)	0.22% (6)	100% (2,751)
Evolve Politics	96.3% (2,649)	2.7% (73)	0.7% (21)	0.29% (8)	100% (2,751)
Novara Media	96.7% (2,661)	2.1% (58)	0.9% (25)	0.25% (7)	100% (2,751)
The Canary	93.7% (2577)	4.9% (136)	1.3% (31)	0.25% (7)	100% (2,751)
The Skwawkbox	97.8% (2,691)	1.5% (42)	0.62% (17)	0.04% (1)	100% (2,751)
The London Economic	87.1% (2,397)	10.3% (283)	2.2% (60)	0.40% (11)	100% (2,751)
Right-wing sites					
Breitbart	96.3% (2,649)	2.8% (77)	0.8% (23)	0.07% (2)	100% (2,751)
Conservative Woman	97.2% (2,675)	2.1% (59)	0.6% (15)	0.07% (2)	100% (2,751)
Guido Fawkes	92.1% (2,533)	6.0% (164)	1.6% (44)	0.36% (10)	100% (2,751)

low across all sites, but there was a small but highly active group of alternative media users.

The results of alternative media consumption should be viewed in a broader context. When Oxford University's annual Reuters Institute news survey asks respondents to reveal their weekly use of mainstream news media outlets, it is only broadcasters, in particular the BBC, which have a relatively high level of users regularly accessing coverage several times a week (see Table 7.4).

For newspapers and their digital news sites, the percentage of respondents who stated they accessed this content weekly was between 2% and 5%. But perhaps due to the design of the survey question, this could understate the consumption of mainstream media and, in turn, alternative media sites. This is because many people may inadvertently encounter news sites and channels – across social media networks sites or with the television or radio on in the background – without being fully aware of the source of the media. In other words, caution needs to be exercised when interpreting self-declared media consumption habits because they risk minimising the influence of sites. In the case of alternative media, audiences may be exposed to their content without always being conscious of a site's title.

So, for example, Ipsos iris data, which uses nationally representative data from 10,000 people from 25,000 personal devices to measure how long people engage with websites and apps, discovered that alternative media sites were some of the most consumed formats of political media in the UK (see Table 7.5). The right-wing site, Guido Fawkes, for instance, was the most widely read– with 3.3 million page views in July 2022- beating the mainstream political sites, Politics Home and Politico.

TABLE 7.4 The percentage of public using different mainstream news outlets in the UK

Site	Weekly use	At least 3 days per week
BBC News (TV and radio)	50%	40%
ITV News	27%	16%
Sky News	15%	9%
Channel 4 News	9%	4%
Daily Mail/Mail on Sunday	9%	4%
Commercial radio news	7%	5%
Regional or local newspaper	7%	2%
Metro	5%	2%
GB News	5%	2%
The Times/Sunday Times	5%	2%
Sun/Sun on Sunday	5%	2%
Guardian/Observer	4%	2%
Channel 5 News	3%	1%
Daily Telegraph (and Sunday)	3%	1%
Daily Mirror (and Sunday)	3%	1%
The i newspaper	2%	1%

Source: Reuters Digital News Study 2022 (Newman et al. 2022).

TABLE 7.5 The percentage of users of political media including total monthly time used in July 2022, average minutes per person, and page views

News brand	Total mins	Average mins per person	Page views
Guido Fawkes	4.5m	16	3.3m
Politics Home	3.4m	2	385.1k
Politico	3m	4	2.5m
The London Economic	1.5m	3	1.1m
The New European	1.4m	3	1.1m
Conservative Home	1.4m	6	1.2m
The Canary	929.6k	1	2.3m
Skwawkbox	782.9k	10	159.3k
Byline Times	725.6k	7	210.2k
Novara Media	324.1k	3	292.6k
Politico.co.uk	250.4k	1	365.2k
Labourlist	211.2k	3	183.6k

Source: Majid (2022).

Meanwhile, the left-wing site, The Canary, had 2.3 million page views and almost a million total minutes of use, while Skwawkbox, which regularly publishes long blogs (see Chapter 2), had users spending, on average, ten minutes on its site, far more than most other political media sites. But even despite these relatively high audience figures, alternative users may be understated in nationally representative polls. This is because they are made up of niche audiences, which are concentrated, say, in capital cities like London with high levels of political interest, which will be under-represented in statistically constructed national polling. Tracking alternative media use on websites may offer a more accurate way of measuring engagement than conventional opinion polls (Majid 2022).

Where and why do people use alternative media?

To specifically explore regular users of alternative media sites from the survey of 2,751 people, those respondents who had engaged at least one site once a month or more were examined more closely. Their level of engagement with alternative media was assessed by giving each respondent a score. For each site they used once a month, a score of one was calculated. For each site used once at least weekly, a score of two was calculated. For each site they used on a daily basis, a score of three was added. Anyone with a score of one or less was excluded from the study. This created a potential sample of 401, who were contacted to participate further with the research. Since most of these respondents had indicated a willingness to engage in a second survey when they completed the first survey, a relatively high response rate was achieved. A sample of 303 regular alternative media users – defined either by consuming content weekly, daily, or monthly – was generated, providing a relatively large group of active users to study.

Of the 303 participants who completed the survey, 32.1% were aged between 18 and 29, 42.6% between 39 and 49, and 25.4% aged 50 or over. For gender, 50.5% identified as female, 47.5% as male, 1.3% as binary while 0.7% opted not to answer the question. In terms of education, 28.7% had qualifications up to secondary school, 35.3% at the college level (typically A Levels taken between the ages of 16 and 18), 23.1% had an undergraduate degree, while 3.9% had some kind of postgraduate degree. 0.3% indicated they had another type of qualification, while 0.7% preferred not to say. Finally, 7.9% of respondents indicated they did not have any formal qualifications. Participants overwhelmingly identified as English, Welsh, Scottish, Northern Irish, or British (83.2%). In Chapters 7 and 8, when individual survey respondents were identified, their ethnicity was abbreviated to White UK. There were also a number of respondents with different ethnic backgrounds including Asian (4%), Chinese (1.7%), African (1.3%), Pakistani (1.3%), White and Black Caribbean (1%), Bangladeshi (0.7%), other White (0.6%), Caribbean (0.3%), White and Black African (0.3%), White and Asian (1%), other mixed or multiple ethnic backgrounds (1%), and other ethnic groups (0.6%). 1% preferred not to state their ethnicity. Taken together, the profile of alternative media users was not that different from the overall sample of 2,751 people in the survey but with just slightly younger and more educated respondents.

There was some imbalance in the consumption habits of the sample (see Table 7.6), with more participants who only used left-wing sites (39.3%) rather than just right-wing sites (10.6%). However, contrary to alternative media users living in so-called filter bubbles or echo chambers, the survey revealed that many of them regularly used

TABLE 7.6 Percentage of regular alternative media users who engaged with right-wing and left-wing sites (frequency in brackets)

Regular alternative media users who engaged with right, left, and left-centrist sites	Percentage of users
Users of left-wing sites	39.3% (119)
Users of right-wing sites	10.6% (32)
Users of left-wing and right-wing sites	50.1% (152)
Total	100% (303)

a mixture of sites with different ideological perspectives. Over half of the respondents, for example, regularly accessed both left-wing and right-wing alternative media sites. As explored below, this reveals a complexity and fluidity in alternative media use that challenges the conventional wisdom of how they are often understood (BBC 2019; Robinson 2017). Given most users drew on a range of alternative media sites from across the political spectrum, the analysis in the book does not isolate users according to those just relying on either left-wing or right-wing sites. However, throughout Chapters 7 and 8, when a survey respondent is quoted, their preference for either right-wing and left-wing alternative media sites, or both, has been included.

The aim of the targeted survey of 303 alternative media users was to interpret how respondents used and understood different sites, along with their broader relationship with mainstream media. The survey began by asking qualitatively – in an open-ended question- whether they could recall how they first encountered alternative media sites they regularly used today. Just over half – 50.7% – specifically referenced search engines or social media sites, most often Twitter and Facebook, but also Instagram and Google. This reinforced the importance of social media networks, which many editors and contributors emphasised was significant to attracting traffic (see Chapter 6). Meanwhile, just under one in four respondents – 24.3% – indicated they had encountered alternatives more casually, such as from consuming media content generally.

Almost one in five respondents – 19.9% – revealed that they encountered sites due to personal recommendations from followers or friends endorsing stories produced by alternative media sites on various social media networks. Responses included:

On Twitter, with stories retweeted into my feed by people I follow.
(Male, 40–49, College/A Levels, White – UK, user
of left-wing sites)

It was an article that a friend of mine shared on Facebook.
(Female, 18–24, Secondary school/GCSE,
White – UK, user of left-wing and right-wing sites)

Friend's recommendations, usually through sharing their pages on Instagram.
*(Male, 40–49, Undergraduate degree, White and
Asian, user of left-wing and right-wing sites)*

I came across The Canary whilst reading a post on Facebook posted by a friend
and on visiting and exploring I found a lot of items on environmental issues and
health issues which I found very interesting.
*(Female, 60–69, Doctorate degree, White – UK,
user of left-wing sites)*

From what I can remember, it was a link a friend sent me via Facebook mes-
senger that first directed me to Breitbart.
*(Male, 30–39, College/A Levels, White – UK, user
of right-wing sites)*

There were also some respondents who indicated they encountered alternative
media directly with people they knew outside of their social media networks. This
ranged from word of mouth, friends, or relatives, with some personal anecdotes
about recommendations:

I first came across evolve politics because my 27-year-old daughter mentioned
it to me and she is very politically minded. I first came across Another Angry
Voice because a friend mentioned it to me.
*(Male, 60–69, Secondary school/GCSE,
White – UK, user of left-wing sites)*

Alternative media sites were encountered by Internet searches by over one in five
respondents. Finally, there were some idiosyncratic ways of accessing alternative media sites, whether through podcasts or through contacts with people at
university.

Taken together, the findings demonstrate the importance of social media networks, which make alternative media sites visible to potential users. If users
were not recommended alternative media sites or inadvertently came across
them on sites such as Facebook, Twitter, and Instagram, very few would have
been exposed to them in the same way people encounter mainstream media. In
short, social media is clearly a gateway to users regularly accessing alternative
media.

What issues and topics matter to alternative media users?

To assess what kinds of issues alternative media users considered to be important,
they were asked to list two or three topics of interest. These qualitative, open-ended

responses were then systematically classified and quantified into broader generic categories. Since respondents did not all provide the same number of responses, the analysis focussed on the overall proportion of topics and issues, rather than the total frequency of them. Respondents ranked politics and the environment as the most important issues followed by health, mental health, the National Health Service (NHS), and Covid-19, while economy and social justice issues (including welfare and equality) made up 10% of responses. Other issues that received limited coverage included immigration, education, current news, local news, war and conflict, defence and security, terrorism, sports, employment, and crime.

To further explore why users turned to alternative media, respondents were then asked whether they thought alternative media offered coverage of issues and topics that were different from mainstream media. The question was open-ended, generating qualitative responses, with respondents able to list more than one reason. Many of the reasons were overlapping, but an attempt was made to categorise the different themes about why alternative media was considered distinctive from mainstream media (see Table 7.7).

TABLE 7.7 The percentage of reasons why UK alternative media users consider them different to mainstream media

Reason	Percentage
Alternative perspectives	18.6%
Coverage of under-reported issues	11.0%
Tougher more in-depth reporting	10.7%
Unbiased/independent reporting	7.7%
Opposing voices to give balanced perspectives	7.0%
Left-leaning approach	6.0%
Holding government to account	5.4%
Mainstream media poor	5.3%
Coverage of specific topics	4.8%
Truthful/not censored	3.8%
Reflect my viewpoints	3.7%
Right-leaning approach	2.7%
Straight-to-the point news	2.7%
Alternative facts	2.6%
Other	8.0%
Total	100%

Frequency not provided because respondents could list more than one issue.

Above all, users appreciated what they viewed as sites providing alternative perspectives in reporting. Responses included:

> Showing the news from another angle giving a broader picture.
> *(Male, 30–39, Secondary school/GCSE,*
> *Bangladeshi, user of left-wing and right-wing sites)*

I find that independent media offer alternative viewpoints that MSM do not cover.
(Female, 60–69, Secondary school/GCSE,
White – UK, user of right-wing sites)

They offer views which are hardly represented in mainstream media.
(Male, 18–24, College/A Levels, Pakistani, user of
left-wing sites)

They offer alternate viewpoints that are not funded by billionaires.
(Male, 30–39, Undergraduate degree, any other
mixed or multiple ethnic background, user of
left-wing sites)

From another perspective, many respondents revealed that they valued alternative media because they covered under-reported issues not addressed by mainstream media. For example, one respondent appreciated the radical perspectives of alternative media sites even though they disagreed with some of the views expressed:

Often these outlets are further to the left or right of the political spectrum. I find mainstream media to be too centralised and enjoy reading more extreme points of view, even if I don't always agree with them.
(Male, 40–49, College/A Levels, White – UK, user
of right-wing sites)

Meanwhile, sites from both right-wing and left-wing perspectives were singled out for their coverage in comparison to mainstream media. For instance:

Guido Fawkes highlights some issues which seem to be papered over by the MSM. I am not sure if that's because they aren't deemed important, but I am frustrated with the constant ignoring of hypocrites, liars and thieves in our Parliament. This isn't just limited to one party – they all seem to be at it and at least Guido Fawkes picks on all sides equally.
(Male, 40–49, College/A Levels, White – UK, user
of right-wing sites)

Another Angry Voice allows for information that would not normally make it to the news I follow, e.g., BBC. The BBC seems to be under the control of the government, so no way would they share the same details.
(Female, 18–24, Undergraduate degree,
White – UK, user of left-wing sites)

More broadly, many respondents thought alternative media represented tougher, more in-depth journalism when compared to mainstream media:

> I believe that the highlighted outlets (Novara, Evolve and Byline) all carry out thorough investigative journalism better than the mainstream media and are better at highlighting the failings of government. I also enjoy how Novara and Evolve produce short videos on their stories which are still able to go in to some depth on the topic that they are covering. Byline produces very good research based pieces in print.
>
> *(Male, 30–39, Secondary school/GCSE,*
> *White – UK, user of left-wing sites)*

Behind these perspectives was a general suspicion about mainstream media reporting which alternative media was seen to correct (as explored in Chapter 4). They were viewed as independently driven whereas mainstream media were seen as pursuing some kind of political, liberal, or corporate agenda. A flavour of these responses included believing that alternative media represented:

> True impartiality and a perspective that doesn't always pander to big corporations.
> *(Female, 30–39, College/A Levels, White – UK,*
> *user of left-wing and right-wing sites)*

> a non biased explanation of current events and the real impact they might have.
> *(Male, 25–29, Undergraduate degree, White – UK,*
> *user of left-wing sites)*

> Mainly holding the government to account for their actions in ways that the mainstream media can't or won't due to impartiality or special interests.
> *(Female, 30–39, College/A Levels, White – UK,*
> *user of left-wing sites)*

> information (if true) that the mainstream media either won't cover or refuse to cover for political bias reasons. It gives an insight on the typical day to day events that the likes of the BBC will not mention such as for political correctness reasons.
> *(Male, 60–69, Secondary school/GCSE,*
> *White – UK, user of right-wing and left-wing sites)*

While many responses broadly interpreted the value of alternative media, there were some specific sites singled out for their independence and adherence to high journalistic standards:

The Canary and Guido Fawkes offers a different perspective to the likes of the BBC, Sky News. For me they seem to be not as biased.

(Female, 30–39, No formal qualifications, White –
UK, user of left-wing and right-wing sites)

Guido Fawkes offers alternative political views with independent views.

(Female, 40–49, College/A Levels, White – UK,
user of right-wing and left-wing sites)

I like Skwawkbox because it is a totally unbiased view on mainstream topics. They offer a more detailed approach to let you form your own opinion and not have it forced down your throat like the normal tabloids. They also broach subjects the mainstream journalists don't touch and offer a more raw and subjective viewpoint.

(Female 30–39, Secondary school/GCSE,
White – UK, user of left-wing and right-wing sites)

From another perspective, respondents believed alternative media provided more oppositional and critical voices than mainstream media outlets. This meant they often challenged conventional wisdom, delivering a range of opinions, which users appreciated. For example:

The mainstream media is so left wing now and is full of fake news. These outlets give you a completely different side to the story and are full of common sense views.

(Female, 50–59, College/A Levels, White – UK,
user of right-wing sites)

Simply an alternative perspective. The mainstream media is fairly homogenous with one or two exceptions. Having an alternative view on a matter can be extremely useful, even if I don't necessarily agree with it.

(Male, 30–39, Graduate degree, White – UK, user
of left-wing sites)

Once again, specific sites were mentioned with their coverage favourably compared to mainstream media, most often the BBC:

Novara is more critical of the state and often voices people who are considered 'too radical or revolutionary' for mainstream media.

(Female, 18–24, Secondary school/GCSE,
White – UK, user of left-wing and right-wing sites)

The Canary gives a more dedicated left-wing perspective of the news and Guido Fawkes gives a right-wing perspective and I like to get opinions and views from both ends of the political spectrum and these are not as dumbed down as the BBC for example.

(Male, 40–49, College/A Levels, White – UK, user
of left-wing and right-wing sites)

They all offer differing opinions and "takes". Some like Guido Fawkes and Conservative Woman are very right wing and reflect that in their content. Others, like The Canary, Byline Times, and The Skwawkbox are more left wing and the content there very much reflects those views. So, I read them all to get an overall balanced view.

(Male, 50–59, Secondary school/GCSE,
White – UK, user of left-wing and right-wing sites)

Alternative media, in this context, were seen to offer a full spectrum of views, reflecting a wider range of political debates than professional journalists pursued, which delivered more democratically fulfilling news than mainstream media.

Taken together, the top overlapping five reasons why respondents thought alternative media were distinctive from mainstream included: providing alternative perspectives, covering under-reported issues, producing tougher, more in-depth reporting, pursuing independent and unbiased journalism, and offering opposing and critical voices.

Interpreting the complexity and fluidity of alternative media users

Based on a review of the most recent academic studies and new original quantitative and qualitative survey research, the chapter challenged the perception of alternative media users being solely partisan activists divorced from the 'real' political world or mainstream media. Across several countries, research showed many users demonstrated they were highly curious and critical news consumers (Rauch 2021; Schwarzenegger 2022). They displayed strong media literacy skills, with many still reliant on professional journalism even if they expressed mistrust or dissatisfaction with mainstream media. Or, put more simply, alternative media were not used to simply replace the consumption of mainstream media or confirm pre-existing ideological biases.

The study of alternative media users in the UK revealed that they engaged with different sites selectively and self-consciously in order to enhance their understanding of politics and public affairs. In that sense, the study highlighted how motivations for alternative media use were shaped by the wider national media and political environment. For example, left-wing alternative media users were often critical of the UK's right-wing partisan press system, with broadcasters often seen as reinforcing rather than challenging their influence. Meanwhile, right-wing alternative media users often criticised the BBC for their influence on journalism and advancing liberal perspectives. Audiences of both political persuasions, from different vantage points, critiqued the news agenda and impartiality of broadcasters, and their claim to deliver high-quality journalism. In other words, respondents turned to alternative media because they wanted in-depth coverage of certain issues overlooked by mainstream media, and called for a wider range of more critical and diverse voices reporting on politics than many professional journalists supplied. Put another way, users of alternative media wanted a more rounded ideological picture of the political world than mainstream media conveyed, with more independently driven journalism.

The new research in this chapter adds to recent academic literature that has demonstrated the complexity of alternative media audiences in how they pick and choose different media to self-serve their political news diet (Noppari et al. 2019; Schwarzenegger 2022). It moves debates in the field forward, drawing on first-hand observations from alternative media users, which have often been missing from recent studies, shedding light on individual motivations for alternative media use. Above all, it has shown that a combination of quantitative and qualitative research is needed to better understand the fluidity of alternative media users. Nationally representative polling reveals just a tiny fraction of the population regularly accesses alternative media sites even if many people are aware of a range of specific sites. On the face of it, this can risk downplaying the influence of alternative media. After all, studies tracking personal media use or unique web visits have demonstrated that they can attract a high volume of user traffic (Majid 2022). The chapter has argued that more research needs to creatively target users and examine their media engagement. For instance, the UK study showed many people encountered alternative media indirectly, through casual exposure on social networks or endorsements through friends and followers. Again, this may underplay their interactions with alternative media content, since the brand recognition of specific sites will not be as strong as legacy media, such as the BBC or The New York Times.

The next chapter examines how alternative media users engage with and understands mainstream media in greater depth, as well as exploring if their political orientation shapes their news diet. As this chapter has explored, while the latest research suggests that users of alternative media may be disenchanted with mainstream news and the wider political system, many of them remain voracious news consumers and follow party politics closely.

References

Atkinson, J.D. (2010) *Alternative Media and Politics of Resistance: A Communication Perspective*. New York: Peter Lang.

BBC (2019) 'The BBC and the future of news', 20th March, https://www.bbc.co.uk/mediacentre/speeches/2019/tony-hall-lords

Demir, D. (2023) 'A user research on alternative media', *Athens Journal of Mass Media and Communications*, Vol.9, Vol.1: 39–56, https://doi.org/10.30958/ajmmc.9-1-3

Downing, J. (2003) 'Audiences and readers of alternative media: The absent lure of the virtually unknown', *Media, Culture & Society*, 25(5): 625–645. https://doi.org/10.1177/01634437030255004

Harcup, T. (2013) *Alternative Journalism, Alternative Voices*. London: Routledge.

Kalogeropoulos, A. and Newman, N. (2018) 'Who uses alternative and partisan brands?', https://www.digitalnewsreport.org/survey/2018/who-uses-alternative-and-partisan-brands/

Klawier, T., Prochazka, F. and Schweiger, W. (2021) 'Public knowledge of alternative media in times of algorithmically personalized news', *New Media & Society*, 10.1177/14614448211021071

Majid, A. (2022) 'Ranked: Most popular politics news websites in UK', *Press Gazette*, September 1, https://pressgazette.co.uk/media-audience-and-business-data/most-popular-politics-news-websites-uk/

Media Reform Coalition (2021) *Who Owns the UK Media?* London: Media Reform Coalition, https://www.mediareform.org.uk/wp-content/uploads/2021/03/Who-Owns-the-UK-Media_final2.pdf

Newman, N., Fletcher, R., Kalogeropoulos, A., Kalogeropoulos, A., Levy, D. and Nielsen, R.K. (2018)*Reuters Institute Digital News Report 2018*, https://reutersinstitute.politics.ox.ac.uk/our-research/digital-news-report-2018

Newman, N., Fletcher, R., Robertson, C.T., Eddy, K. and Nielsen, R.K. (2022) *Reuters Institute Digital News Report*. https://reutersinstitute.politics.ox.ac.uk/sites/default/files/2022-06/Digital_News-Report_2022.pdf

Noppari, E., Hiltunen, I. and Ahva, L. (2019). 'User profiles for populist counter-media websites in Finland', *Journal of Alternative and Community Media*, Vol. 4(1): 23–37. https://doi.org/10.1386/joacm_00041_1

Rauch, J. (2021) *Resisting the News: Engaged Audiences, Alternative Media, and Popular Critique of Journalism*. New York: Routledge

Robinson, N. (2017) 'If mainstream news wants to win back trust, it cannot silence dissident voices', *The Guardian*, 27 September, https://www.theguardian.com/commentisfree/2017/sep/27/mainstream-news-win-back-trust-dissident-voices

Schwarzenegger, C. (2022) 'Understanding the users of alternative news media: Media epistemologies, news consumption, and media practices', *Digital Journalism*, https://doi.org/10.1080/21670811.2021.2000454

Steppat, D., Herrero, L., and Esser, F. (2020) 'News media performance evaluated by national audiences: How media environments and user preferences matter', *Media and Communication*, Vol. 8(3): 321–334.

8

THE ATTITUDES OF ALTERNATIVE MEDIA USERS TOWARDS MAINSTREAM MEDIA

Over recent decades, there have been increasing fears about a so-called polarisation of media audiences, where people inhabit so-called 'filter bubbles' and 'echo chambers' that reinforce rather than challenge their ideological convictions (Vaccari and Valeriani 2021). But while these terms are widely used in popular discourse and raise alarm bells among media commentators, regulators and policymakers, they are not often grounded in the reality of how people use and engage with news media sources (Arguedas et al. 2022). This is particularly the case when alternative media sites have been discussed because they have been associated with promoting 'fake news' and populism (Marwick and Lewis 2017). The left-wing media commentator, Owen Jones, for example, singled out the UK site, The Canary, for ghettoising political issues and events and polarising audiences. He argued that the Canary "promotes conspiracy theories and a lot of things that just aren't right. I worry about the Canary-isation of the left, where it ends up in a bizarre sub-culture that anyone who doesn't agree is seen as part of a conspiracy" (cited in Jones 2017). Perspectives like these cast alternative media users as largely passive creatures, either blind in their pursuit of partisanship or trapped in an ideological prison they cannot escape. Or, put even more bluntly, alternative media users suck users into silos that limit or entirely block their engagement with any 'real-world' political and societal reality.

This chapter will examine alternative media users' political orientation and whether it informs their consumption of specific sites. It asks, for example, if alternative media users stick rigidly to sites that reinforce their political perspectives, or if they turn to sources that challenge their ideological beliefs. The chapter then explores alternative media users' relationship with mainstream media. It asks, for instance, whether they broadly interpret the mainstream

DOI: 10.4324/9781003360865-9

media, or if they differentiate the quality of journalism between news sources. As Chapter 1 explored, the boundaries between what constitutes mainstream and alternative media have become fuzzier in a high-choice media environment across broadcast, online and social media platforms. Klawier et al. (2021: 13) acknowledged this point in the conclusion of their study about media audiences, advising researchers that "it is important not only to focus on alternative media in isolation, but also to investigate common notions of established, legacy, or mainstream media, and how citizens make use of them". But despite the greater academic focus on alternative media over recent years, there has been limited analysis of users and, in particular, their relationship with mainstream and professional journalists. As the previous chapter acknowledged, without any direct research on alternative media audiences, their characteristics and motivations can become warped by baseless and misleading stereotypes. In doing so, it can shape debates about the role and influence of alternative media that does not reflect how and why people go beyond mainstream media to learn about what is happening in the world.

This chapter will draw on an original UK-based survey of 2,751 people that identified alternative media users. This generated – as the previous chapter explained – a sample of 303 regular users that were further analysed quantitatively and qualitatively. Overall, the aim was to explore how and why alternative media users chose different information sources, and why they interacted with different mainstream media sources. While a perception has grown that alternative media users have been disenfranchised from mainstream media and driven by populist beliefs, there is limited evidence to support this assertation (Noppari et al. 2019). As the previous chapter argued, alternative media users should not be narrowly classified and stereotyped when their consumption practices are complex and fluid (Schwarzenegger 2022). Moreover, their attitudes need to be understood in the wider media and political context in which they inhabit, which varies considerably between different countries around the world. The UK, for example, has a dominant public service broadcaster, the BBC, and a highly partisan right-wing press system, which can inform how alternative media users interpret mainstream media and professional journalists. More broadly, the chapter contributes to wider debates about news media engagement, challenging lazy assumptions that alternative media users can be uniformly labelled as partisan or an activist, or who collectively mistrust journalists and feel ideologically alienated.

The relationship between mainstream and alternative media

Studies of alternative media audiences have historically been interpreted through the prism of mainstream media consumption (Downing 2003). After all, what alternative media users are typically seeking is relative in that they are looking for something 'alternative' to mainstream media. But this alone does not always capture the nuance and complexity of people's relationship with the use of both mainstream and alternative media, or their wider knowledge and engagement with politics (Rauch 2021). For example, to what extent does exposure to alternative media reduce or enhance mainstream media consumption, influence their perceptions towards professional journalism or the political class, or extend their general knowledge about politics? One study considered whether alternative digital media use had any meaningful influence on political knowledge (Lee 2015). While it found no evidence that alternative media sites enhanced knowledge about institutionally-based politics, such as decisions made by government actors, it did increase a greater understanding of what Lee (2015: 318) calls "oppositional forces". This referred to issues typically marginalised by mainstream politics, such as fostering a better understanding of the environment or human rights.

There have been a few cross-sectional studies that have highlighted predictors of alternative media use. Shulze's (2020) cross-national study of Austrian, German, Swedish, and Finnish audiences, for instance, discovered that the use of right-wing alternative media sites was associated with high political interest and engagement with social media networks, but a mistrust in mainstream media. Indeed, a connection between low levels of mainstream media trust and greater alternative media use has long been established in the literature (Tsfati and Cappella 2003). In a qualitative open-ended survey, Kalogeropoulos and Newman (2018) found that users of right-wing alternative media sites in the US mimicked the language of President Trump when discussing their lack of respect for professional journalism and mainstream media. More broadly, the study discovered that users across a number of nations identified that a "rejection of mainstream, 'biased', 'political correct' media was a core reason for using these websites" (Kalogeropoulos and Newman 2018). Yet it did not explain how all alternative media users' interpreted and interacted with mainstream media or their perceptions and understanding of politics more broadly (Schwarzenegger 2022). More qualitative follow-up research is needed to unpack the characteristics of alternative media use. As the previous chapter established, it is easy to stereotype alternative media users as highly partisan activists who reject mainstream media sources. But, as recent studies have highlighted, this does not accurately characterise their engagement with alternative media, meaning more research is needed to understand users' relationship with mainstream media and politics more generally (e.g., Nappari et al. 2019).

Over very recent years, there have been a few large-scale, quantitative studies that have *longitudinally* explored the relationship between mainstream media and alternative media consumption, as well as their wider connections to political interest, engagement and knowledge. This has helped identify and isolate more specifically the reasons for (dis)engagement with mainstream media and politics among alternative media users over specific time periods. Reiter and Matthes (2021), for example, drew on a two-wave panel survey at the beginning and at the end of a six-week election campaign in Austria in 2019 in order to explore changing perceptions of mainstream media. Their study of 524 people discovered some significant findings for both high and low consumers of alternative media. First, that political interest in the election increased when alternative media was not used. Second, greater exposure to alternative media was associated with declining levels of trust for those also consuming mainstream media. Third, no connections between political knowledge with mainstream or alternative media use were identified. But, fourth, they discovered that more consumption of alternative media over time may generate greater political interest. Overall, they concluded that

> Alternative digital media may not only be "correctives of the mainstream media" but also erode the democratic function of mainstream media. That is, mainstream media may still be associated with political interest (and by doing so, potentially also political knowledge in a second step) but only when citizens are not or only marginally exposed to alternative digital media.
>
> *(Reiter and Matthes 2021: 16)*

In other words, alternative media use was viewed as a corrosive force in terms of advancing democratic citizenship.

Similarly, Anderson et al. (2021) developed an extended longitudinal survey of 1,567 people to explore alternative and mainstream media consumption in Sweden. Their four-panel survey conducted between 2018 and 2020 revealed three striking findings that reinforced the conclusions of Reiter and Matthes's (2021) study. First, that those seeking alternative media over time recorded declining levels of trust in mainstream media. Second, that alternative media did not replace mainstream media use as many respondents continued to consume both. And third, they identified alternative media users were mainly young males, with low levels of education and low trust in media, society and politics. But they were also highly interested in mainstream media. Taken together, they concluded that

> mainstream media trust further decreases as a consequence of alternative news orientation. Thus, although alternative media create a more diverse media environment where people can nurse special interests and connect with like-minded people, it also comes with the risk of polarization.
>
> *(Anderson et al. 2021: 15)*

However, there was no clear connection between alternative media consumption and the creation of ideological filter bubbles or echo chambers.

Both surveys of alternative media users (Anderson et al. 2021; Reiter and Matthes 2021) acknowledged their analysis was limited by a number of factors. Neither included any analysis of media content, limiting the assumptions they could make about effects. Both surveys did not separate the consumption of left-wing or right-wing alternative media either or specified what alternative media represented. This meant respondents could self-define alternative media, which, as the previous chapter explored, could lead to some confusion about how people interpret mainstream media and alternative media, and disagreements with how researchers might classify different news sources. In short, relying on quantitative surveys that can pose relatively crude questions about media consumption cannot always unpack the nuances and complexity of how people engage with mainstream and alternative media. There is a need for more targeted sampling of alternative media users based on a close analysis of their consumption habits. Moreover, more combined quantitative and qualitative audience research with users would shed more light on how people use and engage with mainstream and alternative media.

This chapter now turns to original audience research introduced in the previous chapter that carried out both quantitative and qualitative survey analysis with regular alternative media users. Having identified 303 regular users of alternative media from a survey of 2,751 people, a follow-up study was conducted in order to examine the degree to which their political orientation informed their choice of alternative media, their levels of engagement with mainstream media, and their views on mainstream media and professional journalists.

The political orientation of alternative media users and their engagement with mainstream media

To date, there has been limited research exploring the perspectives of alternative media users across both left-wing and right-wing sites. For example, do the political viewpoints of alternative media users reflect the partisan media they consume, or do they disengage from mainstream media as part of their routine consumption of media? Drawing on a targeted survey of 303 users of alternative media sites in the UK, Table 8.1 shows whether users of alternative media favour political parties that reflect or deviate from the political content of sites they routinely access. Needless to say, the survey cannot claim to be representative of users of both left-wing and right-wing perspectives. It is based on a relatively small self-selecting sample, which skews to the left of the political spectrum. While being cautious about the survey's statistical accuracy, it can still provide some insight into whether regular alternative media users stick rigidly to sites that confirm rather than challenge their ideological perspectives.

Contrary to conventional wisdom, Table 8.1 reveals that audiences of both left-wing and right-wing sites were not made up of users blindly following their political agendas. Half of the users on the right-wing site, Breitbart, for example, favoured left-wing parties, while four in ten users did so for Guido Fawkes. To a lesser degree, some users of left-wing sites – for instance, The Canary – favoured right-wing politics, including favouring the Conservative Party, who was in power at the time the survey was conducted. More broadly, left-wing users did not just favour the UK's main left-wing party, Labour, they indicated a preference for either left or centre-left parties such as the Liberal Democrats, The Greens, or the Scottish National Party (SNP). In other words, alternative media sites were not party-political websites that users loyally followed. While users still broadly

TABLE 8.1 The percentage of left-wing and right-wing alternative media users' party-political preferences in the UK

	Site's political view	Labour (left)	Conservative (right)	Lib Dem (centre-left)	SNP (centre-left)	Green (left)	UKIP (right)	Other (including other parties or none, or no response)
Another Angry Voice	Left-wing	67%	5%	5%	5%	–	–	7.6%
Byline Times	Left-wing	52%	2.4%	14%	12%	4.8%	2.4%	11.8%
Evolve Politics	Left-wing	48%	3.4%	14%	14%	14%	3.4%	3.4%
Novara Media	Left-wing	60%	4%	4%	4%	8%	4%	8%
The Canary	Left-wing	55%	13%	13%	8%	6%	–	11%
The Skwawkbox	Left-wing	61%	17%	6%	6%	6%	–	6%
The London Economic	Left-wing	46%	23%	11%	–	6%	–	14.2%
Breitbart	Right-wing	44%	20%	4%	–	4%	4%	24%
Conservative Woman	Right-wing	35%	47%	6%	–	–	–	12%
Guido Fawkes	Right-wing	33%	50%	–	–	7%	–	9.7%

shared the political views of the websites they consumed, there was some ideological divergence demonstrating the diverse ways users turn to them for news and
information.

The survey further asked alternative media users across different sites how
often they consumed different mainstream news sources (see Table 8.2). These
were categorised across five sources – the BBC specifically, any other broadcaster,
a current affairs magazine, and a broadsheet or tabloid newspaper. Once again, it
is important to acknowledge that the survey was not representative of alternative
media users. Responses for some sites were relatively low, but taken together they
help generate new insights into whether alternative media users live in filter bubbles or have more diverse diets than conventional wisdom holds.

Above all, Table 8.2 shows that far from alternative media users divorcing
themselves from the world of mainstream media, the vast majority of users regularly consumed a diverse range of news produced by professional journalists.
Like the UK population, alternative media users relied more heavily on the BBC
than other mainstream media sources. With the exception of Breitbart News, the
vast majority of alternative media users from both right-wing and left-wing perspectives either watched or read BBC News regularly. To a lesser extent than
the BBC, all alternative media users relied also on broadcast news, including
Breitbart users.

Once again, across the right-left spectrum a majority of respondents regularly read broadsheet newspapers, but to a lesser degree than broadcast media.
There was some variation with alternative media audiences accessing specialist
current affairs magazines, with roughly two to four in ten regularly using them.
Meanwhile, a majority of right-wing alternative media users regularly read tabloid
newspapers, whereas a minority did for left-wing users. But despite some minor
differences in mainstream media use, the bigger picture clearly showed the vast
majority of alternative media users from across the political spectrum regularly
consumed broadcast news, especially the BBC, along with other professionally
produced news sources.

But this only paints part of the picture of alternative media engagement with
mainstream media. More research is needed about how users think about mainstream media and specific journalists, in particular BBC journalism, which the
chapter now addresses by examining follow-up qualitative responses of the 303
alternative media users.

Alternative media users' attitudes to mainstream journalism and journalists

To explore how regular alternative media users' perceived mainstream media
journalists, the survey asked them in an open-ended format. It elicited a lot of
overlapping responses, with respondents supplying sometimes multiple rather
than singular reasons for explaining their attitudes toward professional journalists.

TABLE 8.2 The percentage of alternative media users' engagement with different mainstream media sources in the UK

Site	Level of access	BBC	A main broadcaster	Broadsheet newspaper	Current affairs magazine	Tabloid newspaper
Left-wing sites						
Another Angry Voice	Regularly	82.1% (32)	71.8% (28)	53.9% (21)	25.6% (10)	23.1% (9)
	Not regularly	18.0% (7)	28.2 (11)	46.2% (18)	74.4% (29)	76.9% (30)
Total		100% (39)	100% (39)	100% (39)	100% (39)	100% (39)
Byline Times	Regularly	90.5% (38)	76.2% (32)	66.7% (28)	26.2% (11)	14.3% (6)
	Not regularly	9.5% (4)	23.8% (10)	33.3% (14)	73.8% (31)	85.7% (36)
Total		100% (42)	100% (42)	100% (42)	100% (42)	100% (42)
Evolve Politics	Regularly	82.7% (24)	75.9% (22)	65.2% (19)	37.9% (11)	37.9% (11)
	Not regularly	17.2% (5)	24.1% (7)	34.5% (10)	62.1% (18)	62.1% (18)
Total		100% (29)	100% (29)	100% (29)	100% (29)	100% (29)
Novara Media	Regularly	87.5% (28)	62.5% (20)	71.9% (23)	37.5% (12)	28.1% (9)
	Not regularly	12.5% (4)	37.5% (12)	28.1% (9)	62.5% (20)	71.9% (23)
Total		100% (32)	100% (32)	100% (32)	100% (32)	100% (32)
The Canary	Regularly	86.8% (33)	81.6% (31)	60.5% (23)	39.5% (15)	44.7% (17)
	Not regularly	13.2% (5)	18.4% (7)	39.5% (15)	60.5% (23)	55.3% (21)
Total		100% (38)	100% (38)	100% (38)	100% (38)	100% (38)
The Skwawkbox	Regularly	66.7% (12)	72.2% (13)	61.1% (11)	33.3% (6)	38.9% (7)
	Not regularly	33.3% (6)	27.8% (5)	23.9% (7)	66.7% (12)	61.1% (11)
Total		100% (18)	100% (18)	100% (18)	100% (18)	100% (18)
The London Economic	Regularly	88.7% (63)	80.3% (57)	63.4% (45)	35.2% (25)	45.1% (32)
	Not regularly	11.3% (8)	19.7% (14)	36.2% (26)	64.8% (46)	54.9% (39)
Total		100% (71)	100% (71)	100% (71)	100% (71)	100% (71)
Right-wing sites						
Breitbart	Regularly	48% (12)	64.0% (16)	60.0% (15)	20.0% (5)	56.0% (14)
	Not regularly	52% (13)	36.0% (9)	40.0% (10)	80.0% (20)	44.0% (11)
Total		100% (25)	100% (25)	100% (25)	100% (25)	100% (25)
Guido Fawkes	Regularly	75.9% (41)	77.8% (42)	53.7% (29)	20.4% (11)	53.7% (29)
	Not regularly	24.1% (13)	22.2% (12)	46.3% (25)	79.6% (43)	46.3% (25)
Total		100% (54)	100% (54)	100% (54)	100% (54)	100% (54)
The Conservative Woman	Regularly	88.3% (15)	76.5% (13)	52.9% (9)	23.5% (4)	64.7% (11)
	Not regularly	11.8% (2)	23.5% (4)	47.1% (8)	76.5% (13)	35.3% (6)
Total		100% (17)	100% (17)	100% (17)	100% (17)	100% (17)

TABLE 8.3 The percentage of alternative media users' attitudes towards mainstream journalists in the UK

Reason	Percentage[a]
Biased/lack impartiality/one-sided/politically tied/not fact-based/untruthful	17.9%
Pushes leading ideology/ownership/agenda	12.0%
Too populist/sensationalist	5.9%
They are untrustworthy/selfish	5.4%
It depends on the journalist	5.0%
Used to be good/deteriorated over time	4.4%
Omit stories/important details	4.2%
Too careful/soft news/lack opinion	4.1%
Don't hold authorities to account/not critical enough	4.1%
Do a good job/competent/professional	3.5%
I trust them	3.0%
BBC is too tied to government	2.6%
MSM journalist frame the stories as they suit them	2.6%
Fair/balanced/impartial/not biased	2.4%
I don't trust media in general	2.1%
Too much opinion/not balanced enough	2.1%
Other	18.7%
Total	100%

[a]Frequency is not provided because respondents could list more than one issue.

Table 8.3 groups together some of the dominant categories about these perspectives towards mainstream media.

Above all, Table 8.3 demonstrates that a diverse range of perspectives inform
how alternative media users think about mainstream media journalists. These
were difficult to classify into unique themes, which explains why 'other' was the
largest category of responses. While respondents were mainly critical of mainstream media, there was a small but vocal minority that positively evaluated journalists. It should be noted, in this context, that research has long shown public
attitudes towards journalists generally typically elicit negative responses (Cushion
2009). In other words, although alternative media users chose to be largely critical of journalists, it does not necessarily mean they are distinctive from how the
public think more generally.

Of the wide range of responses, by far the most common – representing 17.9%
of themes identified – was alternative media users believing mainstream media
journalists were either biased, politically driven, lacked impartiality, not fact-
based, or considered untruthful. For example, one respondent believed that professional journalists were "bloody awful, they are biased and more than happy
to do a hatchet job on a politician if he/she doesn't follow the msm viewpoint"
(Male, 50–59, Graduate degree, White – UK, user of right-wing sites), while

another said: "Mainstream journalists tend to have bias which favours the ruling party" (Male, 25–29, College/A Levels, White and Asian, user of left-wing sites). But beyond some of the broad criticisms of mainstream media, there were more nuanced answers that critiqued journalism differently according to how they perceived their standard of reporting in areas such as being impartial. For example, one respondent said:

> BBC in particular are influenced by the government in how they report. Channel 4 are more independent and do challenge status quo. Red top newspaper journalist such as sun are gutter press and should be better regulated.
>
> *(Female, 40–49, Undergraduate degree,*
> *White – UK, user of right-wing and left-wing sites)*

In other words, respondents not only developed their own critique of mainstream media by separating broadcast and press media, they drew a distinction between specific outlets, such as the BBC and Channel 4 News. Moreover, the perspective that Channel 4 tended to challenge government claims more than the BBC is supported by an analysis of how they reported the coronavirus pandemic at the start of the health crisis (Cushion et al. 2022).

Another common charge – representing 12% of responses – was that alternative users thought professional journalists reinforced the ideology of the government of the day or the perspectives of their media owners, pursuing their own agendas as opposed to an independent assessment of newsworthiness. These responses give a flavour of perspectives:

> I greatly admire the BBC journalists, but they increasingly seem constrained by the control of government, which I find distressing.
>
> *(Male, 50–59, Undergraduate degree, White – UK,*
> *user of right-wing and left-wing sites)*

> They are governed to an extent by the political views of their owners so cannot freely report their own opinions to an extent I believe. I also think they are selected just as much for their political beliefs as well as their journalistic abilities.
>
> *(Male, 60–69, secondary school/GCSE,*
> *White – UK, user of right-wing sites)*

> I hesitate to call them journalists. They seem to report virtually everything along the same narrow establishment and political guidelines. They appear to have very little integrity and they are certainly not open minded or thorough in their enquiries.
>
> *(Male, 60–69, secondary school/GCSE,*
> *White – UK, user of right-wing sites)*

There was, among many respondents, an appreciation of the structural and editorial constraints the media operate under, in particular the BBC. This informed their criticism, which was not just directed at individuals but external pressures to conform to an agenda or follow editorial guidelines that mitigated the production of high-quality journalism. Take, for instance, this critique of impartiality and lack of diversity in party-political coverage:

> They are stuck in a hegemonistic perspective which makes a lot of assumptions about how the world works, what is important, what is interesting etc. What's worse is that they're not aware of this, so for example when they attempt to report "without bias" they often fail badly because they're not aware of their own biases. Reporting two or even three perspectives of mainstream political parties is seen to be unbiased.
>
> *(Female, 40–49, Secondary school/GCSE, Any other white background, user of left-wing sites)*

At the same time, there was some criticism that the media had, over recent decades, changed and become populist or sensationalist in their reporting. For example:

> I think that the quality of mainstream media journalists has declined in recent years and there seems to be more opinion and less reporting.
>
> *(Male, 25–29, Undergraduate degree, White – UK, user of right-wing sites)*

> 15 years ago, I would have said "yes, the MSM in the UK is for the most part, fair and balanced" but it seems to be shifting further and further towards propaganda. The news cycle moves too quickly for any one story to actually have any effect.
>
> *(Male, 30–39, graduate degree, White – UK, user of left-wing sites)*

Following this perspective, some respondents considered mainstream media untrustworthy with journalists pursuing a selfish, self-centred brand of journalism often for financial rewards that did not serve audiences. For users of both right-wing and left-wing sites, this was evident as the following examples illustrate:

> They are mostly just interested in making money rather than reporting the news in an unbiased way.
>
> *(Female, 40–49, College/A Levels, White – UK, user of right-wing sites)*

> I think a lot of them are worried to go against the status quo and the money driven greed of their employers. They're in comfortable positions (this is coming from supposed left wing independent publications too), hence they have less of an economic reason to represent the true impact of the Government's

acts on the public. They seem out of touch and mostly Oxbridge graduates (which says it all). They don't seem to represent people like me.

(Female, 18–24, College/A Levels, White – UK,
user of left-wing sites)

However, some respondents were selective with their criticism of journalists, praising some reporters while criticising others. On occasions, users of right-wing and left-wing alternative media sites singled out the same journalist but had entirely contradictory views about their political agendas. Take, for instance, the following two examples:

I don't particularly like or trust them. They all seem to have agendas but never come out and say it and instead hide behind their organisation. Laura Kuenssberg of the BBC is probably the worst; a closet Labour supporter who tries to put her point across as news.

(Male, 25–29, Secondary school/GCSE,
White – UK, user of right-wing and left-wing sites)

The BBC journalist Laura Kuenssberg is probably the most prolific of all the mainstream media journalists, who very rarely questions what the government are actually doing. She has in the past defended the likes of Boris Johnson, when it is impossible to defend him. She has blatantly spouted lies about the left wing and especially Jeremy Corbyn, who was always described as anti-Semitic when there is no evidence whatsoever.

(Male, 50–59, College/A Levels, White – UK, user
of left-wing sites)

In other words, some users appeared to be critiquing journalists through their own ideological prisms. Their views, in this sense, were far from broad generalisations about professional journalism. Many respondents pointed to differences between mainstream media sources rather than just broadly using the MSM classification. So, for example, one participant stated:

I think for reporting the MSM is reasonably accurate – obviously tabloids, including the Daily Mail, are terrible propaganda rags most of the time! But for analysis I look elsewhere. Far too often you read an opinion piece and then read the byline and realise the writer is connected to a party or politician and therefore they're just parroting.

(Female, 40–49, College/A Levels, White – UK,
user of right-wing and left-wing sites)

Many respondents also drew on specific examples of coverage to evidence their criticism of mainstream media, and contrasted different outlets and professional journalists to justify their responses:

I do believe that mainstream media are really controlled, the best example is the BBC when Naga Munchetty was warned after she called somebody out for racism. I felt she was in the right, but she was not allowed that freedom of speech, however ITV who are not controlled by the government have staff that more often than not state their opinion. So overall I do not trust the media that I have access to – BBC, but know that it is based on fact, and that other things may not be covered because they don't want to state the fact.

(Female, 18–24, Undergraduate degree,
White – UK, user of right-wing and left-wing sites)

Users' critiques of mainstream media and professional journalists were, at times, quite sophisticated and evidence-based. In many ways, this reflected, as Chapter 4 explored, the agenda of many alternative media sites, which often focussed on correcting media and pointing out factual flaws or poor journalistic standards. Like many alternative media sites, users were often critical of the BBC for not holding the government accountable and highlighted some dubious editorial decisions.

Although much of the responses were critical about journalists working for professional news organisations, a significant minority of comments – almost one in ten overall – were positive towards reporters working in mainstream media. These ranged from users' trusting particular journalists or news organisations, especially the BBC, or praising their journalistic standards such as their impartial approach to reporting.

Think most mainstream journalists do a great job, people like Laura Kuenssberg and Robert Peston give a real good insight into what is going on in British Politics, they seem to have their finger on the pulse and I really enjoy listening to them.

(Male, 40–49, Secondary school/GCSE,
White – UK, user of right-wing and left-wing sites)

I personally believe that mainstream media in our country is beneficial. The journalists appear top notch and it seems to be regarded as prestige within the journalism industry. If someone works for BBC, ITV, SKY etc. I would trust them to be a competent and clever individual. I have only ever had good experiences with mainstream journalists and struggle to fault the majority.

(Male, 25–29, College/A Levels, White – UK, user
of left-wing and right-wing sites)

The only news organisation that I trust to make extreme efforts to present the facts without any bias is the BBC. I find comfort when both Governments and oppositions complain that the BBC is biased.

(Male, 70+, Secondary school/GCSE, White – UK,
user of left-wing and right-wing sites)

The BBC, in particular, was often singled out either for criticism or, in this case, praise, which runs counter to the fiercely critical agenda most alternative media sites pursued against the broadcaster (see Chapter 4). Given the editorial focus on the BBC, particularly its news output, the survey asked alternative media users specifically about their views on the UK's main public service broadcaster.

Alternative media users' attitudes towards BBC News and the BBC generally

When asked about their views on BBC News and the BBC more generally, regular alternative media users largely accused the public service broadcaster of advancing some kind of political bias or displaying a lack of impartiality in political reporting. Once again, their responses were categorised into specific themes, but there was some overlap between them (see Table 8.4). Moreover, it was difficult to classify responses into specific themes, which explains why 'other', once again, represents the second largest category.

TABLE 8.4 The percentage of alternative media users' attitudes towards BBC News and the BBC generally

Reason	Percentage[a]
Political bias/lacks impartiality	16.2%
Pushes specific ruling ideology/too tied to government	8.9%
It is fair/balanced/impartial/not biased	7.3%
Important stories are omitted	6.7%
Don't hold politicians/government to account	6.7%
The BBC may do a good job	6.3%
Good range of programmes/provide good news	6.1%
It is reliable/trustworthy/factual	4.8%
Too careful/soft news/lack opinion	4.0%
Not fact-based/untruthful	3.1%
Don't like it/trust because of specific journalists	3.0%
None/I trust the BBC	2.8%
Unprofessional/corrupt	2.7%
They should remove/reform the licence fee	2.4%
Used to be good/deteriorated over time	2.4%
Don't trust it	2.1%
Other	14.5%
Total	100%

[a]Frequency is not provided because many respondents listed more than one issue.

Like with their views about mainstream media generally, 16.2% of responses related to the BBC being biased, often directly questioning the impartiality credentials of its news agenda and reporters:

> I'm not convinced they're as impartial as they claim to be. Sometimes it is appropriate to make a stand and call out unacceptable behaviour.
>
> *(Female, 40–49, No formal qualifications,*
> *White – UK, user of right-wing and left-wing sites)*

The BBC is not impartial. There is too much interference by government, in particular Conservative government.

(Male, 50–59, Secondary school/GCSE,
White – UK, user of left-wing and right-wing sites)

Many respondents referred to a lack of journalistic independence and impartiality because of the financial relationship the BBC has with the government of the day. The following responses reflect this perspective:

The BBC is not state owned but is operationally dependant on the government so how can they be impartial?

(Female, 50–59, Undergraduate degree,
White – UK, user of left-wing and right-wing sites)

They are the government's mouthpiece presenting opinion as fact without holding them to account all the while presenting a distorted view of the other political parties and the less fortunate in society.

(Male, 60–69, Undergraduate degree, White – UK,
user of left-wing sites)

it tells you what the government wants you to hear.

(Male, 30–39, undergraduate degree, any other
mixed or multiple ethnic background, user of
left-wing sites)

At times, criticism of the BBC was focussed on the public service broadcaster being either too left-wing or right-wing in its coverage of politics:

The BBC is no longer deemed as neutral as a liberal/lefty influence dominates it now plus it is so constrained by going down the Political Correctness route and full of journalists who many would describe as "Wokes".

(Male, 60–69, Secondary school/GCSE,
White – UK, user of right-wing sites)

I think BBC in the main is controlled or at least heavily influenced by the Tories.

(Female, 50–59, College/A Levels, White – UK,
user of left-wing and right-wing sites)

In questioning the BBC's independence some respondents pointed out specific examples of so-called bias reporting and name-checked journalists, most prominently, Laura Kuenssberg. Or there were accusations from respondents of stories being omitted from news agendas for ideological reasons.

At the same time, over a quarter of responses about the BBC were broadly positive about the public service broadcaster being impartial and balanced, that they generally do a good job, produce a range of quality programmes and pursue news reporting that, for the most part, is factual and trustworthy:

> BBC News is the only outlet I visit that isn't classed as "alternative media". The BBC comes across as very neutral, there to only deliver the information needed.
>
> *(Female, 30–39, Secondary school/GCSE,*
> *White – UK, user of left-wing and right-wing sites)*

> I do follow news on the BBC and generally appreciate their coverage, as it focuses on being impartial and tends to have higher standards of morality and values compared to other broadcasters.
>
> *(Male, 40–49, Undergraduate degree, White – UK,*
> *user of left-wing and right-wing sites)*

Taken together, alternative media users' attitudes towards the BBC were somewhat distinctive from their views about mainstream media. This was because there was a greater focus on a perceived political bias or lack of impartiality rather than on declining journalism standards, such as pursuing sensationalist or 'click-bate' news. Yet there was also a greater proportion of responses that praised BBC journalism and its news service than mainstream media generally, making up roughly a quarter of perspectives about the UK's main public service broadcaster.

Beyond echo chambers and filter bubbles: towards a sceptical media savvy user

Over recent years, fears have grown that alternative media help ghettoise audiences, pushing them into so-called filter bubbles and echo chambers. But far from being trapped in ideological prisons, this chapter has shown that most users do not turn to alternative media to *replace* their consumption of mainstream media. Instead, users engage with a range of mainstream media in addition to either (or even both) left-wing and right-wing alternative media sites. As the UK case study demonstrated, not only were regular alternative media users heavily reliant on a rasp of mainstream media sources – from broadcast, print, and online outlets – some even used alternative media sites that were ideologically opposed to their own brand of politics. The targeted survey of alternative media users revealed that many read both left-wing and right-wing sites (particularly users of Guido Fawkes) and regularly consumed mainstream media content. These findings challenge claims about ideological echo chambers and audience segmentation emanating from the use of alternative media sites.

In exploring alternative media users' relationship with mainstream media sources, the UK case study found many were highly sceptical of professionally produced journalism. But, significantly, they still relied on a range of mainstream media outlets to understand what was happening in the political world. They justified their scepticism according to a wide range of often complex issues, including the structural and political constraints journalists work under. From sometimes crude accusations of political bias to sophisticated accounts of broadcasters breaching impartiality, alternative media users were not uniformly partisan in their engagement with mainstream media. They often drew on examples to illustrate specific instances of poor editorial decisions or standards or where profit and partisanship trumped journalistic integrity and professionalism. For example, when critiquing the BBC, while many respondents mistrusted its journalism, their views were not just vacuous partisan attacks from either left-wing or right-perspectives. Many were justified by the BBC's lack of independence due to its reliance on the government of the day for future funding. In fact, despite the obvious hostility many alternative media sites held towards the BBC (see Chapter 4), over a quarter of responses from users about the UK's main public service broadcaster praised its impartiality, journalistic standards, and breadth of programming.

Far from alternative media users being passively partisan creatures, blind in their pursuit of ideologically driven news, the chapter showed that many were highly literate if sceptical users of alternative and mainstream media. Or, put another way, across the political spectrum alternative media users were not sucked into silos that mitigated their engagement with mainstream media or alternative political viewpoints. Needless to say, most alternative media users were distrustful and, in many cases, dissatisfied with different mainstream media, but they were not monolithically motivated. Users selectively critiqued and praised different mainstream media sources and journalists across a range of issues and events.

Viewed in this light, users of highly partisan alternative media were, on some occasions, motivated by the same ideological beliefs as the sites they consumed. But some users also engaged with sites that ran counter to their own political views. Meanwhile, the vast majority of users consumed a variety of mainstream media outlets that, by their own admission, informed them about what was happening in the world even when they questioned the quality or integrity of reporting. In order to identify the sometimes complex and nuanced relationships between alternative media users and their engagement with mainstream media, the findings point towards the importance of understanding national media environments. As previous chapters have explored, sometimes idiosyncratic national media and political ecosystems can produce user dynamics that make it difficult to generalise beyond the nation state. This was displayed by many users' engagement with the BBC in the UK's political media landscape. While many had a progressive alienation from the BBC, they did not switch off entirely but continued to rely on the UK's main public service broadcaster – even if sceptically – to understand politics and public affairs. In other words, regular users of alternative media were not trapped in a partisan prison, but their wider media consumption habits were driven by an ideological understanding of their national media environments.

Taken together, the body of research drawn on throughout this chapter has demonstrated the importance of understanding cross-national differences in alternative and mainstream media user engagement. The final chapter of the book develops a cross-national review of alternative media research that explains the (trans)national influences and ideological boundaries that police user engagement with alternative and mainstream media. It also considers how national media systems shape the production practices and editorial content of alternative media.

References

Andersen, K., Shehata, A. and Andersson, D. (2021) 'Alternative news orientation and trust in mainstream media: A longitudinal audience perspective', *Digital Journalism*, https://doi.org/10.1080/21670811.2021.1986412

Arguedas, A.R., Robertson, C.T., Fletcher, R. and Nielsen, R.K. (2022) 'Echo chambers, filter bubbles, and polarisation: A literature review', https://reutersinstitute.politics.ox.ac.ukki/echo-chambers-filter-bubbles-and-polarisation-literature-review

Cushion, S. (2009) 'FROM TABLOID HACK TO BROADCAST JOURNALIST', Journalism Practice, Vol.3(4): 472-481, https://doi.org/10.1080/17512780903259358

Cushion, S. Morani, M. Kyriakidou, M. and Soo, N. (2022) 'Why Media Systems Matter: A Fact-Checking Study of UK Television News during the Coronavirus Pandemic', *Digital Journalism*, Vol. 10(5): 698-716, https://doi.org/10.1080/21670811.2021.1965490

Downing, J. (2003) 'Audiences and readers of alternative media: The absent lure of the virtually unknown', *Media, Culture & Society*, Vol. 25(5): 625–645. https://doi.org/10.1177/01634437030255004

Kalogeropoulos, A. and Newman, N. (2018) 'Who uses alternative and partisan brands?', https://www.digitalnewsreport.org/survey/2018/who-uses-alternative-and-partisan-brands/

Klawier, T., Prochazka, F. and Schweiger, W. (2021) 'Public knowledge of alternative media in times of algorithmically personalized news', *New Media & Society*, https://doi.org/10.1177/14614448211021071

Lee, F. (2015) 'Internet alternative media use and oppositional knowledge', *International Journal of Public Opinion Research*, Vol. 27(3): 318–340.

Jones, S.M. (2017) '"Canary-isation" of the media is a concern for the left, says Owen Jones', *PRWeek*, 9 January, https://www.prweek.com/article/1420048/canary-isation-media-concern-left-says-owen-jones

Marwick, A. and Lewis, R. (2017) *Media Manipulation and Disinformation Online*, Data & Society Research Institute. https://datasociety.net/library/media-manipulation-and-disinfo-online/

Noppari, E., Hiltunen, I., & Ahva, L. (2019) User profiles for populist counter-media websites in Finland. *Journal of Alternative and Community Media*, 4(1), 23–37. https://doi.org/10.1386/joacm_00041_1

Rauch, J. (2021) *Resisting the News: Engaged Audiences, Alternative Media, and Popular Critique of Journalism*. New York: Routledge.

Reiter, F. and Matthes, J. (2021) 'Correctives of the mainstream media? A panel study on mainstream media use, alternative digital media use, and the erosion of political

interest as well as political knowledge', *Digital Journalism,* https://doi.org/10.1080
/21670811.2021.1974916

Schulze, H. (2020) 'Who uses right-wing alternative online media? An exploration of
audience characteristics', *Politics and Governance,* Vol. 8(3): 6–18. https://doi.org/10
.17645/pag.v8i3.2925

Schwarzenegger, C. (2022) Understanding the users of alternative news media—Media
epistemologies, news consumption, and media practices, *Digital Journalism,* https://doi
.org/10.1080/21670811.2021.2000454

Tsfati, Y. and Cappella, J. N. (2003) 'Do people watch what they do not trust?: Exploring the
association between news media skepticism and exposure', *Communication Research,*
Vol. 30(5): 504–529. https://doi.org/10.1177/00936502032533

Vaccari, C. and Valeriani, A. (2021) *Outside the Bubble: Social Media and Political
Participation in Western Democracies.* Oxford: Oxford University Press.

9
ALTERNATIVE MEDIA AND THE FUTURE OF JOURNALISM

Alternative media have historically operated at the margins of power, with their ideological goals largely associated with promoting a progressive brand of left-wing politics designed to challenge the hegemony of mainstream media (Downing 1984). But, as this book has empirically revealed, today's alternative media do not *solely* exist to be in opposition to mainstream media nor do they *all* occupy a radical space outside of media or political power. Alternative media have evolved over recent decades into an array of online and social media networks that intersect with mainstream media, and address a wide range of subjects from right-wing and left-wing perspectives. In other words, they cannot be narrowly or uniformly categorised, or pigeon-holed as being the preserve of left-wing activists. In more recent years, right-wing alternative media have attracted scholarly attention because they have become aligned with the rise of populist parties and candidates (Benkler et al. 2017; Thompson and Howley 2021; von Nordheim et al. 2021), and been criticised for spreading disinformation and legitimising dubious political claims (Marwick and Lewis 2017; Mourão and Robertson 2019). To different degrees cross-nationally, many (mostly right-wing) alternative media sites have moved from the margins of power to more prominent positions in Western media landscapes.

This book focussed on *alternative online political media from across the political spectrum*, examining their production processes, editorial agendas, and output over recent years, along with user engagement. Taken together, it found some editorial similarities between different sites, but there were also considerable differences and variations in their production, output, and engagement with users. Drawing on the latest scholarship and original UK case studies, different chapters revealed that alternative media sites have embraced the practices and conventions

DOI: 10.4324/9781003360865-10

of mainstream media and professional journalism. Or, put more broadly, a mainstreaming of alternative media was identified in many national media environments because the editors and contributors of sites were drawing on sophisticated production processes and legitimised their journalism through external regulation. Operating like conventional newsrooms but in virtual forums, many sites have developed highly focussed and streamlined publishing strategies that sought to influence the agendas of political parties and mainstream media. For example, some sites created carefully crafted headlines to bypass social media algorithms that once limited their reach. In different ways, editors and contributors of alternative media sites today now mimic the rhythm and routines of professional journalists but without having anywhere near the same level of resources as most mainstream newsrooms.

While the audience reach for most alternative media sites remains relatively low, the book challenged the perception that this was solely limited to partisan activists dissatisfied with mainstream media. It revealed many users do not live in ideological filter bubbles or echo chambers, and still relied on mainstream media while some consumed alternative media sites from across the political spectrum. In short, the book has demonstrated that alternative media sites do not operate outside of mainstream media nor do all their users exclusively inhabit an alternative media universe. Needless to say, most alternative media sites continue to editorially strive to correct or oppose the agendas of mainstream media. But many have accepted the production logic of professional journalism in order to enhance the quality of their content in ways that were consistent with their ideological goals.

In understanding alternative media, this book has argued that it is necessary to analyse the wider national media system and political environment they routinely inhabit. Only then can scholars interpret the editorial motivations of alternative media production, the type of agenda pursued and why users engage with different sites. This is because alternative media editorially operate within the worlds of mainstream media and institutional politics rather than in isolation from them. But there has been limited academic attention paid to exploring the relationship between alternative media, national media systems, and political environments. Yet national media systems have long been theorised as reflecting the social and political characteristics of the country they inhabit (Siebert et al. 1956). Hallin and Mancini's (2004) 18-nation widely referenced study of countries from Western European and North America developed three media systems – liberal, democratic corporatist, and polarised pluralist – that connected specific countries with political and journalistic identities. But there was no sustained discussion of the role of alternative media in their classification of national media systems.

Since media and political systems shape the development of alternative media, this chapter will explore some cross-national differences in order to help understand how they influence production processes, editorial agendas, and engagement with audiences. In doing so, it goes beyond the key findings of the book and considers broader questions about the wider ideological influence of alternative media and, importantly, what future role they will play in the world of politics and journalism. In comparing and contrasting alternative media cross-nationally, the chapter explores five inter-related areas. First, it begins by examining under-researched media environments around the world from Latin America, to Turkey, Iran, and China. It suggests a de-Westernisation of alternative media scholarship is necessary because many nations have political structures that limit or entirely censor any form of independent and critical journalism. Second, the chapter argues for a decentring of alternative media studies, with less emphasis placed on sites from the US because America has an exceptional media and political system that creates more opportunities for (far-right-wing) alternative media to thrive than most other Western nations. Third, the chapter examines the implications of more people turning to alternative media as an information source. It reveals that regular exposure to alternative media can enhance public disaffection with mainstream media, particularly public service journalism. Fourth, the chapter analyses the rise of right-wing alternative media and the role played by corporate donors sustaining an infrastructure of partisan journalism. Fifth, the chapter concludes the book by re-imagining how left-wing alternative media can expand their audience reach beyond a limited ideological base. Ultimately, it argues that if alternative left-wing media maintain a professionalised approach to production and engage with mainstream journalism – rather than operate at a distance away from it – they will expand their ideological influence on the world.

De-Westernising alternative media studies: understanding differences in cross-national media and political environments

Waisbord (2022: 1431) has recently suggested "that alternative [media] refers to the communicative politics of contestation which take different interpretations across political contexts", as well as being "understood in relation to other media". In other words, it is difficult to uniformly define alternative media – they instead need to be understood in their media and political environment. In doing so, Waisbord (2022) further argued that alternative media studies should de-Westernise scholarship in order to more accurately understand and interpret their production, content, and users. This was due to 'alternative' being viewed as a relative concept, defined, and interpreted in often idiosyncratic local contexts. In Waisbord's (2022: 1432) own words:

> "Alternative" takes different meaning in countries and regions. Their analysis taps into different uses of "alternative" to denominate certain media/journalism as mainstream, especially as used by media workers/journalists and audiences. Because the 'mainstream' is quite different terms of media, journalism and politics across countries, such as Germany and Turkey, "alternative" only makes sense in relation to particular positions and definitions by various actors.

As explored in Chapter 5, some Turkish alternative media sites viewed themselves as professional journalists, replicating the editorial practices of mainstream media, and respecting rather than rejecting journalistic norms such as impartial reporting (Ozul and Veneti 2021). Their 'alternative' approach to Turkish journalism was borne out of political developments over the last decade or so, and the wider influence this had on the national media environment. More specifically, the growth of alternative media in Turkey can be attributed to a new authoritarian political system, putting constraints into place that limit journalistic freedoms and public debate. As Asker and McCollum (2018: 1) have observed, "alternative media is used to report news otherwise blocked by censorship or other restrictions on media in contemporary Turkey". They argued this generated two types of alternative media. On the one hand, it led to alternative media being produced by former professional journalists who were frustrated by the constraints imposed by the government but motivated enough to deliver independent reporting. This helps explain why many sites embraced rather than resisted long-standing editorial practices of mainstream media (Ozul and Veneti 2021). On the other hand, new alternative media arose from dissatisfied citizens who considered themselves poorly served by national media. According to Ataman and Çoban (2018: 1025), in Turkey "business relations, commercial risks, and enormous political pressure compel the national mainstream media to be pro-government and partisan. Thus, most of the professional and independent journalism that holds power accountable has disappeared". They carried out interviews with activists producing alternative media that demonstrated how their news-making was editorially driven by the desire to oppose authoritarian politics.

Similarly, in Iran, long-standing authoritarian regimes have created an environment where the purpose of alternative media – or what are known as 'small media' – has been to counter repressive politics. As Koo (2017: 23) has observed, "small media refers to the alternative media vehicle that counters the state authority or companies' big media (national broadcasts or public television)". She concluded that "Just as small media led the Islamic Revolution to success in the past, personal and new media in contemporary Iranian Society are becoming consolidated into a political public space of their own" (Koo 2017: 23). Over the last decade or so, social media networks have become critical platforms for people to access news and information not controlled by the state. But while there have been moments when Twitter and Facebook have been able to disseminate critical content, within Iran alternative media have struggled to bypass government censorship and regularly reach large swathes of the public. Apps such as Instagram and Clubhouse have opened a "new public sphere", but authorities often temporarily tolerate and delimit their use so they can monitor citizens and identify influential actors (Khalaji 2022). Al-Rawi's (2022) analysis of media use in Iran has suggested it is foreign rather than domestic media that offer alternative perspectives to government propaganda. In his words:

The intention of alternative media outlets such as BBC Persian, VOA Farsi, Radio Farda, and Iran International is to create a personalized venue that can assist Iranians in navigating news about their own country and the world, while simultaneously offering them news from the perspective of these channels' sponsors.

(Al-Rawi 2022: 964)

Rather than national political and media contexts largely shaping alternative media, in authoritarian systems the wider international environment becomes an important source of alternative perspectives.

In China, where the media operate under tight state control with online and social media use limited by government censorship, alternative media have also struggled to become widely accessed sources of news and information. While there have been specific contexts or time periods where critical perspectives have overcome state repression (Yin 2018), the degree to which Chinese alternative media can individually or collectively counter government propaganda remains limited. In another authoritarian state, Russia, the inability of alternative media to challenge government perspectives was laid bare when its military was ordered to invade Ukraine in 2022. Since the government controls state television and limits its foreign broadcast and online communication, when the invasion began many Russians relied on the President's largely sanitised version of the war. And when there was any public or media opposition to war, it was swiftly suppressed by the state in the early months of the invasion. Moreover, at the start of the invasion journalists in Russia were told not to call it a 'war', or even an 'invasion' or 'attack'. Instead, they were asked to follow the Russian state script that it was a "special operation", designed for purposes of national security in the face of threats from Nato (Cushion 2022). Alternative and independent sources of news were closed down by authorities, with new legislation enacted to jail any journalists that the Russian state deemed to be reporting 'fake news' about what was happening in Ukraine. In other words, the degree to which an alternative 'window on the world' could be reported was delimited by an authoritative system of government.

In nations with varying levels of repressive state influence on media and political environments, such as Turkey, Iran, China, and Russia, alternative media often operate outside the country, at the very margins of social and online networks, or for fleeting if significant moments in time until state hegemony is re-imposed. This is because, as Waisbord (2022: 1433) has pointed out

"alternative" is a political concept, its meanings are linked to particular experiences in specific contexts. What defines alternative in democracies is different from authoritarianism. What is alternative under capitalism is not the same as in socialism. What characterizes alternative is contingent on its relation vis-a-vis dominant ideologies – liberalism, socialism, conservatism, fascism, racism, patriarchy.

National political environments, viewed from this perspective, help police the boundaries of alternative media across different countries. Waisbord (2022: 1433), for instance, considers alternative media in Latin America to be distinctive from several European countries because it is "associated with grassroots, multicultural, progressive experiences", as opposed to the focus of right-wing politics, such as populist anger with rising immigration. Two decades into the 21st century, Latin American nations no longer have the authoritarian regimes that once limited journalistic freedoms. In the online and social media age, this meant different forms of largely left-wing media sites have emerged and established themselves as alternative sources of news and information, reflecting a new social reality and promoting political participation and protest. However, according to Harlow's (2023) analysis of several Latin American nations over the last decade or so, they should not be crudely classified as alternative media. By drawing on interviews with producers, surveys, and focus groups with audiences, as well as content analyses of websites, she argued that new independent journalism did not represent conventional alternative media sites with partisan perspectives. Just as Chapters 5 and 6 argued in the context of UK case studies, Harlow (2023) discovered a new level of professionalism was shaping the production of alternative media journalism, with practices and conventions more akin to the newsrooms of mainstream media. These sites were championing a progressive form of left-wing politics, pursuing issues that personally motivated them and challenged mainstream politics. In other words, a new form of journalism had evolved across American Latin nations, reflecting sometimes idiosyncratic political developments and media environments that mark them as distinctive from each other and alternative media more generally.

Taken together, the limited studies exploring alternative media in non-Western nations collectively show that it is the political environment that plays a significant role in shaping the type of journalism produced. In authoritarian systems, such as Turkey, Iran, China, and Russia, repressive political systems limit journalistic freedom of expression. Meanwhile, in many Latin American nations, the editorial character of alternative media was viewed as different from conventional definitions (Harlow 2023) and reflective of the wider political and media system over recent decades. This demonstrates the need to de-Westernise alternative media (Wasibord 2022), challenging crude or lazy assumptions about what alternative media represent and their wider impact on the world. But there is arguably a need to also decentre alternative media studies so that developments in America – which often act as a vocal point in recent scholarship – do not represent or reflect alternative media in all other Western nations. In a variety of different ways, the American media environment and political system is exceptional when compared to that of most other Western nations (Curran 2011). The next section now explores how America's distinctive media and political system has shaped the development of alternative media.

Decentring alternative media studies: why the US's media and political system is exceptional compared to other Western nations

In many parts of Europe, it is predominantly right-wing alternative media sites that have become prominent parts of the media system. Without repressive government-imposed restrictions, many Western democracies have witnessed a rise in new alternative media sites that reflect a diverse range of issues and perspectives unique to their national media and political environments. Over recent years, new alternative media sites have become highly critical of mainstream media, while also pursuing populist political causes on issues such as immigration or Brexit. But their editorial content – as Chapters 1 and 2 demonstrated – has not been widely researched and taken seriously by scholars. As the introduction to a Special Issue of *Alternative Media in Digital Journalism* pointed out, "alternative news media have often been excluded in broader assessments of news diversity, indicating that alternative media have not been defined as 'news media' or seen as important enough to be included" (Ihlebæk et al. 2022: 1270). And yet, as Chapters 7 and 8 explored, many alternative media users across the US and Europe do not always see a clear-cut distinction between the journalism of mainstream and alternative media, particularly in a highly polarised media environment. Steppat et al.'s (2021: 16) cross-national survey of users from Denmark, Italy, Poland, Switzerland, and the US discovered that in partisan environments audiences often viewed alternative media as mainstream sources of information. This was particularly evident in America because, according to the authors:

> the US offers very favourable opportunity structures for alternative media, the audience of self-proclaimed alternative media is the largest of the five countries. The fact that many US respondents also name various mainstream outlets as alternative news options may be the result of many of these outlets adopting features of alternative media to succeed in a fragmented-polarized media environment.
>
> *(Seppat et al. 2021: 16)*

Put bluntly, recent developments in American's media and political environment have led to a convergence between mainstream and alternative media.

While many Western democratic nations have moved towards a more polarised media landscape and witnessed the growth of populist political candidates and parties, it is the US where these trends appear most intense and extreme. Compared to many other Western nations, its media system does not have well-funded and widely consumed public service media (Curran 2011, Cushion 2012). Instead, rampant commercialisation has long defined the US media system, with much of its journalism driven by profits over editorial principles, and reporting of policy debates marginalised for more sensationalist coverage of politics (Cushion and Thomas 2018; Pickard 2020). Since rules about ensuring balance and impartiality in television and radio were rescinded in the 1980s, broadcasting in the US has become a more ideologically driven environment. Channels such as Fox News and MSNBC largely cater to Republican and Democrat supporters respectively, reinforcing rather than challenging their partisanship (Cushion and Sambrook 2016). In doing so, they have gained a significant audience share and helped cultivate widespread disaffection with mainstream media. For decades, they have undermined professional journalism, with right-wing politicians especially lining up to single out instances of bias and misrepresentation in a perceived liberal mainstream media system. Where once ideologically driven cable news channels could claim to operate in an alternative political media environment, today they have become increasingly integrated into the American mainstream media system.

Over two decades into the 21st century, the growth of online and social media networks has further catered to the political polarisation of many Americans. In so doing, it has helped create a thriving alternative media system that has influenced mainstream media and political events, in particular right-wing alternative media. This was well illustrated by Breitbart's influence in the run-up to the 2016 Presidential Election. Benkler et al.'s (2017) study examined the media ecosystem people inhabited by tracking what stories from websites they shared across their social media networks. They compared patterns across those that retweeted Hillary Clinton and those that retweeted Donald Trump to assess how their partisanship informed what stories they shared from different news sources, including mainstream and alternative media. Examining 1.25 million shared online stories, across 25,000 sources, between 1 April 2015 and November 8 2016, Benkler et al. (2017) discovered, in their words, that Breitbart was "the center of a distinct right-wing media ecosystem, surrounded by Fox News, the Daily Caller, the Gateway Pundit, the Washington Examiner, Infowars, Conservative Treehouse, and Truthfeed", which promoted a Trumpian brand of Republican politics. By contrast, Clinton's social media activity was largely shaped by mainstream media sources, rather than a left-wing alternative media system. The influence of right-wing alternative media centred on immigration and direct personal criticism of Clinton and, according to Benkler et al.'s (2017) analysis, influenced the wider information agenda. In their words:

> While mainstream media coverage was often critical, it nonetheless revolved around the agenda that the right-wing media sphere set: immigration. Right-wing media, in turn, framed immigration in terms of terror, crime, and Islam, as a review of Breitbart and other right-wing media stories about immigration most widely shared on social media exhibits.
>
> *(Benkler et al. 2017)*

This convergence between Republican politics and far-right-wing media, and their ability to help set the mainstream media agenda, reveals just how normalised many of these alternative media sites have become in the US. Their convergence and conflation into mainstream media helps explain why many Americans – more so than other advanced Western nations – do not differentiate alternative from mainstream journalism (Steppat et al. 2021).

The implications of Americans relying on partisan alternative media for news were revealed immediately after Joe Biden won the US presidential race in 2020. According to one survey at the time, 88% of Republican supporters believed it was an illegitimate victory (Walsh 2020) when there was no evidence to support this false claim. While this was fuelled by Trump's repeated accusations of electoral rigging, it gained wider traction in much of the news media, especially right-wing partisan channels such as Fox News. But even after Fox News largely accepted Biden's presidential victory, alternative Conservative media sources began to attract far larger audiences into 2021, questioning the US voting systems and undermining democratic institutions, such as Newsmax. In other words, many people continue to go beyond mainstream media – and partisan sources – to relatively obscure far-right alternative media sites for information about politics and public affairs.

Interpreted more broadly, the influence of alternative media appears to be greater in Western nations when there is not just political polarisation but public disaffection with mainstream media, leaving an informational vacuum for right-wing and left-wing sites to attract new audiences (Steppat et al. 2021). As demonstrated in Chapters 7 and 8, this should not be misinterpreted as alternative media creating filter bubbles or echo chambers with users exclusively inhabiting their worlds. The success of many alternative media sites has been to naturalise themselves into the media and political environment, making up a diverse diet of mainstream media and partisan news sources. However, as Arguedas et al.'s (2022) review of research about filter bubbles concluded, the nature of a national mainstream media system can shape the degree to which partisan alternative media influence political understanding. Above all, they found in countries with a robust public service media system promoting impartial journalism, their coverage can mitigate the impact of populist politics and the promotion of polarisation. But there is also evidence to suggest that the continued conflation of alternative media into mainstream media undermines how people perceive professional journalism, especially public service broadcasters. As explored next, a growing body of scholarship suggests exposure to alternative media leads to public disaffection with mainstream media and professional journalism.

The relationship between alternative media use and disaffection with mainstream media

Public scepticism towards mainstream media dates back decades. According to one Gallup poll, two-thirds of Americans had confidence in the news in 1968, but over time it fell to just under a third in 2016 (Jones 2018). Over more recent years, the declining level of trust in mainstream media has grown stronger. A pre-pandemic 2019 survey of 27 nations over five years discovered trust in newspapers, magazines, radio and television, online and other platforms had dropped by a third (Ipsos Mori 2019). Meanwhile, a 2022 survey of 28 countries of more than 36,000 people showed that just under 6 in 10 respondents – 57% – did not trust mainstream sources, while over two-thirds of them thought that journalists were purposely trying to mislead the public by saying things they knew were false or gross exaggerations (Edelman 2022).

Needless to say, public confidence varies across different national media systems, with public service broadcasters more widely trusted than market-driven organisations (Strömbäck et al. 2020). A country's political culture can also shape its relationship with mainstream media. In the US, for example, political partisanship has long been associated with people's trust across different news outlets. In the year Trump was elected president, one survey revealed a sharp fall in Republican party supporters' confidence in mainstream media (Swift 2016). A 2016 report found "Republicans who say they have trust in the media has plummeted to 14% from 32% a year ago. This is easily the lowest confidence among Republicans in 20 years" (Swift 2016). Given Trump has a record of regularly attacking the value of mainstream media, questioning the integrity of journalists on the campaign trail, and aggressively criticising them in press conferences, it is perhaps not surprising many of his supporters shared his views about their trustworthiness.

But beyond Trump, the focus on journalistic standards of news organisations, such as The New York Times and the BBC, has become a widely debated issue over recent years. Of course, where once mainstream media were the monopoly suppliers of news and information, today their grip on the market has diminished with new online and social media platforms challenging their hegemonic power. In doing so, many people's diet of news may have been expanded, with alternative media sites questioning mainstream media coverage and encouraging public scepticism in their journalism. As explored in Chapters 7 and 8, understanding the root cause and effect of people's (dis)engagement with mainstream is complicated and difficult to isolate. But a comprehensive review of academic literature exploring how scholars have traditionally measured engagement with, knowledge about, and attitudes towards, mainstream journalism, concluded that alternative media have played a role in cultivating public attitudes. Strömbäck et al.'s (2020: 151) study is worth quoting at length:

> it is abundantly clear that many people do not trust traditional news media. It is also clear that the transformation into high-choice media environments has brought with it a host of new and exacerbated challenges threatening to undermine news media trust... there are more so-called non-mainstream and partisan media that compete with traditional news media. Such non-mainstream media in many cases even actively engage in attempts to undermine trust in traditional news media.

Recent studies have begun to pinpoint the growing influence of alternative media in shaping public opinion about mainstream media and journalists across different media systems and political cultures.

As referenced earlier in the chapter, Steppat et al.'s (2021) comparative surveys across five nations – including Italy, Poland, the US, Switzerland, and Denmark – explored the influence of alternative media in the context of contrasting levels of fragmentation and polarisation. They discovered that "the higher the level of fragmentation and polarisation, the worse the perceived news performance, especially with regard to journalistic independence and objectivity". In doing so, it was concluded that "The use of alternative news media sources seems to promote people's image that the news media performs poorly" (Steppat et al. 2021: 331). Similarly, Ladd (2013) found that declining levels of public trust in American mainstream media was associated with coverage in alternative media. He discovered that alternative media content encouraged mistrust in mainstream media, especially among conservative media users with right-wing views. He found they were more cynical about professional journalists when compared to liberal audiences with left-wing political perspectives. A high level of political partisanship was also associated with having less confidence in the standards of professional journalism in the UK. For example, Newman et al.'s (2020) representative surveys revealed a decline in trust towards mainstream media among left-wing voters over recent years. Meanwhile, Kalogeropoulos and Newman (2018) showed that although the BBC was the most trusted news organisation, faith in the public service broadcaster fell for those holding left-wing or right-wing views between 2018 and 2020.

In short, there is emerging evidence pointing to the growing influence of alternative media shaping how people value mainstream media and professional journalists. It follows then that the more people are exposed to alternative media, the more likely it is to feed public mistrust and antipathy in professional journalism and mainstream media. As this book has empirically demonstrated, mainstream media have been subject to sustained attacks over recent years from alternative media sites, with public service broadcasters often the main focus of critical attention. Much of the criticism directed at mainstream and professional journalism was not necessarily crude or misplaced. As Chapter 4 explored, an analysis of alternative left-wing sites revealed criticism of mainstream media was often evidence-based, drawing on specific examples of journalism (Cushion 2020).

Viewed from this perspective, alternative media not only aim to cover criticism of mainstream media but to uncover their failures, contradictions, and shortcomings in order to improve the quality and performance of professional journalism. By their own admission, their critique of mainstream journalism is driven by an ideological goal of advancing their own brand of politics and challenging competing perspectives. Chapter Four revealed this can generate well-informed debates, such as the consequences associated with the concentration of media ownership. But the constant surveillance of mainstream media, particularly of public service broadcasters, paints an image – however rare or fair – of repeated instances of sloppy journalism or overt examples of media bias. Moreover, without context and explanation, these isolated criticisms can be rapidly shared on social media and go viral within minutes of them being aired or published. Broadcasters, such as the BBC, have become accurately aware of the instant impact of alternative media, acknowledging the editorial pressure that close scrutiny brings. For instance, when BBC editorial staff anonymously briefed the Guardian's Media Editor after the 2019 General Election Campaign, they revealed "A common complaint was the risk of feeling paralysed by the knowledge that every single piece of television, radio or online output is at risk of being examined in detail on Twitter for allegations of bias" (Waterson 2019). Needless to say, when alternative media draw attention to editorial misjudgements they play an important watchdog function that holds mainstream media to account, particularly BBC journalism which has enormous reach and influence. But arguably this constant scrutiny paints a misleading picture of editorial standards, with isolated moments often decontextualised across online and social media platforms, promoting a relentless agenda of news about deliberate or unconscious mainstream media bias. In other words, it is hard to see how routine exposure to mainstream media failure will not, over time, cultivate negative perceptions of professional journalism, especially public service broadcasters.

This raises a long-term question about the role alternative media will play in not just shaping journalism in the future, but their wider influence in society. The final two sections of the book will consider the systemic impact of left-wing and right-wing alternative media, exploring how they will evolve in the digital age of journalism, and assessing where they will enhance and undermine media environments and political systems. It begins by exploring the growing prominence of right-wing alternative media, along with the funding and politics that drive their influence.

The rise of right-wing alternative media and their opposition to mainstream media

While this book has explored the rise of alternative media internationally, it would be difficult to argue their collective ascendancy has radically revolutionised the media systems of most countries. Sites such as Indymedia were once optimistically heralded as significant sites of resistance and influence that would challenge corporate hegemony globally into the 21st century. As Stengrim (2005: 291–2) observed after the World Trade Organization protests in 2003,

The unique double-gestured makeup of Indymedia, including local IMCs and global Indymedia's online networking, more than the content of the newspapers and newswires, is what provides a democratic answer to a trend in corporate globalization that privileges form over content and process over product.

But alternative media – including Indymedia – have arguably not lived up to their democratic potential. Their ability to meaningfully challenge mainstream politics today remains, for the most part, limited in practice. And yet, given the long-known democratic possibilities of the Internet and the relatively new ability for social media networks to instantly connect on a global scale, why has stronger journalism in alternative media not meaningfully challenged the hegemony of mainstream media? After all, the birth of the internet brought promises of new 'informational superhighways' and 'information revolutions'. But the reality is that most mainstream media agendas have not been radically altered due to the influence of online alternative media sites or by new social media platforms.

At the start of the 21st century, the democratic possibilities of alternative media were associated with a progressive brand of liberal, left-wing websites, supporting activist groups locally and internationally. But more than two decades later, across the Western world, it is conservative, often (far) right-wing media that have usurped the ambitions of left-wing alternative media. But why have right-wing sites become a more prominent part of many national media systems than left-wing sites? Above all, funding lies at the heart of their success. Many right-wing sites have been supported by wealthy individuals and commercial organisations with the aim of championing conservative policies and perspectives. This is evident in many regions of the world, across Europe, Australia, Latin America, and many nations beyond. For example, one UK alternative media site examined throughout this book, Westmonster, was privately funded by millionaires in 2017 in order to promote "pro-Brexit, pro-Farage, pro-Trump, anti-establishment, anti-open borders, anti-corporatism news" (cited in Ponsford 2017). Once Brexit had been achieved, the site ceased operations because its political ambitions had succeeded. By contrast, promoting a left-wing of the world is not ordinarily in the interests of rich, private donors or large commercial organisations. After all, the advancement of social equality or egalitarianism – which typically represents left-wing ideology – can undermine profit margins and promote collective state-led solutions in society rather than support more capitalist and individual entrepreneurship.

It is in the US where private donors have most strikingly funded alternative media effectively, promoting a conservative brand of ideology over many decades throughout the 20th century (Bauer 2022). This has been exacerbated in the age of 21st-century online and social media, with significant resources poured into developing an infrastructure of right-wing media that aims to challenge and undermine the authority of American mainstream media. The Centre of Media and Democracy carried out an investigation into conservative funding streams and concluded that

> the family foundations of Charles Koch and a number of similarly-minded right-wing megadonors, along with two donor-advised fund sponsors that they use to shepherd their charitable contributions and receive special tax breaks,

have donated at over $109 million to media operations since 2015, nearly all of them conservative.

(Kotch 2020)

In doing so, they identified the collective range and reach of right-wing alternative media sites and their agendas:

> The host of conservative media outlets have faithfully met the needs of their often billionaire funders. The Daily Caller, heavily funded by the Charles Koch Foundation, prints opinion pieces from senior fellows at the climate change-denying Heartland Institute claiming the idea that human-caused climate change is destroying the earth is a "delusion." The Media Research Center's CNS News site prints essays by right-wing personality Ben Shapiro attacking critics of free-market capitalism. Reason.com promotes the wonders of capitalism and makes podcasts extolling the legacy of the late David Koch, a longtime Reason Foundation trustee. Project Veritas attempts to smear the presidential campaign of economic populist Bernie Sanders and earns praise from President Donald Trump. The Motion Picture Institute produces films that attack regulation and a children's video series in which an economics professor who is affiliated with several Koch-funded programs teaches kids about the value of free-market economics. And PragerU publishes five-minute videos attacking socialism, climate science, socialized medicine, and the left in general.
>
> *(Kotch 2020)*

This rise of right-wing alternative media not only advances conservative voices, they denigrate and weaken their political opponents and ideological beliefs, portraying the mainstream media as promoting a left-wing bias and undermining their professional journalistic principles and objectivity.

The arrival of online media has intensified efforts to fund right-wing alternative media, and they have been collectively developed in the US to exert greater influence than many left-wing media sites hold around the world. Funding alone, however, does not explain why right-wing alternative media sites wield greater influence in the 21st century. It is the conservative brand of politics they promote that has necessitated the need to bypass mainstream media. Throughout the 20th century, most media systems developed professional journalism that upheld values of impartiality and objectivity that delimited how far a particular ideology could be promoted (Tuchman 1972). From an American perspective, Bauer (2022) believed that the drive to acquire media and create right-wing sites of influence "stems from a desire to promote deeply unpopular ideas to a largely skeptical public". In so doing, he argued, "Hostility toward the mainstream press became a core element of conservative identity". This has been evident over recent decades across Europe, where a new populist brand of conservative reactionary politics has not only led to a rise in right-wing alternative media sites but a collective attack on mainstream media, notably public service media. As Holtz-Bacha (2021: 225) has observed

> There are several reasons why populists zero in on public service broadcasting. One is populists' fundamental scepticism towards institutions that are to set limits on the exercise of power in democratic systems and thus provide for checks and balances. The other is the public service broadcasters' commitment to pluralism which implies an integration function whereas right-wing populism practices exclusion.

The focus on curbing immigration in many right-wing alternative media sites, most strikingly across countries in Northern Europe, represents one issue where populist anger and exclusion contrasts with more pluralist and integrationist perspectives on public service media (Beckers and Van Aelst 2019). Overall, then, attacking mainstream media, especially journalism perceived as liberal and impartial, has become instrumental to the advancement of right-wing politics over many decades. Following this agenda, many right-wing alternative media sites have thrived and become a more vocal voice in Western media systems.

Since the rise and influence of right-wing alternative media have been driven by rich private donors and the conservative politics they want to promote, the next section considers how left-wing media can flourish and become a more prominent and widely used source of news about politics and public affairs.

The future of journalism? The role of alternative left-wing media and their ideological influence

Historically, as Chapter 6 explored, left-wing alternative media have been criticised for their amateurish approach to news production, with short-term partisanship prioritised over pragmatic, long-term decisions about editorial sustainability and strategy (Comedia 1984). But as evidenced throughout this book, many alternative media sites today have become increasingly professionalised, drawing on practices and principles of mainstream media that champion left-wing causes. But to achieve financial sustainability, they have strict ideological parameters that shape their ownership model and funding streams. Accepting advertising or private income from wealthy owners is viewed by many alternative media sites on the left as inimical to the production of alternative and independent journalism. Instead, many alternative left-wing sites have adopted funding models which ask users to regularly contribute money to sustain their journalism. While some sites ask for direct subscription from readers, for instance, other models include a member-style service, inviting users to be part of a cooperative that feeds into editorial policy-making. For example, Price (2020) examined users of a Scottish investigative alternative media site, The Ferret, which adopted a cooperative funding model. His survey of readers concluded that "it is important The Ferret does all it can to stress and foster the inclusive nature of this arrangement [cooperative], making subscribers feel as much like members of a club as possible" (Price 2020: 1334). However, while Price (2020) concluded that The Ferret may be able to sustain itself in the immediate future, it was a relatively small number of mostly old, left, liberal, and ideologically motivated members that supported the site's journalism and objectives. In other words, to generate more investigative resources and wield greater influence, the site would need to go well beyond its core membership to produce the necessary finances.

The degree to which left-leaning alternative media sites professionalise their journalistic practices and adopt mainstream media practices is another factor that could shape their long-term sustainability. After all, the ideological DNA of right-wing sites can easily conform to market solutions, such as accepting advertising or large donations from commercial corporations. But left-wing sites have to balance the need for financial sustainability with their ideological principles about media ownership. Recent changes by a UK left-wing site, The Canary, represent the wider tension left-wing sites have when professionalising their journalism and adopting top-down hierarchical ownership models. In early 2022, the site released a video confidently explaining the "6 ways The Canary is radically different from other media outlets" (The Canary 2022a). It included editorial policies such as writing accessibly, being transparent in reporting, covering local beats, and reflecting the reader's perspective, along with other specific practices and ownership principles. For instance, the site stated "they don't have external shareholders or corporate sponsors to tell us what to do … nearly all our funding goes into paying our staff" (The Canary 2022a).

However, just a few months later, the site underwent a major revolution, developing a cooperative model that challenged The Canary's previous six-year ownership model. It published a story that explained its reorganisation:

> The Canary was founded in 2015 as a limited liability company (LLC), and its founders/directors ran it like a capitalist business – albeit not very well. However, in the summer of 2022, everything changed. A seismic chain of events led to revelations none of us could have anticipated. We uncovered a gulf between directors' and workers' pay and terms that was much larger than any of us had suspected. In light of these revelations … What we have undergone is a workers' revolution. We are now a co-operative with a structure that is run democratically by the people who actually work here. We pass decisions in open meetings, where everyone gets a say and everyone's vote counts – and we make decisions transparently and collectively. For the first time since its inception, the Canary is truly walking the talk – we are embodying the sort of work environment and community spirit that we advocate through our journalism.
>
> *(The Canary 2022b)*

This changing ownership model of The Canary reflects a wider sensitivity about the production of left-wing alternative media. The ideological principles of alternative left media police any hint of capitalistic exploitation, with either contributors themselves or regular users challenging their journalistic principles and questioning their independence. Viewed from this perspective, alternative left-wing media production can only operate within a relatively limited set of financial structures that makes it difficult to create the kind of income that can fund journalism that rivals the newsrooms of many mainstream media organisations. Or, put differently, unless alternative left-wing media generate bottom-up funding from a wide pool of users – whether through director subscription, a cooperative model, or another income stream – it is difficult to foresee how they can wield greater influence in mainstream politics and public affairs.

Where left-wing politics could advance greater ideological influence in journalism is in reforming rather than attacking the existing infrastructure of mainstream media, in particular public service journalism. After all, whether through a licence fee or form of direct taxation, public service media represent a bottom-up funding system that, in theory, is driven by the needs of the public rather than private interests (Curran 2011). This broadly represents the kind of ownership model supported by left-wing alternative media, a citizen-funded solution to delivering journalism in the public interest. Moreover, there is growing evidence to demonstrate the impact public service media have in serving the public more effectively than commercial media. A large body of scholarship literature has shown that well-funded, impartial public service media produce a greater range and depth of news that leads to better public understanding of the world than nations more reliant on market-driven media (Aalberg and Curran 2012; Aalberg and Cushion 2016; Curran et al. 2009; Cushion 2012, 2022; Strömbäck 2017). In short, public service media help create well-informed democracies.

However, there remain critical voices from the left – including coverage in alternative media sites (as Chapter 4 explored) – that have pointed out that the model of public service media has not necessarily led to the kind of independent journalism that effectively serves the public. Freedman (2019: 214), for example, has argued:

> The vision of a truly public media—one that is genuinely accountable to and representative of publics and that scrutinizes elites rather than deferring to them—remains as relevant as ever. The problem is that actually existing public media, including the BBC, have been severely constricted in their ability to realize these ambitions.

Informed by this critique and many others, alternative left-wing media could focus their agenda more centrally on *reforming* public service media rather than relentlessly *attacking* their journalism, and undermining mainstream media more generally. Over recent years, alternative systems of public service media have been debated and specific policy recommendations proposed, with the aim of creating more independent and accountable journalism (see Fenton et al. 2020; Pickard

2020). While Chapter 4 found instances where alternative left-wing media in the UK critiqued the BBC's limited independence from the government of the day, the far more routine focus centred on exposing sloppy editorial decisions, punctuated with accusations of political bias or breaches of impartiality. The implications of constantly criticising mainstream media and professional journalism should not be underestimated. As explored earlier in the chapter, there is growing evidence that relentless attacks on public service media undermine trust and support for this type of media system. Moreover, it reinforces the same ideological ambitions of right-wing media – to discredit and undermine mainstream media and professional journalism. For public service media this represents an existential threat to their future. If public support for this system of funding wanes, rather than reform public service media, the impetus of governments – especially those on the right – may be to downgrade their resources or eradicate them entirely. Once weakened or destroyed, the ability of public service media to regain the same infrastructure and influence is highly unlikely. In an American context, for example, Pickard (2015) has demonstrated the challenges associated with promoting popular support for public service broadcasting in a commercial climate fuelled by partisan media and conservative political scepticism towards this type of funding system. In short, the relentless criticism and opposition to public service broadcasting by alternative media sites risks undermining the politics and journalism left-wing alternative media champion.

History suggests there will always be a market-place for alternative left-wing media, with new online and social media platforms creating favourable conditions for independent sites to thrive and reach audiences beyond mainstream media. Moreover, the evidence drawn on throughout this book has shown their future sustainability appears more assured than past generations. After all, adopting more professionalised production practices represents a break from the criticism directed at the amateurish processes and short-lived ambitions of old left-wing media. But without the resources of most mainstream newsrooms or the financial backing of private donors that sustain many right-wing sites, their ownership model limits how far they can enrich their journalism to attract more users.

In order for left-wing media to expand their audience base and enhance a greater influence on mainstream political debates, arguably their editorial strategy should not be limited to pursuing blind partisanship or hostility to professional journalists. Fenton (2016: 71) has acknowledged the limitations of promoting a radical brand of politics in a digital media environment given the relatively "small, cause-specific and alternative news websites that have emerged online". She argued that "The problem is that counter-publicity [of alternative media] is less likely to be heard and taken account by political elites. Counter-public spheres are by their nature outside of and antagonistic to the dominant political system in any one instance" (Fenton 2016: 71). Viewed from this perspective, in order to become a more influential source in political debates, alternative media need to engage with mainstream media and professional journalists more constructively rather than operate at a critical distant from them. Right-wing media, for example, have been legitimated by mainstream media, such as during election campaigns in the US and UK, by helping to set the broadcast media agenda (Benkler et al. 2017, Cushion et al. 2018). Over recent years, con-tributors of alternative left-wing sites, such as Novara Media in the UK, have begun to appear more regularly on mainstream media, advancing their opinions and debating issues with mainstream journalists and politicians. Their alterna-tive voices, in this sense, have extended well beyond their own online and social media networks, raising topics, and championing causes that might otherwise have limited reach. This intermedia agenda-setting approach – piggy-backing on mainstream media programmes and platforms – represents an effective way left-wing alternative media sites can extend their ideological influence. But it hinges on alternative media maintaining working relationships with profes-sional journalists and editors, and policing robust standards and principles in their journalism. This can help legitimise their perspectives and enhance their journalistic authority, and lead to a normalisation and routinisation of their mainstream media access and engagement. Put bluntly, alternative left-wing media should focus less on attacking mainstream media from a critical distance. A more ambitious editorial goal would be greater convergence into the world of professional journalism in order to promote their politics on the mainstream stage.

References

Aalberg, T. and Curran, J. (2012) *How Media Inform Democracy: A Comparative Approach*. London: Routledge.

Aalberg, T. and Cushion, S (2016) 'Public service broadcasting, hard news, and citizens' knowledge of current affairs', Oxford Research Encyclopaedia of Politics, https://oxfordre.com/politics/view/10.1093/acrefore/9780190228637.001.0001/acrefore-9780190228637-e-38.

Al-Rawi, A. (2022) 'News loopholing: Telegram news as portable alternative media', *Journal of Computational Social Science*, Vol.5: 949–968, https://doi.org/10.1007/s42001-021-00155-3

Akser, M. and McCollum, V. (2018) 'Introduction: Alternative Media in Contemporary Turkey', In Asker, M and McCollum (ed.) *Alternative Media in Contemporary Turkey: Sustainability, Activism and Resistance*. Rowman & Littlefield.

Arguedas, A.R, Robertson, C.T., Fletcher, R. and Nielsen, R.K. (2022) *Echo chambers, filter bubbles, and polarisation: A literature review*. https://reutersinstitute.politics.ox.ac.uk/echo-chambers-filter-bubbles-and-polarisation-literature-review

Ataman, V. and Çoban, B. (2018) 'Counter-surveillance and alternative new media in Turkey', *Information, Communication & Society*, Vol. 21(7): 1014–1029, DOI: 10.1080/1369118X.2018.1451908

Bauer, A.J. (2022) Opinion | Why Conservatives Can't Stop Acquiring Media Companies, Politico, https://www.politico.com/news/magazine/2022/11/02/conservatives-acquiring-media-companies-musk-twitter-00064443

Beckers K. and Van Aelst, P. (2019) 'Did the European Migrant Crisis Change News Coverage of Immigration? A Longitudinal Analysis of Immigration Television News and the Actors Speaking in It', *Mass Communication and Society*, Vol. 22 (6): 733–755, DOI: 10.1080/15205436.2019.1663873

Benkler, Y. Faris, R. Roberts, H. and Zuckerman, E. (2017) 'Study: Breitbart-led right-wing media ecosystem altered broader media agenda', Columbia Journalism Review, March 3, https://www.cjr.org/analysis/breitbart-media-trump-harvard-study.php

Comedia (1984) 'The alternative press: The development of underdevelopment', *Media, Culture & Society*, Vol. 6(2), 95–102. DOI: 10.1177/016344378400600202

Curran, James (2011) *Media and Democracy*. London: Routledge. ISBN 978-0-415-31707-8

Curran, J., Iyengar, S., Brink Lund, A. and Salovaara-Moring, I. (2009) 'Media System, Public Knowledge and Democracy: A Comparative Study', *European Journal of Communication*, Vol. 24(1): 5–26. DOI: 10.1177/0267323108098943

Cushion, S. (2022) 'Are public service media distinctive from the market? Interpreting the political information environments of BBC and commercial news in the UK', *European Journal of Communication*, Vol. 37(1): 3–20. DOI: 10.1177/02673231211012149

Cushion, S. (2022) Russia: The west underestimates the power of state media, The Conversation, 22 February, https://theconversation.com/russia-the-west-underestimates -the-power-of-state-media-178582

Cushion, S. (2020) 'Six ways alt-left media legitimatize their criticism of mainstream media: An analysis of The Canary and Evolve Politics (2015–19)', *Journal of Alternative and Community Media*, Vol. 5(2): 153–171. (10.1386/joacm_00081_1)

Cushion, S. (2012) *The Democratic Value of News: Why Public Service Media Matter*. Basingstoke: Palgrave Macmillan.

Cushion, S. and Sambrook, R. (eds). (2016) *The Future of 24-hour News: New Directions, New Challenges*. New York: Peter Lang.

Cushion, S. and Thomas, R. (2018) *Reporting elections: Rethinking the logic of campaign coverage*. London: Polity.

Cushion, S., Kilby, A., Thomas, R. Morani, M. and Sambrook, R (2018) 'Newspapers, Impartiality and Television News', *Journalism Studies*, Vol. 19 (2): 162–181, DOI: 10.1080/1461670X.2016.1171163

Downing, J (1984) *Radical media: The political experience of alternative communication*. Boston, MA: South End Press.

Edelman (2022) 2022 Edelman Trust Barometer, https://www.edelman.com/trust/2022 -trust-barometer

Fenton, N. (2016) *Digital, Political, Radical*. Cambridge: Polity.

Fenton, N. Freedman, D., Schlosberg, J. and Dencik, L. (2020) *The Media Manifesto*. Cambridge: Polity.

Freedman, D. (2019) "Public Service" and the Journalism Crisis: Is the BBC the Answer? Television & New Media, 20(3), 203–218. https://doi.org/10.1177/1527476418760985

Hallin, D.C. and Mancini, P. (2004) *Comparing Media Systems: Three Models of Media and Politics*. Cambridge, UK: Cambridge University Press

Harlow, S. (2023) *Digital-Native News and the Remaking of Latin American Mainstream and Alternative Journalism*. London: Routledge. DOI: 10.4324/9781003152477

Holtz-Bacha, C. (2021) 'The kiss of death. Public service media under right-wing populist attack', *European Journal of Communication*, Vol. 36(3): 221–237 DOI: 10.1177/0267323121991334

Ihlebæk, K.A., Figenschou, T.U., Eldridge, S.A., Frischlich, L., Cushion, C. and Holt, K. (2022) 'Understanding Alternative News Media and Its Contribution to Diversity', *Digital Journalism*, Vol. 10(8): 1267–1282, https://doi.org/10.1080/21670811.2022 .2134165

Ipsos Mori. (2019) https://www.ipsos.com/ipsos-mori/en-uk/impact-declining-trust -media.

Jones, J.M. (2018) U.S. Media Trust Continues to Recover from 2016 Low. https://news .gallup.com/poll/243665/mediatrust-continues-recover-2016-low.aspx.

Kalogeropoulos, A., & Newman, N. (2018) 'Who Uses Alternative and Partisan Brands?', https://www.digitalnewsreport.org/survey/2018/who-uses-alternative-and-partisan -brands/

Khalaji, M. (2022) Social Media in Iran's Protests: A New Public Sphere? The Washington Institute. https://www.washingtoninstitute.org/policy-analysis/social-media-irans -protests-new-public-sphere

Koo, G.Y. (2017) 'Constructing an Alternative Public Sphere: The Cultural Significance of Social Media in Iran' in Lenze, N. Schriwer, C. Jalil, Z.A. (ed.) *Media in the Middle East: Activism, Politics, and Culture*. Basingstoke: Palgrave MacMillan.

Kotch, A. (2020) Right-Wing Megadonors Are Financing Media Operations to Promote Their Ideologies', 27 January, The Center for Media and Democracy's PR Watch, https://www.prwatch.org/news/2020/01/13531/right-wing-megadonors-are-financing -media-operations-promote-their-ideologies

Ladd, J. (2013) *Why Americans Hate the News*. Princeton: Princeton University Press

Marwick, A. and Lewis, R. (2017) *Media manipulation and disinformation online*, Data & Society Research Institute. https://datasociety.net/library/media-manipulation-and -disinfo-online/

Mourão, R.R. and Robertson, C.T. (2019) 'Fake news as discursive integration: An analysis of sites that publish false, misleading, hyperpartisan and sensational information', *Journalism Studies*, Vol. 20(14): 2077–2095. https://doi.org/10/gftc6p

Newman, N., R. Fletcher, A. Schultz, A. Simge and R.N. Nielsen (2020) Reuters Institute Digital News Report 2020. Oxford: Reuters.

Ozgul, B.A. and Veneti, A. (2021) 'The Different Organizational Structures of Alternative Media: Through the Perspective of Alternative Media Journalists in Turkey and Greece', *Digital Journalism*, DOI: 10.1080/21670811.2021.1943482

Pickard, V. (2020) *Democracy Without Journalism? Confronting the Misinformation Society*. Oxford University Press.

Pickard, V. (2015) *America's Battle for Media Democracy: The Triumph of Corporate Libertarianism and the Future of Media Reform*. Cambridge University Press.

Ponsford, D. (2017) 'Westmonster: News website supporting Brexit, Farage and Trump set up by political donor Aaron Banks', *Press Gazette*, 19 January, https://pressgazette.co .uk/publishers/digital-journalism/westmonster-news-website-supporting-brexit-farage -and-trump-set-up-by-political-donor-aaron-banks/

Price, J. (2020) 'How to feed The Ferret: Understanding subscribers in the search for a sustainable model of investigative journalism', *Journalism*, Vol. 21(9), 1320–1337. DOI: 10.1177/1464884917733587

Siebert, F.S., Peterson, T. and Schramm, W. (1956) *Four Theories of the Press*. University of Illinois Press, Urbana III.

Stengrim, L.A. (2005) 'Negotiating Postmodern Democracy, Political Activism, and Knowledge Production: Indymedia's Grassroots and e-Savvy Answer to Media

Oligopoly', *Communication and Critical/Cultural Studies*, Vol. 2(4): 281–304, DOI: 10.1080/14791420500332527

Steppat, D. Castro, L. and Esser, F. (2021) 'What News Users bookPerceive as 'Alternative Media' Varies between Countries: How Media Fragmentation and journalPolarization Matter', *Digital Journalism*, DOI: 10.1080/21670811.2021.1939747

Strömbäck, Jesper (2017) Does Public Service TV and the Intensity of the Political Information Environment Matter? *Journalism Studies* 18(11), 1415–1432.

Strömbäck, J., Y. Tsfati, H. Boomgaarden, A. Damstra, E. Lindgren, R. Vliegenthart and T. Lindholm. (2020) 'News Media Trust and its Impact on Media Use: Toward a Framework for Future Research', *Annals of the International Communication Association*, Vol. 44 (2): 139–156

Swift, A. (2016) 'Americans' Trust in Mass Media Sinks to New Low', Gallup, 14 September, https://news.gallup.com/poll/195542/americans-trust-mass-media-sinks-new-low.aspx

The Canary (2022a) '6 ways The Canary is radically different from other media outlets', YouTube, https://youtu.be/NLUdEkxg5A8

The Canary (2022b) The bosses are gone! We are now the Canary workers' co-op, *The Canary*, https://coop.thecanary.co/

Thompson, J. and Hawley, G. (2021) 'Does the Alt-Right still matter? An examination of Alt-Right influence between 2016 and 2018', *Nations and Nationalism*, Vol. 27(4): 1165–1180

Tuchman, G. (1972) 'Objectivity as Strategic Ritual: An Examination of Newsmen's Notions of Objectivity', *American Journal of Sociology*, Vol. 77: 660–79.

von Nordheim, G., Rieger, J., & Kleinen-von Königslöw, K. (2021) 'From the fringes to the core: An analysis of right-wing populists' linking practices in seven EU parliaments and Switzerland', *Digital Journalism*, https://doi.org/10.1080/21670811.2021.1970602

Waisbord, S. (2022) 'Alternative media/journalism and the communicative politics of contestation', *Digital Journalism*, Vol. 10(8): 1431–1439.

Walsh, J. (2020) Poll: 88% of trump supporters appear to falsely believe Biden didn't legitimately win', *Forbes*, 19 November, https://www.forbes.com/sites/joewalsh/2020/11/19/poll-88-of-trump-supporters-appear-to-falsely-believe-biden-didnt-legitimately-win/?sh=1c73d3d37221

Waterson, J. (2019) 'BBC staff express fear of public distrust after election coverage', *Media Guardian*, 14 December, https://www.theguardian.com/media/2019/dec/14/bbc-staff-expressfear-of-public-distrust-after-election-coverage

Yin, S. (2018) 'Alternative forms of media, ICTs, and underprivileged groups in China', *Media, Culture & Society*, Vol. 40(8): 1221–1236. https://doi.org/10.1177/0163443718754653

INDEX